# It Won't Hurt None

# IT WON'T HURT NONE

## A STORY OF COURAGE, HEALING AND A RETURN TO WHOLENESS

**REBECCA E. CHANDLER**

Rebecca E Chandler
An imprint of The Chandler Group, LLC
Los Angeles, CA
United States of America
www.rebeccaechandler.com

Copyright © 2022 by Rebecca E Chandler

REC

Rebecca E Chandler supports copyright. Copyright fuels creativity, free speech, and enhances every culture. Thank you reader for buying an authorized edition of this book. Thank you for not reproducing, scanning, or distributing any part of this story in any form without permission. The sale of this book without its cover is unauthorized. If you purchased this book without a cover, you should be aware that it was reported to the publisher as "unsold and destroyed." Neither the author nor the publisher receives payment for the sale of any "stripped book."

LCCN: 2022923599
ISBN 979-8-9874797-0-4 (Paperback)
ISBN 979-8-9874797-2-8 (Hardcover)
ISBN 979-8-9874797-6-6 (Hardcover w/Dust Jacket)
ISBN 979-8-9874797-3-5 (eBook)
ISBN 979-8-9874797-4-2 (Audible)
ISBN 979-8-9874797-1-1 (Kindle)

All rights reserved, including the right to reproduce this book or portions thereof in any form whatsoever. Copyright under Berne Copyright Convention, Universal Copyright Convention, and Pan-American Copyright Convention.

No part of this publication may be reproduced, stored in a retrieval system, or transmitted/distributed in any form, or by any means, electronic, mechanical, photocopying, recording or otherwise, without prior permission of Rebecca E Chandler. For all requests, please visit www.rebeccaechandler.com

Ordering Information:
Quantity sales. Special discounts are available on quantity purchases by corporations, associations, and others. For details, contact the author at the address above.

10 9 8 7 6 5 4 3 2 1

To Seven.

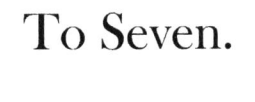

Dear Reader:

This book is a memoir. It reflects the author's present recollections of experiences over time and does not represent word-for-word transcripts. Rather, the author has retold them in a way that evokes the feeling and meaning of what was said and, in all instances, the essence of the dialogue is accurate. While all the stories in this book are true, some names and identifying details have been changed to protect the privacy of the people involved, and some events have been compressed. This is a work of nonfiction. Characters and events are not fabricated. The author recognizes that the memories of real-life family members, friends, and practitioners portrayed in this book may differ from her own.

Please note the following content warning.

This memoir contains detailed references to rape, sexual assault, abuse (physical, sexual, emotional, verbal), child abuse and/or pedophilia, self-harm, depression, suicide ideation, other mental health issues, pornography, death or dying, and pregnancy and/or infertility.

If you feel you would like to speak to someone, please dial 988 to reach the Suicide & Crisis Lifeline in the United States, providing 24/7 service. It is available to anyone in suicidal crisis or emotional distress.

Dial 911 if you think you are having an emergency and are in danger.

If you are being hurt, know someone who might be hurt, or afraid you might hurt another, dial 911 or call the Childhelp National Child Abuse Hotline at 1-800-422-4453 or visit https://childhelphotline.org/. Your chat with one of their professional crisis counselors will be a first step in breaking the silence and getting help.

I like to refer to the professionals who supported my journey as healers. That's my term. They never used that word or implied that they held any healing ability or powers. They are psychologists, psychiatrists, doctors, nurse practitioners, holistic practitioners, guides, empaths, energy workers, neurologists, TCM practitioners, massage therapists, somatic practitioners, astrologists, and mediums.

Please remember I am not a doctor, therapist, counselor, or any other sort of medical professional. I hope that sharing my experiences may be helpful while you work to heal your life and your symptoms. Please know that no information published in this book should ever take the place of professional care, diagnosis, and treatment. Any/all opinions captured in this narrative are my own and do not intend to imply or offer any medical opinions, facts, or diagnosis.

# Contents

| | |
|---|---|
| Preface | 1 |
| Acknowledgements | 3 |
| Introduction | 4 |

**Collapse**
| | |
|---|---|
| Chapter 1 | 9 |
| Chapter 2 | 17 |
| Chapter 3 | 25 |

**Agency**
| | |
|---|---|
| Chapter 4 | 35 |
| Chapter 5 | 49 |
| Chapter 6 | 59 |

**Flight**
| | |
|---|---|
| Chapter 7 | 73 |
| Chapter 8 | 81 |
| Chapter 9 | 95 |

**Transformation**
| | |
|---|---|
| Chapter 10 | 115 |
| Chapter 11 | 135 |
| Chapter 12 | 145 |

**Reconciliation**
| | |
|---|---|
| Chapter 13 | 155 |
| Chapter 14 | 169 |
| Chapter 15 | 179 |

**Freefall**
| | |
|---|---|
| Chapter 16 | 191 |
| Chapter 17 | 207 |
| Chapter 18 | 213 |

**Recovery**
| | |
|---|---|
| Chapter 19 | 227 |
| Chapter 20 | 237 |
| Author's Note | 240 |

| | |
|---|---|
| Epilogue | 242 |
| Special Thanks | 243 |
| Resources | 244 |

# Preface

WHEN I FIRST started to hear voices interrupting my daily thoughts, it was clear they weren't my usual, stressed-out, high school student inner dialogues. Each voice had a tone and vocabulary. Their chatter became an uncomfortable and, at times, dangerous chorus in my mind.

Eventually, I gave each voice a name. After listening intently to their language, tone of voice, and intention, I decided to identify them by their ages. They were Thirteen, Seven, Five, and Six.

Collectively, I called them my fragments, created for my protection when my mind chose to dissociate during years of childhood sexual abuse. Each piece stored horrific details of various assaults at arm's length so that I could survive.

Decades passed before I received the official diagnosis of Dissociative Identity Disorder, or D.I.D., previously referred to as multiple personality disorder. There is significant and unfortunate stigma around those diagnosed with D.I.D. For me, the diagnosis simply meant my mind functioned on a level most will never have to experience. Living with D.I.D. was complicated, but it never stopped me from finding success, being creative, or leading a fulfilling life.

Dissociation is disconnection. Most people experience some level of disconnection in everyday life, such as when they sit at a traffic light and daydream or lose track of time and end up parked in their driveway. However, such moments are short-lived and don't typically involve multiple identities.

The level of dissociation, or disconnect, I experienced was multilayered and much more complicated than a simple daydream at an intersection. My dissociation became habitual during years of abuse, and I disconnected whenever any environment made me feel as though I was in danger. I still feel tempted to dissociate in social situations from time to time.

After years of therapy, somatic coaching, and meditation, I reconciled with Thirteen, Seven, Five, and Six. We came to an understanding, and I resolved all their pain. In our resolution, and ultimately their release, I was allowed to finally live wholly complete and in the present.

My journey reflects a healing approach and experiences particular to me. Each person has to discover the best techniques for them to heal. I often hear "my trauma isn't nearly as bad as yours so I don't think I need to get help." Some believe if their experiences weren't, say, as violent as mine, their healing journey is somehow less challenging, less of a priority.

The truth is: Trauma isn't experienced on a sliding scale. Your trauma, or the trauma of someone close to you, is as serious as mine. We are equally affected in our minds and bodies. The details may differ, but your truth carries the same weight.

I hope my story of surviving trauma and healing encourages you to tend to your wounds. *The poet Rumi says, "The wound is the place where the light enters you."* Let your wound open because when it is visible, it's vulnerable. Look at it, communicate with it, learn from it, and heal it. We do not have to live broken by shame and in the shadows. I believe we all have the ability to heal.

It won't be easy. It's uncomfortable, horrible, perhaps a bit scary, and exhausting. But always remember, you are not alone. You are a survivor among many. You can do the work. You will heal your fragmented soul.

You are courageous because you survived. So stand in your truth, acknowledge all your wounds—even the ones you've never talked about—and find the strength to let them open and let all the healing light shine in.

# Acknowledgements

There's no way to properly express the gratitude and love I hold for Shawna, Wanuri, Breanne, Lily, Lynda, Aparna, Monali, Fatuoh, Denise, and Theresa. I aspire every day to mirror their loving, brave, funny, creative, intelligent, and exceptional selves. Their patience, generosity, laughter, and wisdom guide me, and I am better every day when I follow their example.

I owe a debt to my siblings for loving, trusting, and encouraging me to write this story. They have seen me through life's detours with grace, patience, and a wonderfully twisted sense of humor only we can fully appreciate. I cannot imagine a world without them.

To my nieces and nephews, in America and around the world, thank you for sharing your cheeky humor, sense of adventure, and wondrous inquisitive nature.

Thank you Dr. D, Amelie, Natalia, and Hana for hearing me, seeing me, validating my truth, and guiding my healing journey.

To friends far and wide who call every part of the world home, thank you for inviting me into your lives and sharing your humor, creativity, hospitality, and sense of adventure.

Finally, there is one person who inspires me to find joy every day. My late Granny Chandler, Inez, born October 18, 1914, made life bearable, filled it with love, and infused it with hot chocolate and Rice Krispy treats. The magic dust we mixed in our imaginations and sprinkled into the night sky at bedtime fed my curiosity and creativity. She illuminated a dream world full of vibrant color and possibility. When I wasn't sure I could hold on, Granny Chandler showed me how to be strong. Her beauty and wisdom are forever with me.

# Introduction

**H**OUSE GUESTS CAN be a blessing or a curse. And sometimes, they can be both.

A great house guest waits for an invitation to visit. They knock on the front door and offer warm embraces, laughter, chocolate, wine, gifts, and treats for the pet. They're considerate and respect the house by contributing groceries and changing the beds before they leave.

A miserable house guest arrives uninvited and barges through the front door announcing they have some dirty laundry and their children are just "getting over" the flu. Every morsel in the cupboards and fridge is devoured. They overstay their welcome and refuse to depart until everyone is sick and exhausted, finally leaving the house in disarray.

Trauma was never invited into my home, my body, or my mind. Instead, it crashed into my body and mind when I experienced the first sexual assault at the age of Five. The sexual violence shook my foundation. My mind buckled and the beams cracked. The bearing walls shielding my body broke. Trauma's force was so powerful I became unhinged. My nerves frayed. The house, my soul, was nearly destroyed.

In an effort to protect me, my mind developed multiple fragments, pieces of me trapped in time and circumstance. Each one claimed a different room for itself. I was no longer the sole owner and occupant of my life. I became a dissociated, early childhood sexual assault survivor.

My identities inhabited and punished me with nagging conversation, "chatter," in my head, obsessing over every decision, thought, and action. Restless, they created space for other uninvited guests, like depression, who I also called Darkness. They all took residence among the rubble that was my existence. I became their host and hostage and nearly succumbed to their ransom demands with my life.

Escape seemed impossible. But a part of me, the bit trying to live my life each day, clawed through the destruction and escaped my captor's grip to find healers. In time, I learned to negotiate with the fragments and reconcile the traumatized pieces of myself, eventually integrating, and then evicting, my uninvited guests.

My structure, my mind and body, is sound once again. The remodel is nearly complete as I am slowly retrofitted with self-love and acceptance one brick at a time. Healthy energy, like water, flows through my pipes, and my voice has restored my power. The deep, shameful cracks and fissures in my walls, in my wounds, feel gently repaired but require lifelong maintenance. I check in with my mind and body daily to nurture the ongoing repairs and healing they require.

Today, the foundation, the underpinning, is strong and fortified by my truth. My house is in order, and I am clear.

Trauma hates to lose, and it still lurks around my house hoping to find a window, unlocked door, or vulnerable piece of me to exploit. I no longer fear the interloper because I've done the work.

I am strong.

I am courageous.

I am whole.

# Collapse

*"This is a time for healing deep emotional trauma. Situations you thought you cleared are coming up again for more awareness. Healing is done in layers. You have to continue to spiral through the same emotional experiences until there is no electric charge left to trigger you."* (Anonymous)

## Chapter 1

**T**HE WORST KIND of traumatic event is the kind that doesn't sound like it will be particularly traumatizing. Keyhole surgery sounded tidy and simple. Unfortunately, keyholes can be deceptive. A house can look good from the outside. A few nails here and there and a fresh coat of paint and it's good as new.

But once the keyhole is unlocked, the front door groans as it creaks open, revealing the truth. Pipes drip, drip, drip, and the walls are full of holes. Spiderwebs stretch across doorjambs. And the electrical panel, keeping things warm in winter and cold in the summer, is completely offline.

My body felt good in January 2017. Sure, I had some pain and the plumbing leaked a little, but I didn't take any of it seriously. I thought I just needed a simple repair.

At the time, I lived in Kenya and experienced sharp, cutting pain throughout every menstrual cycle. A visit with a local doctor revealed a fibroid tumor sitting on my left side, just above my bladder. Additionally, I was also warned I had "prolific and severe" endometriosis contributing to the pain. My doctor in Nairobi recommended I consult with a Dubai surgeon. Just a few weeks later, I met with The Cutter, a tall, glamorous, and determined woman whose offices overlooked one of the city's premiere golf courses.

"The scans show that the fibroid tumor is about the size of an orange," she explained. "It's sitting on your bladder, which explains the urgency issues you mentioned."

"What do you suggest?" I asked.

"When they start to hurt, it's time to take them out," she said confidently. I agreed. The fibroid was an uninvited guest, and we made plans for surgery.

A month later, I left my house in Nairobi and traveled back to Dubai and had one last consultation with The Cutter in her luxurious, chic office.

"We're going to conduct a keyhole, laparoscopic procedure and remove the fibroid," she explained. "We'll also check your uterus, ovaries, and fallopian tubes. It's a common procedure, and you shouldn't have any problems."

"I was diagnosed with severe endometriosis as well. What if you decide during the procedure that it is a more serious issue? What if you find early signs of cancer, for example? I don't want to have two surgeries," I said. I was always thinking proactively and negotiating for the best deal. A film and TV producer, it never occurred to me that I shouldn't treat my body like another project.

"Well, okay, that's a fair point. I recommend that we leave an option open for a partial hysterectomy where I would potentially remove your uterus but leave your ovaries and cervix. You need to sign a release authorizing me to remove your uterus if I find anything that I think is dangerous."

I asked her about the post-surgery effects and complications in the same mind frame and tone of voice that I used when I spoke to my blessed mechanic about my 2012 Mercedes C-Class.

"If you yank that old part out, will it still run the same? I don't have time for more repairs."

The difference was that I was talking about my body and the removal of a major organ. The conversation with The Cutter was a symptom of classic detachment and I was going through the motions.

"It's a simple procedure. The uterus doesn't really serve a purpose once you get beyond childbearing. You may have increased hot flashes and other perimenopause symptoms," she explained. "We can manage all of it with the HRT (hormone replacement therapy) that you're currently using."

"That makes sense. But you'll only remove it if you feel like it's really necessary, right?" I asked.

"Of course," she replied.

It sounded simple. I reassured myself the operation would go well and left The Cutter's office to enjoy a gorgeous, Dubai spring day. When I got to my friend

Sandy's house to spend the night, I did my best to relax. I ignored some of the alarm bells going off in my head and dismissed my anxiety as normal pre-surgery nerves.

"So how are you feeling about tomorrow?" Sandy asked as she poured us a special blend of iced tea.

"I feel good. I mean, I'm a little afraid, but that's normal," I replied.

"Yeah, I mean from what you've told me, the surgeon makes it sound like a pretty straight forward operation. I'm sure it will all go well," she said to reassure me.

Early the next morning, I sat in bed and had a conversation with the fragments.

*"How are we feeling?"* I asked, perhaps a bit too enthusiastically at 5 a.m. Almost immediately, there was a lot of "chatter" in my mind.

*"What if something goes wrong? Who is this doctor? How long will it take to recover? Are you sure you want to do this? Do you really want a hysterectomy?" they asked in a chorus.*

*"Well, if there's something wrong with my uterus, and it's dangerous, then it needs to come out,"* I explained.

*"It's scary,"* Five whispered.

*"What's the rush? Why now?"* Seven pressed.

*"It's not a rush. I've been in pain for years. It's time to get rid of the tumor. It's fine. I trust the surgeon. She might not even need to remove my uterus,"* I replied hoping to calm their nerves.

The fragments pumped more fear and adrenaline into my body once I left Sandy's house at 6 a.m. and headed to one of Dubai's private women's hospitals. After checking in, I lay in the hospital bed while they started the IV. I kept reassuring myself the surgery was necessary. In hindsight, I wasn't present and paying attention.

My mind and body frantically waved a flag back and forth, but I ignored their warning. Normally I would read everything Dr. Internet had to say about a particular procedure, medication, or diagnosis before making any health decisions. And yet, for reasons unclear at the time, I skipped over my usual "protocols." *It's too late to turn back*, I told myself as the anesthesiologist delivered the first round of sedatives and I was wheeled into surgery.

I woke up a few hours later in a lovely, peach-toned, private hospital room on the maternity floor. The view out the window captured a beautiful grove of bright-green trees, healthy from the latest rainstorm. I slowly regained my senses and recognized the sound of the newborn babies crying down the hallway. Once more lucid, I started pressing my nurses for information.

"Do you know if she removed my uterus?" I asked the nurse who was checking my IV. She gave me a confused look. "She didn't know if it needed to be removed before the surgery. I want to know if she removed it," I said in a slightly panicked tone.

"I don't know," the nurse replied. "You need to wait for your surgeon to call."

"Okay," I said, "please tell her to call me now. I need to know what happened to me."

"I'll call her office and leave a message," the nurse said on her way out of my room. I stared at the clock, walls, and out the window for what seemed like hours before The Cutter finally called me.

"Hello, Rebecca," she said. "I hear that you're asking questions about your surgery."

"Yes, well, I thought that you would stop by today. The nurses don't seem able to tell me what happened."

I felt her rolling her eyes at me over the phone. After a pause, I detected a bit of agitation in her voice. "Okay, well, I don't normally speak to my patients the day of their surgery. But you seem to be recovering very quickly."

*My* eyes started rolling. Did she think she was doing me a favor?

"Well, thanks. So how did it go?" I asked in my "Don't you dare screw with me right now" voice.

"The fibroid was removed without any issues. I didn't see any abnormalities."

I took some deep breaths. I didn't care about the fibroid. It was harmless. I knew that. I wanted to hear about my womb. Sighing heavily into the phone, I felt as though I had to drag the most critical information out of her.

"That's great. And what about my uterus?"

"Well, when I examined the uterus, it was severely damaged from endometriosis," she said. "In fact, you had a lot of endometriosis outside of your uterus as well. It didn't look healthy, and I made the decision to remove it."

My throat tightened. I started to feel tears form. I didn't understand what was happening. *Why am I sad?* I asked myself. It was just a simple operation.

"Are you happy with the result?" I asked The Cutter.

"Yes. I don't expect you to have any issues. It was a straightforward procedure."

Fibroid gone. Uterus was out. No signs of cancer. I kept telling myself it was a good outcome. I wasn't in too much pain. The call ended but the ache in my throat and chatter in my mind wouldn't stop.

*"What have you done?" my body asked. "We can't ever have a child now. You've ruined us."*

*"What? How in the world did I ruin us?" I asked.*

*"I wasn't finished. I wasn't ready to stop trying for a baby. I wasn't ready to close that door forever. I never gave up hope. It was my dream. I just wanted to be a mother. I was going to keep our child safe and love it forever."*

*"I get that, but our chances of having a child ended long before this operation, and you know that," I replied impatiently.*

*"You've ruined us," my body responded through tears. "You took away the one thing that guaranteed we would not be lonely. Our womb. Who is going to love us now?"*

There was a familiar anguish in the voice. Two years of failed attempts to get pregnant dragged me through two years of grieving until I was finally able to grow comfortable in the knowledge I would not have any children. Did the voice, now back with fresh torments, lay dormant the whole time? Why did my body still want to be a mother? How would I get it, me, to accept the fact that I allowed our womb to be removed?

The voice, like the surgeon's blade, cut deep when it asked, "Who is going to love us now?" I sat alone in the darkened hospital room in the middle of the night, listening to the newborns crying. An overwhelming sense of loss filled the space where my womb once resided.

The next morning, I was discharged, and I settled back at Sandy's house where I went for walks along the beautiful track, passing by kids on the playground, birds enjoying water fountains, and gorgeous spring flowers. Walking a little further a few times each day, I congratulated myself for my resilience. *"I'm feeling good. I'll get through this."* I told myself proudly.

Just a few days later, though, my confidence quickly evaporated as extreme hot flashes engulfed my entire body. I felt like I was immersed in a boiling pot. I reassured myself it was all part of the side effects The Cutter mentioned until the hot flashes escalated and sleep became impossible.

A little more than a week after the surgery, my symptoms grew even more severe, and I finally consulted with Dr. Internet about "What to expect after a hysterectomy."

The news wasn't hopeful. I read the removal of my womb could potentially deliver me into metabolic syndrome. Other risks, like premature menopause and other post-menopause complications were also common. The Cutter never mentioned any of it to me. I became increasingly worried about the hot flashes and sleeplessness that continued to escalate as I made plans to return to Nairobi.

Within a few days of getting home, my mental health began to decline sharply. Darkness, like a fog silently creeping into a forest, pushed into my mind. I sat on my porch one morning and stared at the trees surrounding my small, stone cottage in Kenya as my thoughts unraveled.

*The Cutter took my womb, and I'm going crazy,* I said to myself. *No. Stop.* I had to admit that it wasn't true. I willingly surrendered my womb. I gave it away voluntarily. I didn't protect my body. I had to take responsibility and accept whatever came my way.

My mind was breaking while massive hormone shifts pulsed through my flesh. Absent sleep, I became obsessed with the pursuit of information. I conferred with Dr. Internet as my symptoms worsened and research revealed The Cutter lied when she told me the uterus didn't play a significant role in the body beyond childbearing. The Cutter wanted to cut. The truth was somehow extraneous. The uterus, I learned, plays a significant role within the entire endocrine system. It's where every hormone and biological process is regulated.

My symptoms escalated and bore no resemblance to the days of relatively gentle perimenopause. Where I used to experience an occasional hot flash before the surgery, they now set me ablaze and drenched me in sweat in seconds, multiple times an hour. At night, my sheets became soaked as I lay naked under the constant blast of a large fan. Sleep came in short bursts that only served to intensify the Darkness growing in my mind.

I became completely untethered as my mind and body replayed every painful step of my infertility. The failed attempts to get pregnant, the discovery of no ovarian reserve, and the sting of a formal rejection of my adoption application as a single parent jabbed at me. Every emotion I ever felt about not having a child circled back, bigger, darker, and more hurtful than ever before. Unlike other bouts of depression, this species of Darkness draped over me like a wet, weighted blanket.

The "routine keyhole procedure" devastated my entire endocrine system. My body quickly surrendered to Metabolic Syndrome. I felt destroyed and refused to leave the house.

Darkness tightened its grip and escalated its forced march across my mind by unearthing my childhood sexual trauma. I stopped obsessing about my infertility as vivid flashbacks of the assaults flooded into my mind. The creak of a doorway, or the sound of my gardener smacking his lips as he ate lunch, were part of a long list of cues, triggers, that dragged me away from the present and into my past.

In the midst of all of my troubles, I had to find a way to get back to work. I had recently shifted to consulting for one of the world's biggest brands after twenty-five years of producing films, TV, and marketing campaigns. My work couldn't be put off any longer.

But nearly a month after the surgery, I was clearly not ready when my manager and friend Monali called me about our television project, and I dissolved during the conversation. I was in bad shape. I didn't know how to describe what was happening to me. I could have asked Monali for help, or just to listen, but instead I lost control.

"Hey," she said, "How are you? I talked to procurement today and they said they're still waiting for you to send in the report. When do you think it will be ready? We need to get the project moving."

"You know what, Monali," I shouted into the phone, "I do not care about the damn budget. I am losing my mind. My body is completely falling apart! I can't sleep! I can't function! I don't care about any of it!" I shouted.

"Wow, okay, I'm going to let you go. You don't sound good. I'll talk to you tomorrow," she said, ending our call.

I felt so embarrassed. Monali was, and remains, a good friend. She was also one of my main client contacts, and I had just lost my shit on the phone and sounded hysterical. I was known for having a short fuse at times, but the exchange that day crossed over so many boundaries I was afraid for my job.

I should have known better. A few hours later, a messenger arrived at my house to deliver an enormous bouquet of flowers. The note read, "You need these. Mo."

When my friend Sam called me at home, she kindly asked if I needed any help. I was ragged and immediately rattled off all my health issues.

"If I do not figure this out, I will not survive," I told her.

"What does it feel like?" she asked.

I know she wanted to help me. I could hear it in her voice, so I tried to explain. I found it so difficult to articulate.

"I feel like I'm going crazy in real-time. I am sliding into some sort of void where I can't think. The last time I felt like this was when I first revealed my abuse to a therapist. My mind literally broke when that happened."

"Jesus. Does it help to work? To keep your mind busy?"

"Work is impossible. I can't concentrate. I sat through a normal meeting earlier today where we talked about production schedules for the next TV series, and I forgot the details. I'm a producer. I live for details. If I can't remember things, execute plans, and focus, I'm no use to my clients."

"Maybe you need some extra sleep," she encouraged.

"Yeah, if only I could sleep. I don't even get the sensation of being sleepy anymore. I've tried melatonin, hypnotherapy, and medication. I think that my body is too angry to let me sleep. It's like a part of me will only let me focus on my abuse." I began to feel exasperated. I wasn't in the mood to explain all the miserable details about my childhood.

"After all this time? I thought you said you went to therapy and sorted that out," she asked.

"I did go to therapy," answering a bit abruptly, "several times. But I don't think that the trauma was entirely healed. I mean, I'm remembering details about the abuse that I haven't thought about for decades. It doesn't make any sense."

"Let's hope your surgeon can sort you out when you get to Dubai," she replied.

"Inshallah," I replied. God willing.

I clung to the hope that a checkup with The Cutter would give me answers and put my body and mind back on track.

## Chapter 2

After flying the all-too-familiar route from Nairobi to Dubai, I spent the night at my favorite Sofitel Hotel on the beach. I needed some peace and quiet. There was something really wondrous about Dubai in late spring, when the sea was 85 degrees and well before the monstrous summer heat took over the city. After an evening swim, I went to bed early, hoping The Cutter would offer solutions and life would return to normal.

"So, Rebecca, how are you doing? Your incisions have healed really well," The Cutter observed.

"Well, sure, that's the easy part, isn't it? The other side effects of the surgery have been disastrous."

"Tell me. What's happening?" she said, settling back into her overpriced chair. It was white leather, like the rest of the furniture in her office. The environment I once thought was European chic flipped to overpriced and tacky in my mind. My throat tightened as I started to speak.

"I feel like I'm losing my mind," I said, noticing my tone sounded rather desperate. "I am incredibly depressed. Irritable. I cannot sleep. I don't even feel tired. I have brain fog and it's affecting my work."

"Well, Rebecca," she said condescendingly, "there's absolutely no correlation between a partial hysterectomy and insomnia or depression."

A surge of anger filled my veins. My anger was always fueled by a fragment I called Thirteen. Whenever I became annoyed or pissed off, Thirteen took over. We had a complicated, and completely unhealthy, relationship. *"Thirteen, would you like to have a go at her?" I asked, prepared to unleash hell.*

*"Yes, I would. Get the fuck out of my way," she snarled as her energy took over.*

"Right, well, I wasn't depressed or an insomniac before the surgery. Now, I am. And you think you're going to sit there and tell me that none of these issues are related to my surgery? It's all a coincidence?"

She flashed her best "I'm a doctor and you're not" look at me and said, "Removing your uterus had no effect whatsoever on your sleep or mental health. It says in your chart that you have a history of depression."

"Yes, that's true," Thirteen replied with a thick layer of disdain. "But this depression is different. I haven't felt this depressed in decades, if ever. Something is wrong."

"Honestly, Rebecca, you sound a bit hysterical." Her derision made me want to punch her in the face. "I'm going to write two prescriptions for you. One is a mood stabilizer, and the other is a sleeping pill."

"Wait a minute. You want to medicate problems that you claim don't exist? Is that right? Keep your prescriptions. I won't take them. You're throwing a Band-Aid at me while I'm bleeding out."

Her overfilled lips remained pursed. Perhaps her malpractice insurance provider was lurking around the corner, making her incapable of speech. I'll never know. After what felt like a full minute of silent staring, Thirteen and I had enough.

"We aren't getting anywhere. You're not listening," I said to The Cutter, completely exasperated.

"It's only been a month. Your body is going to settle down in a few weeks. This is all normal," she said in a slightly less offensive tone.

"Normal? Right. I can't sleep and I'm dangerously depressed. My memory is fading. And you think that it's all normal? Or I'm hysterical. Which is it?"

I stood up and left her sitting in her diploma-laden office and walked to the front desk.

"Hi. I'd like copies of my entire file, please," I said to the office manager. "I won't be back."

There were plenty of moments when Thirteen's anger served a solid purpose, and my final meeting with The Cutter was just such a moment. The ability to summon Thirteen from within and channel her into my immediate thought process was a great tool; but Thirteen's sharp barbs extracted a price. She didn't easily back off after I set her free. It took me several hours of swimming in the ocean and relaxing in my hotel room the rest of the day to calm down and focus.

I spent the evening consulting Dr. Internet to find a new OB/GYN and specifically looked for a woman who was at least my age. Early the next morning, I found "Dr. Sensible's" listing in an expat chat room and called to make a same-day appointment. A mid-fifties woman who studied in Beirut, Dr. Sensible had a calm, sophisticated energy about her that all women from Lebanon seem to share. Her office wasn't chic, and that comforted me. I'd had enough of chic. I needed pragmatism, experience, and intelligence.

"Of course you have insomnia. Your entire system is in shock. You're going to have a lot of side effects for a long time," she explained after listening to my story.

"What do you mean?" I asked, confused. She was so matter of fact that it caught me by surprise.

"The uterus is a major organ. It helps regulate your endocrine system. It's all connected. You can't just remove an organ without disruption. Your body is going to have to recalibrate. The depression and brain fog you're experiencing are common for women who have a partial or total hysterectomy. Why did she remove the uterus?" she asked, glancing through my file.

"The report at the back says that the endometriosis was severe and that it greatly affected the uterus," I replied.

"Yes, I see it. I mean, that's probably true, but that's not life-threatening. It might be painful, at times, but I don't see anything in the report that suggests your uterus needed to be removed," she commented.

Her words hit me like a full body blow. I was embarrassed and I felt stupid. I couldn't tell her it was all my fault.

"My surgeon called me hysterical," I told her.

"You're not hysterical. It sounds like you're experiencing a possible system collapse, and you've every right to be upset," she explained. "I don't think the insomnia and other symptoms will last for more than a year."

"Did you just say that I was going to be miserable for a year?" I asked in shock.

"Yes. This is a massive disruption. The body doesn't recover from this very quickly, even when everything goes perfectly. And your body isn't handling it well."

"Should I take HRT (hormone replacement therapy)? Will that help?" I asked.

"Probably not," she replied. "It will complicate your body's natural ability to balance. Get out and walk. Eat healthy food. Give yourself time."

I left her office and felt a bit reassured. It was helpful to speak to a woman who had herself gone through menopause. She understood my symptoms and feelings, which made a difference.

I also felt anger growing inside of me. I was in a thermonuclear meltdown and it was entirely my fault. I signed the paperwork. I didn't research the removal of my uterus. As a result, I was going to have to live with the consequences of my actions for a very long time. The thought of not sleeping properly, feeling depressed, and fighting through brain fog for years overwhelmed me, and I started to think of resources in Kenya that might be able to help.

After a final night at the Sofitel, including a stop at my favorite gelato shop, I boarded the flight to Kenya and prayed my body would find balance. I've never been naturally inclined to feel hopeful. That's one of the many side effects of being abused. My mind jumped from the beginning to the end of the story in one big leap, and the finale is always an apocalypse. The worst-case scenario was the only option.

It's called "catastrophizing," and it made me a great Executive Producer, granting me the "sight" to see all the way down the pipeline to the end of the project and identify roadblocks long before they occurred. It was going to be difficult to see a rainbow at the end of the journey I was on, but I tried. *I'm going to heal. I will meditate on my healing,* I said to myself in the car on my way home from the airport. *I will focus on the positive.*

Unfortunately, Darkness didn't care about my hopes, positive affirmations, meditations, or prayers, as it marched relentlessly deeper into my mind. The sexual violence of my past became wholly intertwined with my everyday life. I began to hear whispers in my mind—my grandfather's whispers. Words I'd not heard for years echoed in my head like some sort of macabre performance from the past.

*"Do you like that? You love me, right? You feel good. Touch me. You're a good girl."*

My mood became increasingly darker and I knew I was in trouble. I didn't want any more traditional talk therapy. I wanted to explore a different approach to unwrap, yet again, my childhood trauma. In April 2017, I booked a session with an incredibly gifted, empathic healer, Amelie, who I had met in Nairobi just a few years prior in 2015. I knew instinctively she was the person to help me.

Vulnerable and on the verge of tears, I wasn't sure I would be able to talk to her as we sat down in her office. She took a long look at me and immediately sensed things were off.

"What's going on with you? You're shaking," she said to me while holding my hand.

"I need your help. There's a lot of chatter in my head," I replied.

"What do you mean by chatter? Remember, I'm French—you Americans say some strange things," she said with a smile, lifting my spirits.

"Do you remember a few years ago when I told you about the fragments in my mind? The alters? I need them to settle down. They're all in an uproar because I had a partial hysterectomy about six weeks ago," I told her, before breaking down into tears.

"Oh no! I'm so sorry. What do you mean by a partial hysterectomy?"

"They removed my uterus but I kept my cervix and ovaries," I answered.

"Your womb? They removed your womb!" she repeated in shock. "That's why your energy is so confused. What happened? Did something go wrong?"

I exhaled and explained through intermittent sobs all the horrible details. I cried from the center of my soul with Amelie. After every deep inhalation, I wailed some more. A lifetime of tears poured out of me. She listened intently and helped me calm down.

"Rebecca, you're in mourning," she said. "You've lost a huge part of your identity. Your womb. You need to forgive yourself for signing the release. It was a mistake. It's over. Accept what has happened so that you don't get more depressed or angry. Make space to give yourself time to grieve."

"I will try to accept it," I said through fresh tears. "It's so complicated, Amelie. I never had a great relationship with my womb. You know that I was sexually assaulted as a child. I had terrible period pains my entire life. I wasn't able to get pregnant. Why am I grieving for a body part that betrayed me?"

"Betrayed you?" She looked at me in surprise. "Your womb didn't betray you. Your womb likely suffered during the abuse—perhaps beyond repair. Your womb was part of you. You didn't betray yourself."

I took a breath and held it for a beat. I was trying to connect all the dots. "What am I grieving about?"

"You're not grieving for the actual body part. You're grieving the loss of motherhood," she explained, breaking my heart into a million tiny pieces. Amelie's words pierced my soul, and the truth nearly pulled all the air from my lungs.

"Motherhood? I processed all of that when I found out I couldn't have children in 2012. I grieved my infertility profoundly for two years," I told her as flashes of doctor's reports, ovarian reserves, the news I would never get pregnant, and the adoption rejection filled my mind.

"How? *How* did you grieve for it?" she asked.

"I cried a lot, and then I got angry."

"Ah, well, I know you, Rebecca. Be honest. You probably got angry and stayed angry," she pushed back. She knew me too well.

"Maybe. But it's in the past. What more do my mind and body need from me? I cannot have children. Full stop. That was true in 2012, and it's still true in 2017."

"You only mourned infertility. That's only one part of your mother journey. Adoption was the second part," she clarified.

"Okay. And I was sad about that—and angry," I explained.

"Yes. More anger. The removal of your womb is the final end to the entire cycle because it's the gathering point for all of your experiences and expectations. It feeds your own life and is attached to your mother self—the part of you that still wants a family," she explained. "And now it's gone. It cannot be fixed. The source at the center of your soul is trying to understand the unexpected and devastating loss," she explained.

"What can I do?" I asked her.

Amelie knew me well enough to know I healed through ceremonies. "You're a writer. So write a letter to your womb. Write whatever you want. Say everything you've ever felt. Read it out loud, and then burn the letter."

The conversation with Amelie gave me some relief. I knew if I continued to meet with her, I could unravel the truth of what was happening in my mind. Later that afternoon, I sat at my desk overlooking the garden and watched the beautiful Kenyan sunset and wrote a farewell letter to my womb.

*"You were my source—my power—and now you're gone. How do I mourn the loss of the part of myself that made me a woman? Does a womb make me a woman? I didn't know that I needed you until you were gone. It seems like such a natural thing–that my womb would be my friend. But we weren't ever friends. Endless cramps. Tormented by pain. Why is that? I assumed pregnancy would be easy. But it wasn't. I tried to get pregnant, but you left me childless. Barren. Why wasn't I good enough for children? I still feel jealous of my friends who have swollen bellies or already have children. I so wanted to have a family, but you made it impossible.*

*Somewhere in my head, I've decided that half of my sex is gone. Now I'm afraid to even touch myself. Am I still female? What am I? Half a woman? How can I find anyone to grow old with if I'm incomplete? Is that fair? What is a woman? Do I decide if I'm still female even though I don't have a uterus? Without a womb? I don't think I know anymore.*

*Will men notice that I have no womb? Will they sense that I am somehow 'incomplete' and avoid me? Embarrass me? The thought terrifies me. I am afraid of growing old alone, and yet I feel sentenced to a life of isolation because I am incomplete.*

*When I say that I had a hysterectomy, I cry. I'm so sad. Shattered. But there's no turning back now. It's final. I have to find a way to say goodbye to you and be okay with that. I have to say goodbye to my womb—my mother self—and accept the loss.*

*So this is goodbye. Goodbye motherhood. Goodbye to the center of my source. We were never really friends, and I'm sorry. I didn't trust you, and I'm sorry. I didn't consult with you, and I'm sorry. I didn't protect you, and I'm sorry. I didn't listen, and I'm sorry. But it's over now, and I need you to release me.*

*Please, I beg you, please release me, motherhood, because I can't mourn you forever. I can't be punished for my decisions forever. It's done. It's my fault, and I'm so sorry. I made a terrible decision. I broke my body. Please release me from this anguish so I can heal."*

I printed the note and made a small fire in the outdoor chimney just a few steps from my front patio. Listening to the Kenyan night full of owls, frogs, crickets, and some errant monkeys, I sat down and stared into the hot fire for quite some time until the wood burned down into orange and red embers glowing against the dark night sky. My cheeks turned red and tears rolled down my face as I contemplated my womb.

My mother self.

No longer residing within me.

I cried for my body, my health, and my happiness, all destroyed in an hour at the hand of a surgeon.

Night grew late, my favorite big dogs lay beside me, and I read the note out loud several times until the pain within the words had finally extinguished. And then, I tossed the note into the flames and watched it burn. The ceremony was cathartic. It established the beginning of my healing journey. After sitting in the dark for several hours, I decided to wait for the sunrise. Just as the equatorial sun rose over the treetops, my mind whispered, *Start writing. It's time to tell your truth.*

I walked back into my cottage, grateful it was Sunday and the house would be quiet. Sitting down at my desk, I powered on my laptop, took a deep breath to clear a bit of the anguished cobwebs out of my mind, and typed: "My Womb."

## Chapter 3

**T**HREE INSOMNIA-FUELED DAYS later, I checked the manuscript and discovered I wrote twenty-thousand words. It was the beginning of my truth.

"I started writing my story," I told Amelie the next time we met. "It's helping me to calm all the chatter in my mind."

"What exactly do you hear?" she asked.

I knew I could trust her and that it was time to share.

"I hear my grandfather's voice. It's disgusting the things that he used to say to me. There's also a vicious Darkness—depression—circling around. Telling me the abuse was all my fault. It sort of hisses at me. I heard it when I first revealed my abuse to my therapist when I was nineteen. There's a connection between the surgery and my abuse," I explained.

"Let's talk more about the fragments. We spoke about them a few years ago when we first met but didn't really get into the details. When did you first realize they existed?"

"I don't know how to explain when they started because, technically, each fragment began at the moment of trauma. I didn't hear them until I was a teenager. Every fragment is a traumatized piece of me frozen in time."

"So would you say that they're stuck? Maybe they don't know that you're not being traumatized anymore? They're trapped in a loop," she asked.

"I guess so. I never thought about it that way. They take over one at a time and fill my mind and body with fear, anger, or sadness. I heard the angry one first when

I started high school. Over time, I heard the others. I couldn't make them stop, so I decided to listen to them in my sophomore year. That's when I figured out that they each had a different personality. That they were different versions of myself."

"Do they have names?" Amelie asked.

"They do have names! It took me a long time to sort that out. I mean, what do you call a fragment in your mind that's always crying or shouting? Is Betsy crying? Is Sue angry? It sounded weird," I said, laughing.

"Yeah," Amelie said, laughing. "Betsy sounds funny."

"Right! I figured out the age of each voice, and I started using their ages as their names. Thirteen is angry, and she's uncontrollable. Seven is sad and always crying. The third one is Five and is always afraid, but I don't hear from it very often. Once I named them, I could more easily figure out when I was thinking as Rebecca, my present self, in the moment, instead of some fragmented version of myself in the past."

"The names gave you a sense of control," Amelie observed.

"Yes. And I need some sort of control because I'm always in a battle with my fragments. It's really horrible when I blend with one of them and it takes over. You know, even when I don't need or want to feel angry about something, Thirteen's rage boils over. The trauma takes over, and my adult self just sort of steps aside."

"Do they ever tell you to harm yourself?" Amelie asked with a touch of caution in her voice.

"Yeah. It feels like they join forces with my depression at times. They become self-destructive. Dangerous."

"Wow, that's a lot. What should we focus on today to help you?" she asked.

"Let's focus on breath work and building up my meditation skills. If I can learn to regulate myself more, then I can tune them out and stop blending with them. That will make me happier. It's impossible to get anything done with all the noise in my head," I explained.

"Sounds good. At some point, we can also work more on integrating them back into yourself," she explained.

"Really? I never thought about that before. I mean, I've spoken to them in my head, but actually integrating them takes things to a whole new level."

Amelie's words stayed with me after our session. I loved her approach to healing because it felt and sounded limitless. My meditation and control over the fragments improved, and time passed. It would take a lot more time before I was able to finally meet the fragments and reconcile. Work kept me busy, and eventually, my mood stopped spiraling. I traveled extensively, working on global projects, and the demands on my schedule served as a happy distraction.

Working across Africa, the Middle East, and Asia-Pacific, I spent most of my time analyzing budgets, negotiating costs, working with legal teams to draft documents, and providing technical expertise. I compensated for the premature-menopause-induced brain fog by taking copious notes and saying less in meetings. I'm sure people noticed I wasn't as "tack-sharp" as in the past, but I blamed jetlag, language barriers, and the errant "lost email," and it worked most of the time.

Every trip out of Kenya was an opportunity to get new blood work and seek consultations with doctors, the "White Coats," in a global search for answers. Six months after the surgery my body wasn't recalibrating. My new normal meant I had to take sleeping pills, raging with hot flashes, and experiencing memory issues. Adding insult to injury, I was also rapidly gaining significant weight.

Never a petite frame, at first, I thought, yeah, it's just the usual stress. I can lose it. I always did in the past. My new menopausal body was a beast with claws working on an entirely different level. Every pound was permanent and as uncomfortable as the thoughts swirling in my mind.

I grew a stomach. A gut. A belly. I said goodbye to ever seeing my toes, or my vagina, without a mirror ever again. My boobs became huge. Not super fun huge, but all new bras huge—and that's just annoying. My ass, an ass I do not share with anyone else in my family, grew, and even a great airplane seat became tight.

No amount of exercise or diet changes helped stop, much less reduce, the unwelcome transformation taking over my frame. I pursued answers and consulted with White Coats around the world, and they all ordered new lab work. Every result came back "normal," and they all told me that nothing was wrong.

"You look perfectly normal on paper, Ms. Chandler," the White Coat in India reported.

"Yes, but do I look normal to you in person?" I quipped.

"No. I understand your concerns. But I cannot identify anything in your labs to suggest that there's a problem."

Have you ever just known when something was off with your body, but it seemed like nobody was listening? The White Coats were gaslighting me. They were an exhausting blend of male and female doctors, specialists, gynecologists, aging experts, and clinicians in Dubai, London, Manila, Mumbai, Johannesburg, New York, Hong Kong, Los Angeles, and Nairobi who didn't have any answers. Not one of them looked at my extensive and costly lab results, food logs, and exercise reports and offered even a guess, much less a diagnosis.

Every consultation ended with, "I'm not sure what's happening. Your labs are normal, but clearly things aren't quite right." In lieu of help, all I got was a charge on my credit card.

The White Coats were failing me, so I decided to retool. I educated myself about hormones, stress, cortisol, liver function, and adrenals. The entire endocrine system was my assignment. Creating an information folder with articles and spreadsheets, I "produced" my health journey and invested every spare hour learning how all the body systems are codependent. I became a graduate of the "Internet School of Medicine". I was confident if I spoke the right language, then perhaps the "specialists" would actually hear me and help me.

I was wrong. No amount of study facilitated a diagnosis. Rather, it left me feeling defeated. Absent a medical explanation, I started to doubt my own feelings. I asked myself some tough questions at the end of 2017, almost a year after the surgery.

*Was I a hypochondriac? Was the weight gain just a natural part of aging? Was the sleep disruption permanent? Maybe there was nothing wrong. Every report and specialist said my body was normal. It had to be me, right? Was it all in my head?* After a few months of debating my own sanity, I finally regained my sense of self. *No! Oh, Hell no! I am not hysterical.* I drilled down and kept hunting for answers.

The search continued, but no matter how many degrees I earned from the "Internet School of Medicine" and "Dr. Internet," I never felt heard by any of my physicians and certainly never healed. Every White Coat functioned from the same script as if they all went to the exact same medical school which was, of course, impossible. But they did all graduate from the same system that spent almost no time whatsoever teaching about women's health beyond childbearing.

When I learned that most medical schools and residency programs don't teach aspiring physicians anything about menopause, or trauma informed care, I became furious and gained a whole new perspective. It's no wonder that when I said, "I have a trainer and I am at the gym five days a week but my cholesterol and triglycerides keep pushing up," the medical professionals heard, "I walk on the treadmill for fifteen minutes every few days and eat chocolate cake and cheeseburgers for breakfast."

The White Coats, with little to no training, chose to see and hear an obese thing. Not a person. And certainly not a middle-aged, post-hysterectomy woman. I was the problem because they couldn't come up with a diagnosis.

"You really have to lose some weight. I'm concerned about your A1C progressing into Type 2 Diabetes," a White Coat said in his posh Los Angeles office.

"I hear you. You all say the same thing. What am I doing wrong? I eat clean and exercise with a trainer every day. The pounds won't come off. In fact, I keep gaining—particularly around my middle."

"Yeah, well, you had a partial hysterectomy. You can expect to have a weight issue for quite a while," he replied.

"How long?" I asked.

"Ten years," he answered casually.

I felt my body start to vibrate sitting in the exam room. I recognized that Thirteen was willing and able to launch my curvy self across the room to pin down the so-called expert. I grabbed both of the armrests to keep myself seated as pure frustration and anger rippled throughout my body and endorphins filled every cell. Thirteen and I were ready to attack the guy talking out of both sides of his mouth.

*"Is it wrong to call him Dr. Motherfucker?" I asked Thirteen in my head while I watched his mouth open and close.*

*"No," she snapped back. "Call him Dr. Motherfucker while I choke him with his stethoscope."*

I regained control over the impulse to attack him, and I asked the obvious question.

"So you're telling me that I won't be able to shed any excess pounds for ten years. You're also telling me to lose the excess weight so I don't get Type 2 Diabetes. You see the problem, right?" I asked him.

"Well, yes, but the tests are normal. Just try harder," he quipped.

In London I heard, "All of your ranges are normal. If you reduce your caloric intake and walk an hour a day, your body will settle down. Have you tried intermittent fasting?"

"Yes. I've tried everything. Do I look normal to you? My stomach and ass just keep getting bigger no matter what I do."

*Someone please send me a new definition of normal!* I shouted to myself.

In Manila, the White Coat tried a new approach. "I can't help you, Rebecca. Maybe you should try plastic surgery."

Their inability to see and hear me is the only explanation I have for all their failures. I was eating less and moving more. I became obsessed with everything that went on my plate and literally drank vegetables.

Meals were categorized into "good food" and "bad food," which was a whole other problem that I had to solve. It took me years to acknowledge that food had no morality. It was just food. A full year after the surgery, in February 2018, I ignored Dr. Sensible's advice about HRT and started taking hormones. I also started taking thyroxine and more supplements than my pill organizer could store.

None of it worked.

My body slowly evolved into an entity I no longer recognized. I officially became morbidly obese, treated like a subset of the human race. My shape became fodder for jokes. It didn't help that my ass continued to grow exponentially along with the rest of me. I'm talking about ass. Serious junk in the trunk. Sales clerks in clothing stores looked at me and walked away. I felt embarrassed asking for a seat belt extender on flights. Trapped in a body I did not identify with, it felt like I was living in a world that did not see me as a person.

Where does one turn in a time of crisis when flying from Africa to Asia for yet another film shoot? Social media, of course. Somewhere between Dubai and Manila, I came across a hysterectomy support group, and it created some sense of clarity and calm. My new "Hystersysters" confirmed that, yes, my weight gain, insomnia, depression, severe hot flashes, and brain fog were all normal.

The hystersysters offered a safe space to ask questions, share my story, and even offered some advice based on my own experiences. I was finally heard. When I told my hystersysters I didn't like the broken, childless, wombless, extra-large image in the mirror, hundreds of women understood and shared their empathy and camaraderie with me.

My body was the biggest version of myself I had ever known. I was unwell and unhappy.

The search for answers continued, and I learned to function on three or four hours of sleep per night. I never felt good, much less great, but my work schedule was incredibly demanding, and I didn't have any more time for working with Amelie. The work to integrate the fragments would wait a bit longer.

Eighteen months after the surgery, around September 2018, the fragmented chatter continued to mingle and swirl with Darkness in my mind. There was a non-stop barrage playing out, always with the same script.

*"Why did you have the surgery? You look horrible. You're fat. You're so stupid for signing that paper. Life is not worth living. You're pathetic."* The Fragments and Darkness ranted.

I did my best to ignore all of it as much as possible. Eventually, I think I just became comfortable being depressed, sad, and angry. I simply didn't have any more bandwidth, time, or money for my mind and body.

In February 2019, two years after the surgery, my body continued to defy nutritionists, private trainers, meditation, hormones, thyroid medication, diet plans, and endless, expensive tests. Accepting that the wholly uneducated and grossly negligent decision to remove my uterus was the most detrimental health decision of my life took a long time.

Medicine failed me.

I failed me.

Joy left me.

The traumatized fragments in my mind became stronger, like thick, tangled old-growth vines. They bound themselves tightly around me. Nourished by the single truth that my maternal grandpa was a pedophile and sexually assaulted me from the age of Five until the age of Thirteen, I sensed my foundation cracking.

I was at a breaking point. I had to revisit my childhood trauma to heal.

The need to talk about the years of sexual assault didn't frighten me. Rather, it almost annoyed me. I was in my late forties, and once again, I had to travel back into my own timeline to resolve my present day issues.

Trauma felt like a curse.

But where would I start? Unlike some sexual assault survivors, I didn't repress my memories. (I still don't know if that's a blessing or a curse.) So where in my history was the right moment to start another exploration of my trauma?

I gave myself time to consider the question, and a singular answer kept coming to me. The fragmented chatter really started, and largely consumed everyday life, just after graduating high school, when my days were no longer filled with the distractions of yearbook editing, sports, student government, and classes.

I wasn't going back to when the abuse started. I was going back to when the trauma first took hold of my daily life.

# Agency

*"You're not a victim for sharing your story. You are a survivor setting the world on fire with your truth. And you never know who needs your light, your warmth and raging courage."*

*(Alex Elle, Author of After the Rain)*

# Chapter 4

HIGH SCHOOL IS something most people survive. Self-doubt, bullying, body issues, shame, acne, break-ups, achievements, grades, college acceptances and denials, teasing, economic disparity, and other torments are all part of the journey. It's a miracle any of us come out of the experience intact and functioning.

"Rim", as it's called, is a typical blend of long hallways fitted with endless rows of lockers on either side, the occasional series of windows to gain a view of current weather conditions (snow, rain, sunshine, fog), and the everyday activities of high school students.

Every day, I was dropped off at school, played sports after the last bell rang, and then headed home to finish mounds of homework. I had the typical insecurities of most teenagers my age, except mine rode shotgun with my trauma. If I felt awkward about my clothes, trauma held tight to me and reminded me I was broken. Disgusting. Ugly. Every negative thought I had about myself was doubled.

I was suffering from what would now be diagnosed as complex PTSD (post-traumatic stress disorder) related depression, anxiety, suicidal thoughts, and undiagnosed D.I.D. (Dissociative Identity Disorder). I never felt like I could share my truth with anyone. I felt ashamed and afraid people would judge me if they knew that I was raped. It was 1988. Well before the breakthroughs and conversations around trauma and PTSD were well documented and part of everyday conversation.

The first fragment to grab my attention was angry. Over time, I tried to talk to Thirteen whenever she shouted at me or forced me to blend with her. I quickly learned that if I wanted Thirteen to settle down, I had to agree with her opinion or her demands. More importantly, I had to succumb to her energy in every situation where she felt slighted or threatened.

"*Tell her she's an idiot,*" she demanded for something as slight as a store not having an item I wanted to buy.

"You're an idiot. I'll never shop here again," I would say to the clerk.

When I demonstrated obedience, she went quiet for a short time. Thirteen demanded respect and attention. In exchange, she would never let us be hurt by anyone ever again. She, I, was a bully. We were pissed off most of the time. The more I let her lead my everyday life, the more her intensity took over. I went from resenting and fearing her to embracing her anger. It felt good.

Thirteen became useful.

I was thirteen when the sexual abuse ended. Whenever I visited my grandparents' house, Thirteen dressed in full body armor and assured me she was ready for battle. "*We will beat his fucking head into the ground and kill him if he tries to touch us,*" she declared. I had to admit that she was destructive and dangerous. But she was also the fearless protector and dedicated defender my body needed.

She was everything I believed I wasn't. Strong, smart, clever, and beautiful. Thirteen was a goddamn warrior. Tough as nails, she radiated "fuck you" energy during soccer games when I played goalie, kicking the ball at the back of a player's head. I felt her strength when I served a powerful ace while playing tennis. I used her vocabulary to bully my peers in school. I could be ruthless.

I got to where I didn't mind Thirteen's behavior, even when she embarrassed me.

"*That girl is a bitch,*" she hissed.

"*Who? I don't even know her. She's fine,*" I pushed back.

"*Look at her. She just thinks she's special because she's got nice clothes. Did you see her in class today? Everyone likes her. But she's not special,*" Thirteen argued.

"Yeah, you're right. She thinks she's really something. She's such a bitch."

"*Tell her she's a bitch. She has things that you want, and she doesn't deserve them.*"

"You're a bitch!" I shouted at the girl in the school hallway between classes. I was known for being tough and outspoken, and such outbursts were common.

I became an uncomfortably opinionated, abrasive voice, insisting I was right about everything in every conversation. Surrendering to Thirteen and channeling her intensity and foul mouth seemed like a small sacrifice to pay for the protection she offered.

When she went quiet and I felt like I needed a source of strength, I used to say, *Hey, Thirteen, I need you right now,* in my mind and she showed up immediately, fueled with a sense of fight. Helping me get through a class presentation or social situation where I felt insecure, she was a solution as much as a problem.

I earned a reputation for being brash and I was voted "Most Outspoken" in my senior year of high school. In retrospect, it was not a vote of distinction. Life was black or white without any shades of gray. Thirteen existed as a parasite feeding off me and she weakened my structure.

I realized I didn't need, or want, an inner warrior, but Thirteen didn't know how to relax. After all, gladiators are always prepared for the next battle. Our toxic symbiosis destroyed relationships at work and school. It simply wasn't fun to spend time with me when I was always ready for a fight. I had no soft curves—only edges.

Girls around me were put off by my abrasive nature and high school boys largely just couldn't be bothered to get close to me. Those that approached did manage to break through my tough exterior and unknowingly pierced my heart far too easily. Beneath the bravado lived a girl who really just wanted to be loved and feel safe.

I spent most of high school surviving off a combination of good friends, great teachers, sports, a part-time job, alcohol on weekends, occasional prescription medication I stole from my mom, and a pretty keen mind.

And then, my grandpa died.

It was a surprise to everyone. By the time I arrived at the hospital, he was slipping in and out of consciousness and his life was ending. I looked down at his semi-comatose body lying in the hospital bed and felt sadness, anger, and shock. In the early morning hours, after participating in an overnight family vigil at the hospital, the rapist died.

"Yes! The monster is dead! Yes! Let's celebrate!" Thirteen shouted.

"Shut up! I don't feel like celebrating," I replied.

"I'm really sad," Seven said with a quiver in her voice. "He taught us how to swim in the ocean and took us to Disneyland."

"What the hell? How can you possibly be sad?" Thirteen growled. "That thing in the coffin raped you. He never loved you. Monsters don't know how to love."

"She's allowed to be sad. Stop it. I don't know how to feel," I answered.

*"You're pathetic. Good riddance. I hope he's slowly roasted in hell."*

Thirteen rejoiced, but I wasn't able to celebrate with her. A few days later, I stood in front of his casket and cried hot tears as my anger boiled and hissed inside me. I was never going to get a chance to confront him. He would never answer for his crimes.

My senior year, like so many other years of my life, was stained yet again by him. There was a lot of debate in my head about whether or not I should feel anything for the dead man in the ground.

I drifted through most of the remaining senior year busy with college applications, exams, and yearbook editor duties. A year after graduating, I was ready to move beyond the boundaries of my parents' house and our small town. I was ready to leave. I wasn't the exception. Most of the kids I graduated with eventually moved away to pursue a new life "down the hill." But where would I go next?

I decided finding a full-time job was the first step. Once I had work, I would know where to live. Scanning the classified ads in the newspaper for a few weeks, I turned my well-honed, sixth grade typing skills and high school Mac classes into a salaried position at a large advertising agency.

"So, Rebecca, what can you tell me about marketing and advertising?" my potential new boss, Mike, asked.

"Not much. Honestly, I just know that advertising and marketing people make commercials for TV and billboards. But I'm not sure how it all comes together."

"That's true. It's also print and radio and a bunch of other things. You'll be working with the film and video producers who make TV and radio commercials," he explained.

"Wow, that sounds exciting. I'd love the job."

"It's exciting and a lot of hard work and long hours. I think you're a perfect fit. I'm excited to have you join us. You start Monday," Mike said as he stood up to lead me out of his office.

I left the interview excited. I had a new job but was completely in the dark about "commercial production." I had no idea what that meant. What do producers do? More importantly, I asked myself how I was going to find an apartment in two days and get moved in over the weekend. Thirteen kicked into overdrive and her anger transformed into tenacity.

I scanned the classifieds and found a room for rent in a cute, but small, two-bedroom apartment built over a garage. After speaking to my new roommate, Jeff, and taking a look at the place, I wrote a check for the deposit and first month's rent. Home was about two hours away from my parents' house. It was affordable, comfortable, close to the beach, and safe. A new foundation.

The excitement of it all wore off pretty quickly as I drove home dreading that I was going to have to tell my mom the news. She could be a bit complicated to navigate. I never knew which "version" of her I was going to get, especially when sharing unexpected news. It felt like my mom had a plan for everyone's life. If they veered off course, it was difficult for her to accept, more so with her children. I was supposed to go to junior college and graduate from a local university while living at home. That was her plan. I was about to toss it all out the window.

"So I have some news," I said nervously standing in her office.

"Yes, what's up?" she asked.

"I just accepted a job in Santa Ana. I'm moving to Huntington Beach this weekend," I announced. All of the air in the room left. "I'm working for an advertising agency and I start Monday," I added cheerfully. This was great news!

"Well, that's interesting," she said, forgetting to offer any note of congratulations while she navigated the detour from the plan in her mind.

"Yes, it's great! I'm really excited. Can I use the truck to move on Saturday and take my bed?" I asked, bracing for impact.

"Yeah, I guess so," she said softening, much to my relief. "I think I have some things in the donation pile that you can use. There's a comforter and some sheets," she offered.

Our conversation was short. There wasn't any excited chatter about my new job or the little apartment I was about to call home. I was disappointed and hurt. I drove home, pushed my feelings aside and started packing all my earthly possessions. Early Saturday morning, I moved myself to the beach.

When I finally got everything into my new bedroom, I made my bed and lay down to take a break. My entire body exhaled. *"I'm out,"* I said to myself.

Five, the fragment who held all of my fear, immediately worried.

*"What if that guy isn't nice? Is there a lock on the door?"* she asked.

*"Jeff? He's cool. I don't think he's going to bother us. But yes, there's a lock on the door."* I felt a little bad for her. I was so busy moving and getting ready for my new job that it never occurred to me that moving into a shared space with a strange man might be a problem.

Monday came far too quickly, but I still managed to get to the office at 8:15 a.m.—about forty-five minutes early. My boss, Mike, greeted me in the lobby before walking me back to our department. My desk, one of many in the open concept "cubicle farm," was sandwiched between two other women who worked with legal and finance.

About an hour into my first day, I felt completely out of place. I didn't have proper office clothes, and I was still sporting the high school blue eyeliner and blow-dried, feathered hairstyle that did not compare to the smart, crisp style of my coworkers. I reassured myself I'd find a way to buy some new clothes, and black eyeliner, once payday rolled around.

The first few weeks went by so quickly I felt like my feet never touched the ground. I answered multiple phone lines, organized information for all the producers, and learned as much as possible as quickly as possible.

I didn't have any space in my mind, much less time in my life, to entertain any of Thirteen's, Seven's, or Five's conversation. They were simply no match for the amount of information streaming into my learning center every day while I tried to absorb every detail in every conversation and document so that I could learn the ways of the marketing world.

Life at home was great. Jeff proved to be a kind, older brother type who was respectful and funny. I started summer school at the local junior college, and my schedule became full with competing commitments. I enrolled in the marketing and communications program, hoping to glean some information that might prove helpful at work.

I didn't have a lot of free time for the beach, sun, or fun. Between long work hours and night and weekend classes, my move to the ocean seemed silly because I rarely saw the water. No matter, I loved my job in commercial production. I grew to really admire the producers, who were kind enough to teach me the finer details of creating an advertising campaign.

About two months after I started my new career and life at the beach, I hoped all my hard work might make it possible for one of the producers to invite me to be on set during a film shoot.

"We have three different shoots coming up. I really want to go on set. Do you think I should ask one of the producers if I can join them for a day?" I asked my slightly older coworker, Carol.

"A secretary like you will never go to a shoot. I've been here for two years, and I have yet to get invited to a shoot," she replied.

That's all Thirteen needed to hear. I welcomed her chatter.

*"What's the point of working sixty hours a week if we're never going to get a chance to go on set? We work harder, longer, and ask questions every day. We say yes to every request," Thirteen stated factually.*

"Exactly. What was that little sneer when Carol said, 'a secretary like you?' What the fuck does that even mean?" I replied. "She sits at her desk all day balancing her checkbook, and we run up and down the stairs and hallways all day long."

*"Yeah. She's a piece of work," Thirteen clamored.*

"I'm going to get on set. I'm going to really show her what this secretary is about."

Four months later, and a grand total of six months after I started as a mere secretary, I was on set, and Carol was still sitting at her desk.

When Thirteen's focus was clearing my path to success, I didn't mind. She was an angry pain in the ass, but she had her moments. Determined and focused, Thirteen pushed me whenever someone in the office said, "No, it can't be done." We refused to listen and worked harder and smarter. Blending with Thirteen and "using" her as a tool to further my career felt good until I couldn't shut her off.

Despite the relief provided by the occasional Cadillac margarita happy hour with my cohorts, the hours and stress at work and school eventually started to wear me down. After twelve months working in advertising, I was twenty years old, tired, lonely, and sad, spending more time in my bedroom and less time out with my friends or my roommate Jeff. While Thirteen obsessed about my professional success, Seven found space to unload her sadness.

*"I'm lonely. Why are we always alone?" she asked late one night after I'd just gotten home from school.*

"I know we're lonely. But I'm tired and exhausted. I don't have time to figure out a boyfriend."

*"We don't have any friends. No one likes us," she mulled. "What are we going to do? This is really making me sad."*

"I don't know," I replied. Everyday life was a lot. Having to find a way through it all and explain every detail about my loneliness was too much.

As exhaustion set in, loneliness converted into isolation. Darkness, the evil creature I call depression, started recycling a familiar round of self-destructive thoughts through my mind. The same loathsome tone I knew briefly in high school felt somehow more serious. I wasn't going to be able to detach, ignore, or eat my way through it.

Increasingly depressed and sad, things began to slip at work and Thirteen engaged in fight mode. I became snippy and bitchy. Eventually, I was written up for speaking in a derogatory tone to a manager in another department and, overall, for having a poor attitude. I was projecting my pain. Thirteen and Seven's overlapping commentary tormented me.

"You're going to lose your job. You're so stupid," Thirteen screamed.

"You didn't do well on the exam. What if we fail?" Seven wailed.

"You're useless. You're getting fat, again. Why did you wear that? Why aren't you tan and skinny like the other beach girls?" Thirteen drilled.

"Life is just sad, and I want to cry all of the time," Seven lamented.

I was stuck between the two and their dialogue beat me down, leaving no room for joy. Darkness, always cunning and looking for an opportunity to destroy, offered the perfect solution. "You know, Thirteen and Seven will never be quiet. You should kill yourself. There isn't any noise if you're dead." At twenty years old, I felt like a punching bag hanging alone in a corner of the gym. Every day, Darkness held me in an icy death grip while the fragments beat the shit out of me with their chatter.

In August 1991, I woke up one Saturday morning and looked at the clock. It was 12 p.m. and a beautiful day, and I was in bed thinking about killing myself. Was a life of exhaustion and mental torment all that I deserved? A few hours later, I told myself No.

In my very pragmatic tone, I talked myself into going to therapy. *Everyone who is abused ends up in therapy, right? I'm supposed to go. That's what people like me do.* Ever the researcher, I went to the library to study the various "schools of psychotherapy." I decided I wanted to find a Jungian therapist who could help me dive into my mind and look at my real self—not the self I showed to the outside world.

Next, I searched through the health insurance approved therapist list and chose Dr. D. That was the easy part. The more complicated part was convincing myself therapy was going to be safe. I didn't know what to expect during a session beyond the comical examples on television where patients lay down on a couch and talked as a therapist took notes.

When I walked into Dr. D's office for our first appointment, I saw a leather couch straight out of a television show. The rest of the room was decorated in muted brown tones and antique furniture, and the windows offered a pretty view of the garden. It was a quiet, inviting space, making me feel comfortable.

"Am I supposed to lie down?" I asked, staring at the couch as I stood in the doorway.

"Nah. Why don't you try the recliner? It's the most comfortable," he replied, much to my relief. The couch, and the idea of lying down in a room with a strange man, made me nervous.

I sat in the recliner, happy it was the furthest away from where he sat. I needed distance. My mind raced with all sorts of questions. *Was he going to somehow read my mind? Did he already know my deepest, darkest, traumatized secrets? Was he going to make me talk about all the things that embarrassed me or made my skin crawl? Was he going to tell me I was crazy?*

Dr. D sat down in a high-backed, leather chair and settled in before asking, "So why are you here?"

I didn't know what to say. *Where do I begin,* I asked myself silently as I stared at Dr. D. *Do I mention the fragments? No. He'll think I'm totally insane. What about Mom and Dad? No. Then what? What in the hell do I want to say to this guy?*

My heart raced and Dr. D sat patiently for what felt like an hour but was likely closer to about fifteen seconds of silence.

*Start at the beginning. Tell him your story from the beginning, I said to myself.*

I took a deep breath and fifteen years of self-imposed silence began to crumble. The untapped longing to tell my truth broke free. Pragmatism (and let's be honest, a bit of detachment so that I could "survive" the moment) joined me, and I looked at him and said, "I was sexually abused as a child by my grandpa," and then broke into tears.

Dr. D let me cry, and he remained quiet for some time. In our shared silence, a safe space was created, allowing me to release the first tears I ever shed about the abuse. All my fear, pain, hate, anger, confusion, and sadness—every single emotion I had stored since the first sexual assault at the age of five—literally poured out of me. My body shook as waves of pent up trauma released. Eventually, I stopped crying and calmed down enough to catch my breath.

"I'm sorry." He said. "You've obviously been through a lot. It seems like you've been hanging onto that for a long time. I need to ask, which grandfather is it? Is he alive or dead?"

"My mother's dad. He's dead. He died during my senior year of high school."

"Thank you. If he were still alive, we would need to discuss calling the police. Why don't I explain the process to you today, and we will leave it there for now?" he asked softly. His voice was gentle and helped me settle down.

"Okay," I responded gratefully. I couldn't say anything else for the rest of the session. His comment about the police stayed with me. It was the first time I even considered my grandfather a criminal. He raped me, but I never thought about it as a crime. He was my grandpa.

*"It's a shame he's dead. He'd have been in handcuffs tonight if he was still around,"* Thirteen snarled as I drove to the office after the session.

"It's not that simple. I can't even imagine that happening," I replied. "No one in the family would ever let that happen to him. He was too important to ever get into any trouble."

My therapy journey officially began, and twice a week, every week, I went to Dr. D's office at 8 a.m. and we talked about my trauma and life in general for about an hour. I built a relationship with Dr. D but remained cautious and strategic about my moves and what I would discuss. It all felt like a chess match.

After three months of working together, we built a rapport, but I found it difficult to let my guard down. I feared discussing the fragments because I felt sure he would tell me I was officially insane. Besides, there was plenty to discuss apart from the fragments like PTSD, my compulsive behaviors, triggers, and depression.

In early sessions, I never started a conversation crying, but I usually left with my makeup in a mess. Eventually, I didn't put any make-up on until I left our appointment and got to the office. Each conversation with Dr. D always started in the same way. I walked into his office, sat down in the familiar leather recliner, pushed the footrest out, and got comfortable.

"So how are you doing?" he always asked as he sat down in his chair and prepared to take notes.

"I'm actually pretty good today," I used to say regularly, hoping I could avoid shedding any tears. I got really tired of crying, but my body and mind needed the release.

Dr. D could always sense when I wasn't being entirely forthcoming or truthful. His notebook fed him prompts based on the last session, and he deftly lobbed questions at me like, "Last week, you were talking about how you were feeling detached from your family. You were feeling lonely. How's that going?"

Boom! No escape.

"I'm still lonely. I mean, there's no one in my life right now to help me." More tears. More Kleenex. "I cry every time I see you. I'm tired of it."

"I understand, but it's necessary. You have a lot of sadness, Rebecca, and it's important that it comes out. Denying it won't make it go away," he explained.

He was right, of course, but I still felt drained by the endless tears. I became a big, raw nerve and everything felt like an intentional slight. About six months after we started our work together, I walked into Dr. D's office, sat down, put my feet up, and said, "My mom and sister went shopping this weekend, and they didn't invite me," and cried.

I knew that my mom and sister had every right to go shopping without me but it didn't matter when all I heard was Thirteen's anger. *"They don't like you,"* Thirteen *liked to say to me. "They don't invite you because they don't love you. You're broken. Who wants something like you around?"*

After discussing the abuse for several more months and exploring my family relationships, I trusted Dr. D and decided it was time to reveal the fragments to him. If he decided I was crazy, I felt ready for whatever was next.

"Good morning. How are ya'?" Dr. D asked.

"I'm good. Today I want to tell you about the voices in my head," I lobbed back at him.

"Okay. Tell me about them," he said calmly. I wondered if he was surprised or expected this next phase of healing.

I explained Thirteen, Seven, and Five all named according to their ages. I told Dr. D that I blended with them and even felt bullied at times.

"Who is the most dominant?" he asked.

"Thirteen is the primary noisemaker. She's nasty but also useful. That one is complicated."

"Well, you can start to tell her to hush up whenever she starts talking," he advised.

"Yeah, I'll work on that," I said. I knew it wasn't going to be that simple.

I left his office that day feeling lighter, having revealed one of my biggest secrets. He didn't judge me or tell me I was crazy, and it was a relief. The fragments were less pleased.

*"You think you can really hush me up?"* Thirteen snarled.

*"I'm going to try. Yes."*

*"Well, good luck with that,"* she barked.

*"And what about me? You want me to stop?"* Seven asked.

*"I need you all to relax. Be less angry, sad, and fearful. Life isn't as miserable as you all want to make it. I'd like to feel happy and not hear from you."*

*"Well, I'm just sharing my feelings. I don't think that you're being very nice to me,"* Five added. *"He didn't tell us we were crazy today, but what if he called the police after you left? What if he told someone you were crazy?"* she whispered.

*"I'm not crazy. He didn't call anyone. There's nothing to fear,"* I pushed back.

My victories in Dr. D's office felt short-lived at times because I always ended up in a conversation with Thirteen, Seven, and Five, who second-guessed everything.

Therapy felt a lot like playing tennis, a sport I played in high school, junior college, and still enjoy. Dr. D hit a decent serve over the net with questions or a prompt, and I hit back with an explanation, digging deeper into a particular part of my life. Once in a while, I didn't hit back. I did my best to let the ball pass me by, telling half of the story or ignoring the question entirely.

That never worked.

Dr. D, a self-described "bull in a china shop," always knew when I tried to stand still on the baseline and inevitably smacked a return right at my forehead.

After eight months of twice-weekly matches (I mean sessions), the tears flowed less frequently, and I felt safe and heard. Dr. D validated my story and my feelings.

"It's time for me to tell my family," I announced one morning as I plopped down into the recliner. I was feeling particularly bold.

"I think you're right. Who do you want to tell?" Dr. D asked as he stopped writing in his notebook. My announcement certainly got his attention.

"My mom, dad, brother, and sister. And then my aunties and maternal grandmother. I'll tell my mom and then my dad." It felt good to map out the process with someone I trusted.

"When do you want to start?" he asked.

"I can tell my mom this weekend at our annual cousin campout. It's maybe not the ideal time or place, but I think that if I don't tell her soon, I might lose my nerve. I'll probably just call my dad after I talk to my mom."

"What about your brother and sister?" he asked intently, making sure I covered all the bases.

"I'll call them after I speak with my parents." Saying the plans out loud made it much more real, and I felt my heart rate pick up.

"I want to make sure that you have a support system. When you share a story like this with your family, you might be ignored or called a liar. Or worse," he explained thoughtfully. "I want you to be cautiously optimistic about what might happen."

"I was a child," I replied, surprised that I felt like I had to defend myself. Would they really gang up on me and deny my truth?

"I know. It's your story, Rebecca. But people can turn quickly. They'll say pretty horrible things when they feel like their own reality is somehow threatened."

"What do you think will happen?" I asked, suddenly feeling very small in the chair. I felt Five's fear rising in me.

"Your mom and dad will probably be in shock and feel a lot of guilt. Your siblings will probably be supportive. The rest of your family is unpredictable."

"Yeah. That sounds about right. I mean, I get that my parents might feel guilty, but how could they have known? It's not like they knew and ignored it. It's strange to think about. I was so confident when I first came in, but now I doubt myself," I replied.

"You've done nothing wrong. Remember that you're a courageous survivor. You have every right to tell your story," Dr. D encouraged me.

"It might just set the whole thing on fire, right?" I asked.

"Yes. Remember, family dynamics are always complicated and unpredictable."

*Author's Note: Not everyone has a therapist to help them plan how they will reveal their truth to their family and close friends. The decision to tell or not tell should be made free of any interference or coercion. My only piece of advice for anyone who is considering telling their story is to make sure you have someone in your corner who believes you, trusts you, and will support you no matter what happens. That person, who is your advocate, can live next door, in another state, or another country.*

## Chapter 5

THE ANNUAL COUSIN campout was a lively event held each year in the Southern California mountains. Strictly invite only for all first, second, and third cousins on my mother's side, we were a raucous group who enjoyed good food, conversation, and fierce volleyball battles.

A family largely born out of a generation of people who moved from Oklahoma and Arkansas, the elders packed fruit throughout California and worked other blue-collar jobs to support their families. Anyone coming into our circle would likely never suspect that at least one childhood sexual assault survivor lived among us. And certainly, whatever generational trauma was passed between us was something hardly ever mentioned, much less openly discussed.

"Hardships" became lessons about perseverance and rarely, if ever, about healing.

Armed with a brand new sense of self, burgeoning definition of right and wrong, and the knowledge I was no longer going to deny my truth, I drove up Hwy 38 to the local campground, not quite knowing if that particular weekend would somehow feel different for me. Was I going to enjoy hearing the same stories about the same people? Was the "hero worship" used to describe my maternal grandfather going to pass by me or disgust me?

I wondered how I would continue to fit into the family if they chose to continue to be part of a lie.

When I arrived at the campground, I was genuinely happy to see my cousins, siblings, mom, and stepdad. All my favorite homemade foods were ready. The campfire was lit and cocktails were flowing. Almost immediately, the fragments chimed in.

*"They're getting drunk, again,"* Five whispered.

*"Yes, but they always get drunk at these things,"* Thirteen jabbed.

*"We're not safe when they get drunk. Remember?"* Seven reminded us all.

*"That's true. They got drunk, didn't pay attention, and we got hurt. But we won't get hurt now,"* I reminded them.

*"Damn right we won't,"* Thirteen added while she put on her armor.

*"We don't trust them!"* they all shouted.

I heard their words and, for the first time, acknowledged I didn't completely trust any of the adults. It didn't matter that none of them had no connection to my sexual abuse. The alcohol on their breath triggered every cell in my body.

Alcohol + adults = sexual assault.

It was a simple equation my body had worked out, and I had finally begun to understand.

I chose to compartmentalize, or dissociate, so that I could try to enjoy the campout. I mentally locked away the fragments for forty-eight hours and repeated some simple information to myself.

*They're drunk. I'm an adult. It's fine. I'm fine.*

That became my inner dialogue, but I found myself sitting on the perimeter of the adults, watching them take yet another drink. It was probably one of the first times I actually paid attention to what my mind and body felt like around family. I felt unsafe. The cues I ignored for years were now fresh in my mind and I felt the need to be hyper-alert.

On Sunday, the group was busy enjoying a final meal around the campfire before we all packed up and headed home. After holding back my story for so many years, it was time to tell my truth. The fragments remained silent. Perhaps they knew I had to stay focused and wholly in the present to be able to speak with my mom.

"Hey, Mom, let's go for a walk," I said.

"Sure," she replied, and we took off down a path toward a vista point. Sitting down under a large tree overlooking the valley, it was time to talk.

"So I wanted you to know that I've started going to therapy," I said.

"Well, I think that's a good thing." Her response struck me as odd. Did she have a concern for my mental health she never shared?

"The reason that I'm in therapy is because Grandpa abused me when I was young," I blurted out, and then immediately started crying.

A glazed look came over her face. She was motionless. We sat next to each other in silence until she eventually wrapped her arms around me as I continued to cry.

"He got others too," she finally replied.

My body and mind recoiled. A powerful sense of betrayal sparked within me. At that moment, the mother I knew no longer existed and the fundamental bonds between a mother and her daughter broke irreparably.

I looked at her through a new, sharper lens and felt nothing. Empty. My tears dried up.

*"He got others too? What the hell does that even mean? Who are the others? Where are they? How does she know?"* the fragments shouted over each other breaking their weekend silence.

I processed her words and moved away from her embrace. I wanted distance. No. I needed distance.

My mother knew he was a pedophile, and she didn't protect me. Was that right? The revelation was absolutely not part of the plan I discussed with Dr. D.

The devastating betrayal I felt after speaking with my mother erased every ounce of nuance I had reserved for the conversation. We walked back to the campfire to join the others. I felt numb. I was watching the family pack up and prepare to leave completely outside of myself. I didn't know how to absorb my mother's reaction. I drove home and got ready to see Dr. D on Monday morning.

"So how did it go?" he asked a bit hesitantly. Perhaps Dr. D understood more about my family than me. Perhaps he knew it was going to be a disaster.

"My mom told me she knew about him - said she knew that he 'got others.' I don't even know what the fuck to do with that information. I mean, I literally have no way to process it or understand it."

"I don't know what to say," Dr. D offered. "Did you get a chance to get more details? Did she ask about your healing? Offer an apology?" he asked.

"No. All I got was an admission of guilt. She knew he assaulted others and did nothing to prevent it from happening to me. No questions about my therapy or how I was doing. It was a fucking nightmare. I'm not going to speak to her. I can't. I honestly don't know what I'm supposed to think about her now," I blurted out. My anger and sadness were coming out of me in equal measure.

"It's understandable. Do you want to hold off telling the others?" he asked.

"No. I need it to be over. This all needs to end," I replied as we completed the session. The next day, I had lunch with my sister in her office.

"I need to talk to you. I'm in therapy now because Grandpa abused me. I told mom, and she said she knew he did it to others. I don't really know what to do." I started crying. Always crying. The weight of my story, and the revelation my grandpa assaulted others, made me feel like my world suddenly closed in on me. I wasn't sure if I could bear any more of the truth.

My sister, my "other mother," who took care of me during my parents' bitter divorce when I was seven years old and for years after, walked over to me and put her arms around me.

"I'm so sorry. You should come live with me for a while," she said.

"I don't want to be in the way."

"You're not in the way. Don't you want to come and stay with me? Somewhere you're safe?" she asked.

The fact she didn't chase me out of the room or call me a liar was an enormous relief. I felt like I had my first advocate. And yes, I did want to be near my sister and feel safe. We decided that I would move into her house a few weeks later.

I called my older brother later that day and told him my story. He didn't ask me for details or call me a liar. He didn't question any part of my truth. I had another advocate. He was worried about me and told me he loved me. My big brother is one of the strongest people I've ever known and one of the most kind and loving. His absurdly dry sense of humor might not reveal the enormity of his heart to those who aren't paying attention.

Just a few days after the cousin campout and speaking to my siblings, I wrote to my dad. My mother's revelation hung over me and telling my siblings drained all my energy. I couldn't speak my truth any longer. I didn't feel brave enough to talk to my dad on the phone. The idea that he might also drop a truth bomb on me, like my mom, was too much to contemplate. It would have been too much to process.

The fragments clamored in my mind. Thirteen's fury rose and she controlled the conversation.

*"What in the fuck did she mean? 'He got others too?'"* she barked.

"I don't know," I said still in shock.

*"She knew. She knew and she didn't keep us safe,"* Thirteen added.

"Yes," I replied somberly.

"What are you going to do about it?" Thirteen asked.

"I don't know. I have so many questions, but I can't imagine speaking to her again. I don't want to speak at all."

"Well you can't just leave it like this—someone owes us an explanation. An apology. A reckoning," Thirteen added. Seven and Five agreed.

"Yeah. Okay. I'll write letters to my grandma, aunties, mom, and dad. I have questions for all of them."

I let Thirteen take control and completely forgot I could call Dr. D for guidance. Thirteen and I wrote letters to my mom, dad, grandma, and aunts, exposing the great big ugly secret kept in our family for far too long. I asked a lot of questions and expressed concern for my younger cousins, who spent considerable time with my grandpa before he died.

Anger flowed through the pen onto paper, and I specifically confronted my grandmother and her role in the abuse. Each note ended with strict instructions to all not to call or speak to me. They all received their notes while I stayed at my friend's house for a few days. No one knew where I was, and no one could reach me. When I got back home to my sister's house Sunday night, I had no idea she'd spent most of the weekend answering calls from some enraged family members.

"Everyone called me," my sister explained as we sat down in the kitchen.

"What are they saying?" I asked. "Why did they call you?" I couldn't figure out why they would speak to her instead of just following my instructions. I also didn't understand why my sister felt like she owed them an opportunity to speak.

"They couldn't reach you, so they called me," she said. "They're all just a little angry. Upset."

"Okay, well, I didn't do anything wrong," I said, getting defensive. *My fucking family. They're angry with me because I dared to stand in my truth and say I was abused,"* I said to myself.

"I know. Mom is upset that she didn't know you were going to send letters. Now everyone knows that she knew about Grandpa and that he did it to others."

"Right. So Mom's upset that the big secret is out. She's not upset that I was sexually assaulted." I think it was the first time I realized I wasn't going to be the priority in my own story. My own mother couldn't figure out how to rally around me. Instead, she joined the other members of her family and immediately focused on protecting the dead monster whose legacy hung powerfully over all of them.

Nothing, not even sexual abuse, would break their devotion to my grandpa.

The disappointment I felt would only continue to grow over the years as my trauma, and healing, would remain subordinate to everyone else's feelings.

"Did you hear from Dad?" I asked.

"Yes. He's obviously upset but more sad than anything else. He didn't know. He knows you don't want to speak to him right now," she said.

I lay in bed later that night getting more pissed off.

Six days had passed between the conversation with my mom up in the mountains and the letters being mailed. Six days. My mom had almost a week to call me, express her concerns, explain herself, and offer an apology.

Instead, I never heard from her.

Her inability to connect with me and parent me through my crisis made the fresh wedge between us wider and deeper.

I no longer subscribed to the family's deep attachment to denial and the nauseating lies they circulated about my grandfather. The family constructs that guided me my entire life broke forever. I was out. I cut off all ties with my grandma and my eldest aunt.

I stood alone in my decision.

My siblings and mother remained part of the family and stayed in touch with my relatives. I still don't quite understand how they didn't immediately know they were supposed to be on my side.

I was abused. I was the victim.

And yet, the uproar over the letters quickly faded and my mothers, siblings, aunties, and grandma all maintained their relationships as if nothing happened. It made me feel like I didn't exist. And in all of that, they made me feel as if they thought I was a liar. Why was it so complicated to choose between me and my abuser? How do you choose to ignore a child's pain and continue to socialize with, say, a child's rapist or a rapist's enabler? I felt my truth alone should have been enough to get their total support. The choice should have been clear—and easy. But it wasn't. Their duplicity shattered me.

A week after the letter drama unfolded, my mind abruptly switched off, and I slid into a total mental breakdown. Normal thought processes, like remembering how to get back home from work, became impossible. It was as if my mind connected to a dimmer switch, and slowly turned all the way off.

I managed to keep essential functions, like breathing, online but nothing more. By the time I realized I was in trouble, I couldn't remember my sister's address or my full name. I called Dr. D's office, and they immediately referred me to a psychiatrist.

I had finally turned the master key and opened every locked room that stored all the memories, emotions—everything. My mind was filled to capacity and simply stopped. A psychiatrist quickly determined I needed time off from work, and medication.

The next two weeks were filled with a lot of sleep, television, and silence. The fragments wanted me to continue the conversation with my family, but I was entirely shut down. Feeling as though I was trapped in a game of tug-of-war between myself and my trauma, I had no ability to attach to either side for several days. Slowly, after two weeks of rest, medication, and therapy with Dr. D, I returned to work and my boss, Mike, greeted me.

"I thought I heard your voice, welcome back!" he said while giving me a heartfelt hug. His friendly embrace didn't feel strange and wasn't out of place at the time. Rather, his wide smile and bear hug soothed me. I needed a hug. I needed kindness. The rest of the team greeted me and it felt good to get back into a normal rhythm once again.

A few weeks after my return to work, I came home to my sister's house to find letters from my mom, grandma, and older aunt. The smart move would have been to take them to my next appointment with Dr. D. Unfortunately, I was still learning how to take care of myself and practicing patience was new. I rashly opened the letters without any consideration, or plan, about how to process what they would say.

There's no one quite as hurtful or disappointing as family members, and that was never more true than when I read their words. My eldest aunt shared a hateful, venomous note blaming me for my grandma's "near stroke" and the abuse. She wrote that I was "a liar," suggesting that "if it was true, I asked for it and wanted the attention."

My maternal grandma simply denied my entire story, which was ridiculous and disgusting. She was witness to his constant ass pinching, crotch grabbing, and our long hours spent away from others. She instigated, and was a party to, his vulgar behavior, never once telling him to stop. Her words didn't surprise me. Denial was the family's preferred salve for most things, and she was a liar. She had everyone fooled.

My mom's letter wasn't healing or helpful. The most striking passage said, "I took your letter to a psychologist. I was worried about you. He said that you would be just fine."

I wondered what in the hell she meant by "just fine." I also knew it was probably bullshit. My mother tried to find words to express that she cared about me but fell well short as her letter did not include a heartfelt, passionate apology or a plea for forgiveness. She didn't tell me she broke from the family and was on my side. Her final insult was justifying my aunt's hateful letter stating that she "deserved to have her say as well."

"So she knew that Auntie was going to write that horrible letter and didn't stop it!" Thirteen barbed.

"Yes. It's just more betrayal, hurt, disappointment. She could have easily called my sister and told her to not give me the letters. I would have never known."

"It's bullshit. Fuck her. Fuck all of them," Thirteen shouted, and I agreed.

"She knows my story is true. She said she knew there were others. But she wasn't willing to fight and protect me. I'm done," I told myself.

My mom and I didn't speak for several weeks and I spent Thanksgiving away from the annual family gathering. Just before Christmas, I finally felt clear enough and summoned the courage to call her from my sister's house.

"Hi, Mom," I said.

"Hello, Rebecca," she replied.

"I think it's time that we talk," I said.

"Yes, I'd say so."

The tone of her voice was the same one she used when I was young and in serious trouble. If either of my parents ever used that tone and said, "Rebecca Elizabeth Chandler, get over here," I seriously considered bolting into the woods. I was in deep shit.

When my mom addressed me as Rebecca in that tone, it was a power play to put me in my place and fill me with fear. And it worked for about a minute. Thankfully, though, Dr. D had prepared me for just such a scenario and told me to write down some notes to help me stay focused.

I regrouped, stopped blending with Five's fear, and closed my eyes to remind myself I was an adult. I held my ground even though my body shook. Still, I didn't manage to ask her all the questions on my list.

Who else did he abuse?
When?
Where?
How many know?
Why did you let us spend time at their house so often?
Why did you let them send me their horrible letters?

Instead, the conversation was disjointed. She spent her time telling me it was time to get over things and how the letters I wrote made her feel.

I felt spoken at, as if I did something wrong. The call didn't last long because my confidence waned. Seven, my sadness, took over, and I started crying. After all my therapy and preparation, I ached to hear a simple apology from my mother and her unwavering pledge to defend me. My sister took the phone away from me, shouted at my mom, and ended the call. She was always much stronger than me. I have always envied her clarity and strength.

My dad and I exchanged letters and cards. In typical Chandler fashion, we used sarcasm and funny notes to connect. When Christmas approached, I picked up my dad's mom, Granny Chandler, from her home, and we drove to his house. When we got out of the car, my dad walked straight past his mother and took hold of me.

Hugging me tightly, I collapsed into his arms crying. I knew he was sad. Unfortunately, much like my mother, my dad never really wanted to spend any time talking about the abuse or my feelings. He never asked any questions, and he never apologized for not protecting me.

Accountability was critical for my recovery, but it proved impossible for my parents to acknowledge their failures and my abuse. Thirteen, Seven, and even Five noticed the absence of apologies and shouted at my parents, in my head, for months.

Seven believed that if my dad had just stayed instead of divorcing my mom, he would have protected me. Thirteen channeled pure indignation and resentment toward my parents in equal measure, and it was impossible to ignore. Dr. D's counsel was the only reason I didn't slip sideways, once again, after the New Year.

I continued to see Dr. D and explored and processed my feelings about the letters, the betrayals, the lack of apologies, the absence of accountability, and the actual trauma. I began to find a tenuous balance. A heavy, toxic load lifted from my shoulders, and life started to feel positive.

Shoring up the foundation, I felt stronger, and I decided to move to my cousin Sonja's house to be closer to work and school. Her generosity gave me another safe space to continue to heal. Sonja's love and patience, and the antics of her cheeky son who was four years old, played a big part in my ongoing recovery. I felt like I was living a more fully conscious life, and the fragments became a dull nuisance.

I took an inventory of my life. I courageously survived years of sexual assault. I found the strength to put myself into therapy and tell my truth. I kept my job and graduated from school.

Courage doesn't come before the pain. Rather, courage comes when we choose to survive. I was courageous but I grew tired of surviving. I wanted to live.

## Chapter 6

One of the most challenging parts about living life in spite of (complex) PTSD is, in fact, finding a way to have a life. I needed more than therapy and fragmented chatter. After putting my love-life on hold after high school, I decided to re-engage with men.

I spoke with Dr. D about my desire to start dating again and what sex had meant to me in the past. I explained that the physical act of having sex was easy for me. Sex felt good even if it was somewhat mechanical. Having sex was a way for me to reclaim the sexual part of myself I felt I lost when I was assaulted. Intimacy, on the other hand, was much more complicated and sat apart from sex.

"I'd like to pick up where we left off last week and talk to you about intimacy," Dr. D lobbed during an early-morning session. "How do you feel about it?"

"What do you mean?" I asked.

"I mean, have you ever known or allowed yourself to feel intimate with someone? A true, deep connection with a man beyond just having sex?"

"Not really. Not yet. If I tried to fold feelings into sex, I couldn't enjoy it. When I was being assaulted, I had to focus-not be emotional. I avoided my feelings. I used to count while I was being raped. Counting helped me detach and leave my body."

"And did you keep counting and detach when you started having sex later in life?"

"No. I didn't need to detach. I liked having sex but never expected intimacy. I suppose that sounds strange," I replied as my throat clenched. I fought an urge to cry. I wasn't sure I could explain my feelings about sex to someone who had never been raped.

"Why do you think it sounds strange?" Dr. D asked, looking up from his notes.

"Because a rape survivor isn't supposed to enjoy sex, right? I'm supposed to fear it. Dread it. Hate it. That's what people assume. Women like me are supposed to curl up and die and never want to be touched again. I hear it all the time. So I get upset when I talk about it because I like sex and I don't want to be judged for saying that. Consensual sex makes me feel alive. I don't ever feel like I'm a wounded person having sex. It's just me, Rebecca, having fun."

"Well. I'm not going to judge you for liking sex. And it's not that unusual for a rape survivor to enjoy it. But I also understand that you have to deal with people's ignorance about rape and sex in your daily life. That's something we should talk about some time. We shouldn't overlook how complicated it is for you to talk with people about your experience," Dr. D offered.

"Yeah. It's beyond complicated," I added.

"So, you can 'enjoy' sex, which is really good. That's a big deal. I think it would be great if we worked on how to establish intimacy with someone you're having sex with—to bond. It requires a lot of trust, and that's something you need to build," he explained.

We spent time talking about sex, my body, and designing an approach to intimacy that left me feeling safe. I had to reprogram my body to trust closeness. I had to de-condition my body's immediate response to touch and learn how to receive touch, sound, and arousal positively. It took a lot of solo sex (masturbation) to learn how to enjoy touch, stay present, and identify what I actually wanted from a partner.

After a few months of working through all the layers of my sexuality, I felt like it was time to put my efforts to the test. I sat in the laundromat one bright Saturday morning feeling particularly good, and I met Surfer Dude.

Amid the constant hum of washing machines, the purr of the dryers, and the total meltdown of a woman's two-year-old who clearly needed a nap, we struck up a conversation.

It was almost romantic.

"So what's your name?" he asked as we both folded our laundry. He was about six feet tall, tan with blonde curls, and had an amazing smile that gave me the tingles.

"Rebecca."

"I'm Surfer Dude. Have you lived in Huntington for very long?"

"A couple of years or so. I live just around the corner. What about you?"

"I've lived here my entire life. What do you like to do? Do you surf?" he asked enthusiastically. It felt good to think I even looked like I might be a surfer girl.

"Not really. I grew up in the mountains, so surfing wasn't a thing. I love the ocean, though. Love to swim and boogie board."

"Cool. Maybe we could go out sometime? Write your number down, and I'll give you a call."

I definitely felt some more tingles! I hadn't been properly asked out on a date since my junior year in high school. I drove home thinking I could be a surfer girl. It didn't matter that I had never surfed a day in my life. My happy, pretty, tanned, hard-working self was ready to enjoy life.

Surfer Dude called me later that night.

"So what's your schedule like?" he asked.

"It's crazy. I work insane hours and I have night school. This weekend, I'm going to my sister's wedding. You should come. It's about an hour away. The reception will go all night, so I have a hotel room. You can stay with me if you like."

"Sounds cool," he added, unfazed by my direct approach.

I may have learned how to connect intimacy to sex, but I was in the early stages of that journey. I hadn't yet learned how to set boundaries, and that explains how I went from meeting Surfer Dude in a laundromat to inviting him to a wedding and a night in a hotel room. Setting healthy boundaries was clearly still in the works.

Truth be told, I wanted an excuse to leave the wedding, and Surfer Dude was a great excuse. The wedding was complicated for me. I was thrilled to see my sister get married to a truly wonderful man, and I was also incredibly pissed off with my parents. Pushing all my disappointment about their response to the assault aside, there was something else that angered me. Just a few years after I was told they couldn't afford to send me $150 a month to help me get through university, I was attending a party worth a year's full tuition.

Surfer Dude met me at the wedding reception. As soon as my maid of honor obligations were completed, we danced and drank along with a swarm of family and friends. When people started to get sloppy drunk, it was my cue to leave. Back in the hotel room, things heated up quickly. The lessons around intimacy were completely forgotten and the fragments were silent.

"Whoa. If we do this any longer, I'm going to want to have sex with you," he said as we made out in bed.

"Well, I'm not going to stop, so I guess we're having sex," I said. Taking control of the situation made me feel powerful and safe. Intimacy was nowhere near that hotel room. It was a setback in my therapy. I had yet to learn I could be with a man without immediately offering my body as some sort of barter. In my mind, that's all I could offer. When it came to men, sex was my only identity.

"So how did it go with Surfer Dude at the wedding?" Dr. D asked.

"It was fine. We danced and had a good time."

"Did you have sex?"

"No," I lied. "But I think he's a really nice guy, and we'll probably end up dating."

Lying in therapy wasn't something I did regularly, but it seemed necessary at times. Part of me felt ashamed I dragged sex into a new relationship before I even thought about what it meant. I felt like I had failed some sort of test, and I didn't want to let Dr. D down.

Eventually, I did speak to Dr. D about "taking charge" during sex, but admittedly, I never told him the truth about the first time I had sex with Surfer Dude.

"So why do you think that you go on the offensive so quickly?"

"It's about control. It's also about self-worth. I need control to feel safe and then I'm just there making sure I do things to make him happy. I never expect to actually get what I need, much less orgasm. I think intimacy is just going to be a challenge for me for a while."

"Do you think it's a good idea to have sex when you don't have the proper boundaries in place for intimacy?"

"I think, for now, it's fine. I can't fix everything all at once. I have to live a little." I answered him in such a way as to suggest I was done with the conversation. Therapy was great, but I had my limits.

Unfortunately, the shine wore off our romance after three months. We were entirely different people. Surfer Dude's idea of a good time was to surf, talk about surfing, watch surfing videos, make plans to surf, and get stoned. His overall lack of passion for anything other than, you guessed it, surfing and getting high stopped being cute or interesting.

Pot smoking was my biggest pet peeve. I grew up with people constantly smoking pot in front of me as a kid. I hated it. When adults got high, I became prey. My body will never forget the many sexual assaults I endured when the adults were busy getting stoned.

Near the end of our lopsided relationship, Surfer Dude did make a solid attempt to bring a bit of balance between us. After telling him I didn't want to talk about surfing, he invited me to go for a romantic walk to the beach where we sat and watched the sunset. It was a lovely, simple moment. It was sweet.

And then he said, "Can I talk about the surf yet?"

"Sure," I replied.

He really did try, and he didn't need to be punished for being excited about surfing. I knew our time at the beach that night was going to be our last as he shouted, "Look at that left!"

Newly single, I began to delve into more traumatic memories with Dr. D.

"How did you feel when you were being assaulted?"

"It depended on what was happening. If he was just grabbing at me, it was over in a second, and I went back to whatever I was doing. If he was pushing me against a wall and shoving his tongue into my mouth and groping my body, my mind went quiet."

"You detached."

"Yes. And when I was being raped, I completely disappeared. I stood outside of myself and watched what was happening."

"And what was actually happening during the abuse?" Dr. D asked.

"I can't tell you," I said. "I can't say the words." I looked at him from my perch on the recliner and my heart raced. Part of me wanted to leap off the chair and run out of the office.

"What scares you about telling me?" he asked in his most gentle tone of voice.

"If I say the details out loud, the memories become even more vivid. I'll blend with the past and feel the details all over again. It's much easier for me to talk about feeling 'dirty' and 'broken' or 'abused' than actually talk about the particulars of the assaults."

"That's understandable but I want to challenge you a little bit today. I want you to consider that the details matter. Being able to remember and not be triggered is the goal," Dr. D said.

I took a few deep breaths.

"I can tell you about one assault that happened when I was Seven."

"Okay. Take your time. Tell me as much as you can."

"My siblings and I were staying with my grandparents in their trailer. I was told to sleep with my grandpa one night. When I got into bed, I lay on my right side. He pulled up my nightgown and masturbated his penis between my legs." That was the most detail I had ever uttered, and it was all that I could share. There was much more to that story but I couldn't go any further.

"Are you clear that your grandpa was a pedophile? He was a grown man sexually aroused by a small child. It wasn't an accident."

"I never thought about it before, but it helps to hear that. If it wasn't an accident, it was intentional. I had nothing to do with it," I said out loud.

"Exactly," Dr. D confirmed.

Until my discussion with Dr. D, I largely skipped over the details as much as possible whenever a flashback came forward. I never invested any time in the idea that my grandpa had an erect, aroused penis as he was thrusting himself between my thighs and into my body. Once I let myself remember at least the mechanics, I was still disgusted, but I was also oddly relieved. I was getting stronger. Acknowledging some of the granular details about even one assault felt like significant progress. Some of the triggering power of a particular attack released.

I realized the sight, sound, touch, taste, and smell of my abuse formed a ragged tapestry woven into knots by the details. Sharing the fine points of just one attack loosened the threads. I alone had the power to pull the entire tapestry apart.

I stood in my truth and accepted that none of it was my fault.

Feeling emboldened, I reached out to talk to a few of my cousins, with whom I was particularly close, about the abuse. I was unprepared for their painfully ignorant notions. One of my cousins, someone who was like a parent to me, asked if the abuse was, "just with his hands, right?" I didn't answer. I hated myself for believing I could find anymore advocates in my family. I got the feeling they believed that if my grandpa placed only his fingers inside my five year-old vagina it was just a little bit evil. It didn't really compare to "real rape." People honestly believed "if it was just his fingers, and not his penis, it wasn't really sexual assault."

I learned a hard lesson. Society spends a lot of time juggling what is "real sexual assault" and "just a little sexual assault." It's bizarre. I met with a small support group of women who survived manual sexual assault (penetration with fingers). Quite a few were told that it "didn't technically count" as rape because their attacker didn't use his penis and/or ejaculate.

It made me furious. The myriad definitions and categories of sexual assault are really just a mental exercise for criminal defense lawyers who pick fly shit out of horse shit for a living while they demean and abuse survivors and enable rape culture. I refused to be part of any conversation about "levels of assault". The details didn't scare me, anymore.

After putting in the work and healing, I could finally say to Dr. D and others, "My maternal grandpa sexually assaulted my entire body with his penis, tongue, and fingers. He used my body, from the age of Five to the age of Thirteen, for sexual pleasure. His arousal and perversion knew no boundaries."

As I accepted the implicit, visceral, tactile, and auditory details of every memory, they lost their power. I grew stronger as my truth became clearer.

"That, to answer your original question Dr. D, is the What," I said in a session several months later.

"That's really powerful. I'm always amazed by your ability to cut through the complicated bullshit pretty quickly."

"Yeah. I'm a survivor. My brain is sharp—it has to be. Fair warning to anyone who ever tries to minimize any of my experiences ever again."

"That's right," he replied. I always knew I could count on him to have my back. No matter what.

Everyone has to find their own way through their truth and the details. What worked for me would not necessarily work for anyone else. My process in my early twenties would likely not be the same for a survivor who is fifty. I don't know. I think the key is to listen to yourself. Get healed. Step by tiny step.

"I created an acceptance mantra that soothes me," I told Doctor D. "I take some deep breaths and say out loud, 'I am not afraid to remember. I am not afraid of the details. I am safe. I love and trust myself just as I am.'"

"Wow. That's powerful," he said with a smile.

"It keeps me focused and grounded in reality. I feel strong when I say the words out loud. I know that I will continue to recall more and more abuse. It trickles in day to day. But I feel like as long as I remind myself that I'm safe, I'll do okay."

"That's huge progress. Speaking of reality, I'd like you to describe your family to me. How do you see your family? How do they get along?" Dr. D asked.

"Before all the current issues, we were always like the Brady Bunch. We all got along pretty well."

"Rebecca, did you just say that your family was like the Brady Bunch?" he asked in disbelief.

"Yes. Why?" I asked.

"Your family is absolutely nothing like the Brady Bunch. The Brady Bunch was a fairy tale about two families turning into one big family that loved, respected, and kept each other safe."

"Right," I said, not at all following his argument.

"You were abused in your family. Your mother knew that your grandpa was a pedophile and didn't protect you. Your dad left you. Your parents dragged you through a toxic divorce. You were never the Brady Bunch," he said, seemingly still shocked by my assessment.

I took a minute to think about it.

"Yeah," I giggled, "I guess I got that one wrong. Some parts of my brain aren't quite up to speed. I guess we need to work on that."

I couldn't blame Dr. D for his candor. He was, of course, right. My mind, for so many complicated reasons, still clung onto a child's fantasy that we were an ideal family. I suppose I needed us to be one in some way. It took several weeks to completely accept Dr. D's analysis. I didn't actually grow up in a fairytale. What can I say? The body knew truths my mind didn't easily accept.

Dr. D and I spent the next phase of our work talking about my parents and the inherent dysfunction in our relationship and the family in general.

"I think that my parents unconsciously parented from their own trauma," I shared with Dr. D one day.

"Wow. That's a lot. How so? What sort of trauma did they experience?"

"I mean, both families were poor and uneducated. Whatever horrible things happened in their households, like alcoholism and abuse, passed straight from their parents to them. They didn't process it and they passed it along to my generation."

"That's important, but I want to make sure that you're not letting that become an excuse for what happened to you," Dr. D. clarified.

"It isn't. If my dad is a thief, I don't get to be a thief too. At some point, we all really do have to answer for how we respond to our own trauma. Everyone has to carve their own path so they don't bleed on to the next generation."

"Maybe they didn't have the resources to break away from their own trauma?" Dr. D asked, playing devil's advocate.

"That was probably true in the seventies when the conversation didn't exist and they were just getting started in life. But I mean, now there are loads of books and newspaper articles talking about trauma and its effects on children. My parents are intelligent and well-read. They could have tapped into the information at any time, but they chose to ignore it."

I recognized that their trauma and the impact it had on their life wasn't my problem to solve. I was not responsible for their feelings, their trauma, or their lives. It was time to stop parenting my parents.

"I am only responsible for my healing," I told Dr. D. "My parents need to step up and get their own healing."

"How do you reconcile the fact that they've never been willing to do any work with you, or just by themselves, to make amends for what happened?"

"I have no idea." Sometimes, Dr. D had some real zingers for me. The question about how to feel about my parents and their role in my abuse and healing would take decades to answer. We explored more about my parents, siblings, stepparents, and my life. After a lot of hard work and healing, I felt better. My body felt healthy, my mind was clear, and I felt pretty. It was time to take a break. During one of our final sessions, I asked Dr. D about my odds of success.

"Am I going to make it? Make it through all of this?" I asked him.

"Yes. You will absolutely make it," he replied quite confidently.

"How can you be sure? What makes me so different? I mean, I know some other survivors who seem like they have it all figured out, but they're really into drugs. What determines if a person like me is consumed by their trauma and never recovers or if they face it and come out the other side?"

"That's complicated. The simple answer is that you have just enough piss and vinegar inside of you that you will not let yourself be destroyed by all of it."

"That's it?" I asked. "Piss and vinegar is the official answer? Grit?"

"That's it," he said. "You're one of the lucky ones."

I'm not so sure I felt lucky.

I was probably going to survive the trauma and (complex) PTSD and it all came down to grit, moxie, pluck, or mettle. Choose your favorite. They all describe the ability to get through tough things and make life bearable.

But grit, friends, is not a recipe for living a great life. Grit is coarse and it produces sharp edges. It does not allow for softness or nuance. I wanted to live a life of light, love, and happiness. Not a life of grit. It took me time before I understood "piss and vinegar" was really just a great way of describing my anger.

"Rebecca, you've done some really amazing work here. You still have work to do. But I think taking a break is a good idea for now," Dr. D shared at the end of the session.

"Yeah. I agree. I think that I need to just get on with living."

I felt healthy and strong and ready to return to an independent life after nearly three years of intense therapy. I sat down in Dr. D's office for our final session.

"Today is the day," I said.

"It is. You've done incredibly hard work over the past few years. Be proud of yourself. You have the essentials with you now. Some really good self-awareness and tools. You need to watch out for depression and work on intimacy."

"Yeah. I will. It feels weird and a little bit scary to walk out of here today knowing I won't be back."

"I know. But you're ready. And I'm always here if you want to come back," Dr. D reassured me.

Life without Dr. D felt like "jumping without a 'chute." When I left his office at the end of our session, I cried for several minutes in my car. Dr. D had saved my life.

Wait, that's not quite right.

We saved my life.

Shortly after I stopped my therapy sessions, a new influence wrapped itself around me. It was Flight, Fight's alter ego. My PTSD was still in my mind and body and it energized Flight, stirring a ferocious desire to insert distance between the geographic center of my trauma and myself.

It was time to leave Southern California. I stood outside of my apartment on Christmas Day, and it was ninety degrees. That was the exact moment I decided to move to a city where there were actual seasons. I wanted to wear a sweater and sit in a rainstorm. I also wanted a new home and a new world, where perhaps I could write the next chapter of my life free from the influences of broken family dynamics.

# Flight

*"You cannot heal in the same environment where you got sick."*
*(Anonymous)*

## Chapter 7

**M**OVING BY COMMITTEE is almost impossible. In late 1992, I spent a lot of time asking myself how and where I would start a new life. The fragments, aware of my inner dialogue, had no issue adding their feelings to the conversation.

"*Where are we going?*" Thirteen's ever-vigilant voice asked.
"*Why are we leaving? Why are we going away?*" Seven asked.
"*This sounds really scary,*" Five whimpered.
"I want to go away," I told them. "I want to build my own life. I need distance."

There were moments when a sharp reply shut them all down. Once my mind quieted again, I started to ask myself more questions.

How do I go about creating a new life? A separate life. Where do I go? Taking a look at the map of the United States, I decided the Midwest was not an option. I couldn't live in a landlocked state somewhere in the middle of America. I was born to live life on the edges.

The East Coast clearly became the prize, but options were limited. I was only twenty-two years old with a few years of advertising on my résumé. My future city needed to be somewhere my "L.A." experience might mean something and a place that housed enough advertising agencies that I had a chance of getting a job.

I really wanted to go to New York City; but I knew I wasn't ready for such a big jump. Boston? Nah, it wasn't the right market.

Looking south on the map, my eyes settled on Washington, D.C. Hmm. D.C.? Maybe. After several nights at the library reading about the nation's capital and the local advertising industry, "the District" started to make sense and I chose Washington, D.C., as home. It was the perfect market to grow my career. Not as big as New York, but it offered a solid list of good agencies winning awards with regional and national clients. I also loved the idea of living in a city immersed in history.

I couldn't find much information about life in the District but felt confident my plan would work. New York remained the end goal, but it would have to wait.

"I decided I'm moving to D.C.," I told a friend. "They have real weather. True seasons. There is a good ad agency industry, and it just sounds cool. I don't know anyone there, but I'm sure it's lively with all the government stuff going on. Meeting people won't be a big deal."

"You're just going to pack up and go?" she asked, understandably confused.

"No. I'm too broke to just pack up and pray it all works out. I have a list of agencies in the region. I'm going to send my résumé and cover letter and see what happens."

"Why do you want to leave L.A.? No one ever leaves. Everyone's always trying to move here."

"I've never loved L.A. Everyone is obsessed with getting a tan, being skinny, and networking. It's never been a great place for me. I want to get away—away from my family and my old life. I feel like I need to get distance from my trauma. I can't continue to heal living where I was hurt."

After jumping from my parents' house to a job and life at the beach, leaping from L.A. into a city on the other side of the country made sense to me. I like to make big changes and sort of assume life will sort itself out. I guess you could say I tend to gut the whole house in lieu of making some minor upgrades. Tearing life down to the studs and building again felt natural. I just had to pluck up the courage to try.

Another friend and I chatted a few weeks later and she couldn't understand my decision. I think my willingness to take such a big leap put her on edge. She couldn't imagine it for herself.

"How do you just decide to go? I mean, you're a little crazy," she said, laughing.

"I know. Sometimes my brain feels like it's broken. Maybe things aren't wired quite right. I feel like I don't have a speed regulator."

"Like you don't ever pause to maybe think about things? Or you don't ever let yourself feel too afraid to try?"

"More like I don't respect feeling afraid, so I don't listen to it. I hate it when

Five starts sharing her fear. Sure, I might be nervous that D.C. won't work out, but I refuse to feel afraid."

"Is the rest of your family like that?"

"No. They're not wanderers. Not in the same way. My family all live within thirty miles of each other."

I went to the office early the next day to take advantage of my computer and draft a résumé and cover letter. It was pure poetry. After printing ten copies on expensive gray, linen paper, I tucked them carefully into matching envelopes. Each packet was addressed to a different advertising agency in Baltimore, Maryland, D.C., and Alexandria, Virginia. Once the envelopes were sealed, I took advantage of my robust friendships with the mailroom guys at the office, and they ran them through the postage machine.

"Tommy Burger next week—right?" Sydney asked with a smile.

"Absolutely. Extra chili on the fries," I replied. Lunch once a month as my treat came with benefits like free postage.

I went to work every day optimistic the universe knew it was time for change, distance, and opportunity. Two weeks after I placed my credentials in the hands of the United States Postal Service, I sat in my cubicle on an unusually slow afternoon and my phone rang.

"This is Rebecca," I answered.

"So I'm looking at this résumé. . ." the voice on the other end of the phone said.

My heart leaped into my throat.

"Uh-huh. Right."

"Well, my name is John. I'm the Executive Creative Director at Big Time Advertising's D.C. office, and we're looking for a new head of commercial production."

"Great," I replied. "Can you tell me more about your productions? Are you shooting on sixteen or thirty-six?" I asked, trying to sound technically impressive. I wanted to find out if they were shooting low-budget 16 mm film or high-end 35 mm. I ended up sounding like a moron.

"You mean thirty-five?" John asked.

"Uh, yeah. Sorry. Thirty-five," I replied.

"I'm a little worried that you don't know the difference. But yes, we shoot on thirty-five," he said.

"No, really, I know it's thirty-five. I'm just nervous. Of course I know it's thirty-five," I blabbed.

We talked a bit longer about my current job, why I wanted to shift from L.A., and specifics about the role in his office. I tried really hard to sound like a seasoned professional, hoping that the whole thirty-six vs. thirty-five moment was behind us.

"Okay. Well. Here's the thing. I can't offer to pay for your ticket to D.C. to interview. We're a satellite office, and there's no budget. But if you can figure out a way to get here, that would be great," he said.

The moment our call ended, I immediately rang the main number at John's agency and asked to speak to the office manager.

"Hi. I just spoke with John about the head of commercial production position. I'm just curious. If I get the job, is the company going to pay for my move?" I asked.

"I don't think so," she said. "They only do that for VPs."

"Okay, thanks," I said, ending the call.

*"Did you hear that? They won't pay. You don't have any money," Thirteen snapped.* Damn, she was such a downer sometimes.

*"Well, I can at least go for the interview. Maybe I'll meet other people there and network,"* I punched back in an unusually optimistic tone.

*"How are you going to network in a city where you don't know anyone?" she croaked.*

*"Oh just shut up, will you?!" I snapped, and Thirteen slithered away.* Sometimes, I just needed her to shut her damn mouth.

I had to figure out how to pay for the trip. Debt choked me, and I had no savings. All my extra money went toward tuition and books (and shoes). I went home a few days later and happened to mention the trip to my stepdad.

"I've been invited to Washington, D.C., for a job interview," I told him. "I'd be the head of the commercial production department, which is a big deal. The trick is that they won't pay for me to fly or stay in D.C."

"Well, this might help. I have some coupons for free hotel nights you can use at a Best Western. There," he said, laying the coupons on his desk, "that's seven free nights. Take them all," he said.

The coupons were like gold to me.

I called the Best Western in Dupont Circle to confirm the coupons were valid. I was thrilled when they said yes! I found a sliver of spending room on one of my credit cards and bought a cheap, $200 ticket to D.C. After organizing all the logistics, it was time to talk to my boss, Mike.

"Hey, do you have a minute?" I asked at the end of a long Monday.

"Yep! Come on in!" he shouted. He was always so positive.

"So I have been invited to interview for a job as the head of commercial production at Very Big Ad Agency's D.C. office. The trick is that I need to take next week off. I have the vacation days, but I also know that it's short notice."

"It's fine. Make your plans, and make sure you list me as a reference. You've been through a tough year, and this is really great news. I'm proud of you."

Mike was a true gem. I called John the next day to say I could travel for the interview. We finalized the logistics and set the date to meet. Just a few months after I decided D.C. was going to be my new home, and just a week after John first called me, I was on my way. I had enough coupons to stay free for a week. If I didn't get the job, I had no idea when I would ever go back so I decided to make a vacation out of the trip.

I landed at Ronald Reagan International Airport on a bitterly cold Sunday afternoon in December 1992. Taking the free hotel shuttle up the George Washington Parkway, I stared out the window at the Potomac River, Jefferson Memorial, Kennedy Center, and other landmarks as we made our way to the city. D.C. was beautiful.

Walking into the hotel to check in, I prayed my credit card wouldn't burst into flames when they ran the room deposit. I breathed an audible sigh of relief when they handed me back my card. I pulled my suitcase into the room (I couldn't afford a tip for the bellman) and I was beyond excited.

*"Lucky that the card worked at check-in. You better have a great interview, or this is all just a waste of time and money," Thirteen quipped.*

*"Oh just shut the hell up, would you?" I snapped.*

*"Is this room safe?" Five asked.*

*"It's a hotel room in a nice part of D.C. Yes, it's safe. Relax."*

After I unpacked my clothes and toiletries I wandered down to the lobby to ask the bellman for directions to the closest grocery store. After a short, ten-minute walk, I found the store and bought bread, peanut butter, apples, and other cheap snacks. Sandwiches and a free hotel breakfast. That was my menu for the week. It was all I could afford.

On Sunday night, I unfolded the spreadsheet I had prepared listing the days of the week, and the various tour times for places like the FBI, Supreme Court, and

National Archives, and double-checked my plans. My producer's brain operated well, and I was in my logistics mode. I would see the archives and FBI on Monday, Supreme Court and rental car pick-up Tuesday, interview and Mt. Vernon Estate Wednesday, Smithsonian and D.C. by Night tour Thursday, and then the Library of Congress on Friday. When it was all organized, I congratulated myself on my scheduling prowess.

On Monday morning, I walked out of the hotel armed with a detailed city map and the day's itinerary. It was wonderful to be in a "walking city," even if it was exceptionally cold. I soon realized I was the only person stopping and waiting for the pedestrian crosswalk signs to turn green. A true local never waited before darting across the street. As a native Southern Californian, I felt rebellious when I embraced the local custom and "walked on red."

I woke up early Wednesday morning and I donned the perfect "East Coast interview" look. The second-hand suit I bought at the Salvation Army (tags still attached) suggested an air of maturity my years did not demonstrate. I put on my favorite pair (only pair) of black riding boots (all the rage at the time) and headed out to my rental car.

The ad agency sat in an office park on the edge of the Potomac River in Alexandria, Virginia. As I walked from the visitor parking to the main entrance, I took a moment to appreciate the Potomac as massive chunks of ice flowed down the freezing waters. After just a few minutes waiting in the lobby, I started to worry about what John, or anyone else, would ask during the interview.

"*What if he asks a really technical question?*" Thirteen asked.

"*Pam at work said it's okay not to know everything in an interview. I'll just say that I don't know,*" I explained.

"*Well, this is a big job. They're going to want someone who knows everything,*" Thirteen snapped back. "*You'll sound dumb.*"

"*What if they don't like us?*" Seven asked.

"*Everyone, just stop. I'm fine. It will be fine. I just need to convince these people that I can handle a senior role. I can do it.*"

"*Okay, well, don't overthink this—just be confident,*" Thirteen offered in a quick recovery.

Mercurial most of the time, Thirteen could change her colors as quickly as a chameleon. Hateful one moment, my cheerleader the next. I was in the middle of yet another conversation with her when I was called into the office for my interview.

John was unusual, funny, and made a lot of bad jokes, but our talk went well. I also met with other members of the creative team as well as with client services. They all seemed like good people. We took a look at their past commercial work and sat down for a final chat.

"So what do you think?" John asked, sitting behind a cluttered desk I really wanted to organize. "I'd like to see some different commercial directors do some of the work," he mentioned before I could reply. It was a subtle way to let me know why the resume from L.A. caught his attention.

"I agree. It would be good to branch out beyond regional directors. There's a lot of new talent out of New York and LA that would love to put a great commercial on their demo reel. I think we can bring them into the mix here," I replied. I did my best to sound like a seasoned pro. In truth, I didn't really know what I was saying.

"Sounds great. Thanks for coming out, Rebecca. I'll be in touch Monday."

I left the office confident. After visiting Mt. Vernon, and surviving a final drive back up the Potomac to the District, I caught myself hoping and praying D.C. was, in fact, my new city.

Friday night, I walked down to a nearby Italian restaurant for dinner. I intended to treat myself to a proper meal to celebrate a great interview and the end of my vacation. It was also a much-needed break from peanut butter sandwiches. Walking in the chilly D.C. night air, I felt radiant and smiled at a man as he walked by me. A few moments later he caught up with me.

"Hello. Excuse me. My name is Raymond. I don't know. It's a little crazy. I thought we had a moment just a minute ago. Would you like to have a drink?"

"Hi, Raymond; I'm Rebecca," I said in a calm, mature voice that did not belong to me. Never in my life had I met a man that was so clear, confident, and handsome. It was too much for me to handle.

"Sorry, I can't tonight," I said. "But maybe next week," I said, knowing perfectly well I was leaving in the morning.

"Sure. Here's my card," he said. "Call me tomorrow, and we can find some time."

"Sounds good," I said and turned back to walk to the restaurant.

Thirty seconds later, the fragments chimed in.

*"Who was that? What does he want? He's a stranger. He wants sex. You can't meet him. That's not safe."*

*"Oh just stop it! We leave tomorrow. I'll never see that guy again. Jesus, you're all just hysterical. Shut up!"*

I wanted to celebrate. A man found me attractive and asked me out! The details were irrelevant. The idea that he made an effort to come and say hello was charming, but I felt totally unprepared for adult, clear communication. I could not imagine actually having someone so sophisticated in my life. How do I have a drink with a slightly older, sexy French man in a city? What does that mean? The more I obsessively thought about him, the happier I was to board the plane Saturday morning.

The good news was that D.C. wasn't just a beautiful city steeped in history. It was also a mythical, magical kingdom where men with sexy accents spoke to me on the sidewalk and asked me out on an adult date. Obviously, I would need to learn how to convert flirtation on the sidewalk into actually saying yes to an invite out, but that would come later. Baby steps.

I flew out of the district feeling like a local, knowing in my bones it was home. Monday morning John called me.

"Well, we'd love to have you come out here and take the job, Rebecca," he said. "You'll be our head of broadcast production. When can you be here?"

We discussed all of the details and as soon as our call ended, I immediately applied and got approved for yet another credit card to pay for the move. I also had to resign from my job.

"So I have some news," I said casually to Mike as I walked into his office during my lunch break.

"Yes?" he asked, with his trademark grin.

"I just accepted the job in Washington, D.C. I'm the new head of commercial production!"

"That's great! Good for you! Congratulations!" he yelled as he got up from his desk to give me a hug.

"Thank you so much. I really appreciate all your support. You taught me so much. I'll never forget how kind you've been to me."

A few friends in the office joined me for drinks after work to celebrate. I was excited. I took a chance and believed that a great change would come my way and it did. I broke the news to my family. A few expressed doubts I would actually make it happen. I didn't listen. I was busy calling a moving company.

## CHAPTER 8

I PRODUCED THE HELL out of my first cross-country move. I negotiated moving costs, finalized my timeline, and signed a lease on a new apartment all within a week. When she wasn't being a self-destructive, bitchy, hateful pain in the ass, Thirteen's focused, hyper-organized (or shall I say hyper-alert) energy complemented my own.

We were indeed a formidable logistics and mobilization team. Her chatter consumed every moment of my waking hours.

*"Right, so the moving company quotes are in. Choose 'JK Moving'. They're the best,"* Thirteen directed. *"They're going to collect everything on Monday, so you better get it packed,"* she drilled.

*"Yes. I am packing. I bought boxes."*

*"Are you approved for the new apartment? It looked nice on the internet,"* she countered.

*"Yes. Approved. They got my deposit today."*

*"Is the car ready? Have you had it serviced?"* she asked. Her attention to detail knew no end.

*"No, but I changed the oil, checked the tires, and it's good to go."*

My chariot was a small, but rugged, Suzuki Samurai convertible, which was essentially a junior-sized Jeep. It rattled like a tin can, but I took good care of it and had no doubt it was up for the challenge.

As I finalized my trip details, my big brother and his wife called.

"Hey, when do you leave?" he asked.

"Next week. The movers come Monday, and I start driving Tuesday morning,"

I answered.

"Yeah," he said, "my wife says you can't drive across the country alone. Talk to her."

"Okay," I said, confused.

"Hey there," my sister-in-law said, grabbing the phone. "I told your brother there's just no way we're going to let you do this by yourself. He's going to take a few days off work and drive with you," she explained. She used a tone suggesting she wasn't negotiating.

"Okay, great," I said, "but I can't afford a plane ticket for him to fly home."

"Don't worry about it," she said. "You're doing me a favor by taking him away for a few days." My sister-in-law was, and remains, a true bright spot in my life. She has a glorious sense of humor, a huge heart, and is incredibly intelligent. There's no way to pick just one story to sum up how I feel about her except to say that her banana bread with dark chocolate chips, rum punch, and pool parties reflect the brilliant spark that we all adore. She is simply wonderful, and we're lucky that she's part of the family.

I heard my brother asking questions in the background, and she quickly returned the phone to him to continue our conversation.

"So when are we leaving?" he asked.

A few days later, my brother and I had finalized packing the car in the early morning light. My brother's wife stood with my mom and stepdad as we zipped the convertible top flaps shut. There wasn't an inch of free space in the back seat.

"Time to go," my brother said at 7 a.m.

"Thanks so much for sending him with me," I said to his wife while giving her a hug. I would miss her.

"No. Thank you! It will get him out of the house for a few days!" she said with a smile.

"Make us proud," my stepdad said as he hugged me tight. My mom gave me a final, long hug before my brother and I finally got inside the car. I was excited. I was ready.

Nearly four years had passed between the moment I told my mom about the abuse and the morning of my departure from California. I never got the apology or support I needed. But, in the end, I wasn't strong enough to stand in my truth and live my life without a relationship with my parents. It was complicated. My feelings about my mother's betrayal and my parents' failures remained unchanged. I wasn't sure how to manage all of it. At twenty-three, that was as good as I could make things. A whole new life waited for me in D.C.

I initially planned to drive about eight to ten hours a day. My brother, however, decided we would drive fifteen hours a day. He wanted us to arrive ahead of schedule to give him more days in D.C. before flying back to Los Angeles. Apart from spending grueling hours in the car, our trek was unremarkable. The only highlights I logged were of a few gross motels, terrorizing my brother as I drove us through a death-defying fog-and-rain-infused trip through the Tennessee mountains, and the convertible top leaking during every storm.

We set a blistering pace across the country, and three days later in mid-January we pulled into the parking lot at my new apartment complex. I was relieved to discover the moving company arrived the day before, as planned, and unloaded my bed and other items into my apartment.

Home was a ground floor, one-bedroom unit with a small patio leading to a pretty, grassy courtyard surrounded by tall trees. All the buildings were made out of red brick. Websites were just getting started at the time, and I only had a single photo of the exterior to consider when I signed the lease. I exhaled a sigh of relief when I discovered the interior was just as nice as the courtyard photo.

It was winter and the afternoon light was fading quickly, so we hurriedly unloaded the car and drove to the grocery store. Groceries were the last big investment I budgeted before payday at the end of the month. Thirty minutes into the "my new apartment needs everything" shopping spree, I called my mom in a mayonnaise-induced panic. For those that do not know, there is only one brand of mayonnaise allowed into a proper household and that mayonnaise, on the West Coast, is known as Best Foods.

"Mom," I said, standing in the condiments aisle. "I'm trying to buy mayonnaise. They don't have Best Foods. I can't eat this other stuff."

"No, you can't. They have to have it," she said, confused. "Wait a minute. I think it says on the jar that it's a different brand name on the East Coast. Let me grab it out of the fridge. Yep, it says that East of the Rockies it's called Hellman's," she read into the phone.

I scanned the shelves and saw a gleaming, wondrous bottle of Hellman's mayonnaise. All was right with the world.

"Found it! Thanks!" I shouted. Crisis averted. My brother and I walked around the store before we both noticed we couldn't find any liquor. Neither of us needed to buy any, but it was odd.

"Hi, can you tell me where the liquor is located?" I asked a clerk.

"Ha, you're from the West Coast. Yeah, so in Virginia, you can't buy liquor in a grocery store. You have to go to the ABC (Virginia Alcoholic Beverage Control) store. You can only buy beer and wine in grocery stores."

"Right. So no vodka in the grocery store?"

"No. Is it true you can buy liquor anywhere in California—in any store?"

"Well, every corner shop, gas station, and grocery store sells liquor. We make it simple."

The vodka could wait. I was doing well with the rest of the shopping until I tried to buy some meat.

"Excuse me, do you have tri-tip?" I asked the butcher. I couldn't really afford it, but I thought it would be nice to cook for my brother before he flew back to Los Angeles.

"You're from California, right? You all ask for tri-tip. That cut doesn't exist in Virginia. It's a West Coast thing."

"Geez. Cows are cows," I muttered to myself. "What do people eat here?"

"Steak."

"Right. Thanks." My cheeks turned red as I picked up two steaks. I felt like a scarlet "I'm from California" was written across my forehead.

After driving a few thousand miles, my life was suddenly all about being able to buy the right mayonnaise, understanding where to buy liquor, and giving up on buying a tri-tip ever again.

Culture shock 1 - Californian 0

It was indeed a whole new world.

I stayed home Friday to unpack while my brother set out to see some of the sights in the district. Later in the afternoon, I drove to the metro station to collect my brother when something hissed and then exploded in the engine. I immediately pulled into the closest service station. I panicked. How was I going to pay to fix my car? My brain sort of switched off as the mechanic did his best to explain the damage to me.

"So, basically, the super important thingy in the engine just blew up. I can fix it tomorrow morning. It's going to cost $250.00."

I'm very sure he used all the correct technical words, but I was about a million miles away in 'I am broke and start work Monday' land. Every single credit card I had was at its limit (and beyond). When I say I was broke, I mean *broke*. Steak and mayonnaise pushed me right over the edge.

I needed a miracle. Naturally, I called American Express. I'm sure they used proper customer service lingo but what my panicked, broke mind heard was quite different.

"Hello, super wonderful credit card people," I chirped once I connected with customer service.

"Hello," customer service replied. Her tone suggested that she was quite aware my credit card was maxed out and I was dead broke. "What do you think you need from us today?" my mind heard her say in an ominous tone.

"I need $250.00 in emergency cash for a car repair. I'm with the mechanic right now, and the thingy blew up. I need my car. I have to get to work on Monday," I pleaded.

"I need to speak to the manager," she replied. "I'm going to verify that you're not just standing in the mall ready to buy yet another outfit or pair of shoes." My inner translation system even managed to add a layer of snark for full effect. I held my breath as I watched the mechanic speak to Amex. Eventually, the mechanic handed my phone back to me.

"Ms. Broke. Yes, I've spoken to the Random Mechanic, and he seems like a good guy. Apparently this purchase is, technically, an emergency, so we will authorize a charge for the exact amount of the repair only. We will not, however, grant any emergency cash. The entire amount will be due in full along with your regular payment at the end of the month."

"Got it." American Express to my rescue.

Feeling completely embarrassed, I turned my bright-red face back to the mechanic and said, "Thanks for speaking to them. I just moved, and they wanted to make sure it was really me."

"No problem," he said in a tone that suggested it was not the first time he had to speak to a credit card company about an "emergency." "Bring your car here tomorrow at 8 a.m. It will be done in about an hour."

I left the garage, engine clanking and hissing, and drove to the metro station to pick up my brother. As I pulled up to the curb where he stood waiting, the car sounded like it was about to explode.

"What in the world is wrong with your car?" he asked after shutting his door.

"Yeah, the thingy just blew up. They're going to fix it tomorrow morning," I told him as calmly as possible.

"The thingy?" he asked.

"Yeah, the whatchamacallit thingy," I said. "Whatever it is, it will be figured out tomorrow morning. It will take an hour."

"Uh, okay," he said, with an evil grin. Only a big brother can make that face when his baby sister describes an engine part as a thingy. I love my big brother more than I can say even when he's making fun of me.

The next morning, the repair was completed, and we headed out on a quick road trip to the nearby mall. We started the drive during a rainstorm. Nearly an hour later, we were stuck in miserable traffic in the middle of a dangerous ice storm. By the time we turned around to go home, the ground was covered in a thick layer of ice.

The parking lot at my apartment reminded me of the outdoor skating rink we used to frequent as kids. Once safely inside and warm, we sat in the living room staring out the sliding glass window at our first ice storm. We definitely didn't have those in Southern California. The arctic blast continued overnight, and it was a miracle my brother was able to catch his flight out of Baltimore Sunday morning.

After dropping him off at the airport, I drove back home and prepared for my first day at the office. I laid out my clothes, planned my breakfast, and packed lunch. I even drove the route to the office following my boss's strict instructions to "come all the way down Duke Street until you see our building," just to make sure I wasn't late on my first day.

On Monday, January 17, 1994, I walked into the office feeling proud I had just navigated a cross-country drive, moved into an apartment, survived driving in an ice storm, and I didn't get lost on Duke Street. Pride was fleeting. It lasted a few hours before impostor's syndrome took over, and I worried I didn't actually know anything about anything.

*"What in the hell are we doing here?"* Thirteen asked.

*"Yeah. This is scary,"* Seven chimed in.

*"I know. I don't know what I'm going to do,"* I answered.

*"We're going to be in trouble. They're going to find out that you don't know how to do this job,"* Thirteen snorted.

*"What if they fire me today and send me back to California? I can't even afford the gas to drive to LA, much less another move,"* I told them. *"I have to make this work."*

The office manager, Mary, greeted me in the lobby, and we walked back to my office. Pushing all the chatter as deep into my mind as possible, the usual buzz and activity of an ad agency took over and my nerves settled. I met John and the rest of the creative team who were eager to welcome me to the circus. I left my first day feeling more confident and relieved.

As the scale and scope of my role took shape, I was unprepared for the lack of proper finance and legal systems in New York's "satellite office." I soon realized I was the departmental secretary, coordinator, assistant, and senior producer for a group of largely government clients requiring a considerable amount of paperwork and attention.

Embracing an entirely different sort of client roster, I had to quickly learn U.S. Government contracting processes and bring organization to the chaos. The job was immediately overwhelming despite my very real skills. I needed some advice.

I decided to ask Robert, the Creative Director, to join me for lunch. As an executive creative director, his ideas were incredibly imaginative and often sprinkled with undertones of his delicious sense of humor.

"So how's it going?" he asked as we sat down to eat.

"It's a lot to manage. I don't think the previous head of production was entirely organized."

"Oh God no. She never worked inside a big agency like you. She had no idea how to keep records."

"Yeah, I've noticed."

"Just take your time. No one is going to notice if things aren't perfect. You can create your own systems—really just do your own thing." Robert's advice, and his friendship, became a lifeline for me in the office as I worked my way through all the projects and processes, eventually bringing order to my office.

Time flew by while I settled into my new life and career. Spring in D.C. was glorious as a bitter winter season finally ended and the cherry trees started to dazzle us all with their blossoms. All the city's charm left when summer rolled into town, turning D.C. into a tourist-besieged swamp. John called us into a creative meeting just as fall approached and the trees outside began to show off their magical colors.

"I'm very excited to announce that we won the pitch for the Quick Car Fix Company!" he announced to applause. "Great job, everyone. Now, they want to move ahead with the creative ideas that we pitched for TV. They loved the dancing tow trucks."

"I'm sorry," I interrupted. "Dancing tow trucks? What exactly are dancing tow trucks? I never saw the creative or the storyboards before they went to the client."

"You'll love it. We want a fleet of tow trucks to do a sort of synchronized dance."

My face remained stoic but my brain felt like it was going to explode. I was from L.A. where I worked on a car account. I knew how much it would cost to get a "fleet" of tow trucks to just show up at a location much less "dance."

"Do they have a million dollars?" I asked with a straight face.

"No. They have about twenty-five percent of that number," our account services director, David, explained.

I spent the next three weeks convincing the best car commercial directors in L.A. that they needed the commercial on their demo reel.

"How many times do you get to shoot a bunch of tow trucks doing 360 turns, going off jumps, and flying through the air?" I asked their producers. I leveraged every contact I had in Los Angeles and found an up-and-coming director and production company brave enough to produce the commercial for about thirty percent of the actual cost.

Delivering the commercial, complete with the grand opening shot of a tow truck launching off a jump and into the air, was a massive achievement. As a bonus, the spot earned a few industry awards. John, Robert, and the rest of the creative team were thrilled and the client was happy. I proved to the office, and myself, that I did have what it took to deliver great work.

I continued to enjoy victories in the office, but privately I buckled under enormous pressure. Part of me wanted to believe I left Trauma in California a year earlier when we drove across I-40. I was disappointed, but not surprised, to discover Trauma moved with me. When I began to feel isolated and exhausted, Trauma came out from its hiding place in the depths of my mind and slithered back into my life.

The debt from moving, the emergency car repair, and getting caught up with life took a toll and added more stress to all the PTSD issues. All my credit cards remained maxed out after making minimum payments for several months. Social norms like trips to the beach my co-workers spoke about weren't even a consideration. A storm in my life was on the horizon.

I met Rock Bottom at an ad industry function. Incredibly charming, funny, intelligent, sexy, and unavailable, he ticked all the right and wrong boxes. I tossed aside the discussions about intimacy with Dr. D and ignored my inner compass to pursue desire.

*"He's perfect for you,"* the fragments whispered.

*"Why? You know he's married,"* I replied to their chatter.

*"Yes, but he's the only man that will ever want you. You're broken. You'll never really be close to anyone,"* Seven and Five added. *"It's better that way. He can't hurt you, too much."*

*"No one else wants you. You should just feel lucky that he said hello,"* Thirteen barbed.

I thought about their rationale for a few days after Rock Bottom and I met. *"You're right,"* I told them. *"I'm garbage. I can't expect much more than this."*

*"No. You can't."* They all agreed and tore into me.

The three years I spent decoding my trauma with Dr. D didn't manifest a strong enough sense of self-worth to avoid disaster. My choice to say yes to Rock Bottom and be in an affair reflected the deep-seated shame still living within me.

Instead of respecting myself and rejecting his advances, I chose to be held in the margins by a married man. My abused, traumatized fragments preferred a relationship rich with detachment. It was familiar and their comfort zone. Our affair offered me a half-life. We never ate out or socialized with friends. Never went on a trip together. Our moments were restricted to a few hours spent on a weekend or occasional weeknight whenever our schedules allowed.

Ironically, the lack of attachment we shared somehow gave me space to thoroughly and patiently explore every layer of my desire. Rock Bottom had no inhibitions, and I felt entirely free when we were together. We embraced every fantasy either of us could imagine and I shed some of my inhibitions.

When Rock Bottom and I were together, I was completely present and felt free from my trauma. When our sexual play ended, Trauma returned and the fragments had a lot to say. It was ironic, of course, that the fragments convinced me an affair was all I could expect only to turn into hateful tormentors after every encounter with Rock Bottom. It was a trap that played out repeatedly throughout my life.

*"You're a whore. He likes you because you're a whore,"* Thirteen snarled.

"He doesn't love you. He's never going to love you," Seven added.

"Maybe. I know that it's a terrible mistake, but I can't stop," I answered. "I feel free with him."

"You'll be crushed by it. You're ridiculous," Thirteen barked. "You sound like a girl at a junior high dance. This is going to destroy you."

Rock Bottom and I laughed a lot. We enjoyed the same sorts of stories and politics. Our "relationship" made sense. Except it wasn't a relationship.

It was a lie.

There is nothing quite as lonely and degrading as the moment just after your married lover goes home after a few hours of fun and you're left alone with the clean-up, guilt, and shameful silence thundering into your mind, knowing you just violated another woman's trust. Our affair, like every affair, was a slow, intravenous drip of false intimacy, denial, and self-destruction. Perhaps I didn't have quite as much grit as Dr. D suggested. I was making all the bad choices of a typical survivor.

Engaging in destructive relationships is just one example of the caustic effects sexual abuse plays in a survivor's life. I was prostituting myself for the detached, temporary affection of a married man. It didn't take long for the imbalance in our relationship to make me unbalanced.

"Dr. D would be pissed," Seven hissed in a rare rebuke after Rock Bottom left one Sunday afternoon.

"Well, Dr. D isn't here and I'm doing my best to hold it together."

"You should go back to therapy. You're going to crash," Thirteen chimed in.

"I have no time for therapy. I work seventy hours a week. I don't know what you want me to do."

Trauma and PTSD are shapeshifters and master manipulators. A power source deep within my cells, trauma sparked every one of my fragments and compulsive behaviors. It worked hard to keep systems offline. The mental gymnastics going on in my head slowly wore me down and turned my life into an unrecognizable story at the age of twenty-five. The work I had done with Dr. D felt almost entirely lost.

I was a living, breathing tornado twirling at 1,000 mph. I couldn't see a way through, or out. I don't think my friends or family ever really knew how far off-center my life became during the D.C. years.

Thirteen, Seven, and Five continued to react to every decision I made with anger, sadness, or fear. We were at war with each other. Every day, I had to step into mental body armor to battle the fragments in hand-to-hand combat as they attacked me.

Thirteen took advantage of my weakened mental state, and I felt helpless when I blended with her anger, constantly releasing it in outbursts about trivial things, like a late fax or report. Darkness joined the melee, throwing uninvited flesh memories and vivid flashbacks of my abuse into my mind in some sort of PTSD horror show.

*"You're so stupid. This client hates you,"* Thirteen shouted.

*"Fuck off. Shut up,"* I barked back only to immediately receive a vignette of a sexual assault flashing across my mind. Cheap cologne and a scratchy wool army blanket took over my senses as I relived my grandpa's hands on my body.

*"You're a slut. You're ugly. No wonder you're still with Rock Bottom. No one else wants you,"* Darkness hissed. *"Why are you even alive?"*

*"It's so sad. I don't want to remember this,"* Seven cried out.

*"Fuck off, all of you! I'm in a meeting!"* I shouted in my mind.

Their combined chatter grew louder. Two years after arriving in D.C., the rigors of work were the only reason I stayed rooted to the Earth. Funny thing about roots. When they're shallow, they can spread out a great distance, but a strong, sustained wind or storm can eventually pull them out of the ground. Deep roots, the type that anchor far underground, are properly supported to withstand even the most severe storm. I didn't till the soil properly when I planted my fragile seeds in D.C., and I sowed shallow roots.

There were, of course, bright spots between storms, and that's important for me to remember. Although everyone at the office had too much work and not nearly enough time, my peers—namely Robert, Bobbi, Tom, Paul, Nora, Sara, Karin, Amy, Doug, and Bryan—made the long hours much more tolerable.

We went out to lunch at least once a week and celebrated birthdays, weddings, and babies. Our camaraderie was a gift. Nora's house, in particular, was a wonderful oasis. I spent several Sundays at her home enjoying her husband Glen's amazing BBQ and relaxing in their gorgeous pool.

D.C. was a politically charged nightlife hot spot. I spent more than one drunken night in an Irish pub or tavern with friends from the office, singing, celebrating mid-term election results, and standing in a hallway waiting to use the bathroom alongside the secret service. Embassy parties, political celebrations, and weekend protest rallies made for an invigorating life in the district.

As work projects pulled me into different states from one week to the next, I became more distracted and unavailable, and the affair finally ended. I didn't feel particularly sad. In fact, I felt free. Shame's chains loosened their grip from around my neck and the fragments lowered their volume. The stress in the office subsided for a while, and I felt better physically and mentally. I was back. As my mind settled, I had time to consider my next steps. Did I want to stay in D.C.? Was I ready for New York City? Staying in one place and settling down felt like surrender while new places and experiences made me feel alive.

Three years after moving to D.C., I finally got a chance to travel to New York for work. After walking the busy streets, grabbing a perfect bagel from a corner bodega, figuring out the subway, and catching my first show on Broadway, I knew the time had come to put moving to the best city in the world on the horizon.

My professional ambition demanded I prove myself in the world's most demanding marketing climate. A new location, and another new beginning, was in order.

Flight agreed.

I took considerable time to research what it would take to move into New York City because I was going to move without a job. I wanted to work as a freelancer. Another jump, parachute optional. After nearly four long years as the head of commercial production in D.C., I gave three months' notice and announced my departure from the agency to pursue a career in the big city.

As I put my plans to shift to NYC into action, the Universe, and a co-worker, brought me a new client and mentor in D.C. The first time I walked into Lynda's office, I carried a bottle of cough medicine, a packet of antihistamines, and a jug of cranberry juice.

"Lynda, so great to meet you."

"Hi, Mark says that you're the best producer he's ever worked with—so it's great that we could finally connect," she offered.

"He's wonderful. Sorry, do you mind, I just need to take some medicine really quick. I'm just getting over a small cold," I explained in a perfectly normal tone of voice.

"Sure, of course," she replied.

Lynda watched me take a swig of the fiery cold remedy straight out of the bottle, followed by a quick gulp of juice to help me swallow a handful of pills.

"Did you just do a shot of cough syrup and choke down a handful of antihistamines and juice?" she asked with equal amounts of shock and awe.

"Yes. Yes, I did. I take it every two hours until the cold goes away," I answered in a tone suggesting that it was perfectly normal.

"Oh my God. You're fantastic! Let's talk about the project," Lynda offered as we walked to the conference room.

We immediately bonded. I gained the Jewish, Pisces, vegetarian, granola-loving mama I never knew I needed. She gained a talented, slightly askew, Pisces, fierce protector of creative work, and excellent producer. She was just "crunchy" enough that it seemed right to officially call her my "Crunchita."

Lynda championed self-help and healing and spoke about it unapologetically. She freely discussed astrology and its connection to personality. In my father's house, such "woo-woo" was frowned upon, as it was a "slippery slope" to evil, according to his Born-Again Christian ideology.

Crunchita turned my world upside down, offering a new lens through which to view life. She is a true creative genius, mother, and friend. Always sure of her center, she is clear about her purpose.

"I'm planning to move to New York," I mentioned to Lynda a few months after our first meeting. We were on set waiting patiently for the director to start filming our commercial.

"Amazing. You absolutely should be there—New York is such a fantastic city. I loved it. I also really loved Hong Kong. Do it all now. Do it before the kids and husband. We can keep working together no matter where you go!" she reassured me.

"You're my inspiration, Crunchita. You've really done it all. And I agree. It's time for me to fly."

"Love it!" she exclaimed.

Lynda's support and mentorship further reinforced my decision to move out of D.C. Her exceptional career, both in the states and internationally, reminded me that no dream was too big. I felt validated and appreciated working with her, which wasn't always the case with my boss, John.

I valued her solidarity, advice, and willingness to share her success and failures as lessons to guide my own choices. In preparation for my move, I spent the next few weeks taking the train to New York to go apartment hunting. After figuring out how to prove I made thirty times the rent to qualify for a lease, I signed the documents and was ready to leap.

I locked in a coveted "917" mobile number and finalized all the familiar moving details. My logistical and planning skills remained in top form. After all, relocating is just another location move in the life of a producer.

"You should take some time to think about what D.C. taught you," Lynda told me one day at lunch. I never knew anyone that enjoyed an egg salad sandwich as much as Crunchita.

"Taught me? That's one way to describe it. It has been an interesting, challenging, fun, and tough four years."

"The lessons you learned here make it possible for you to succeed in New York. Think about it," she challenged me.

When I got home, I asked myself to think about everything I learned from every success and failure living and working in D.C.

When I moved to D.C., I didn't practice any sort of balance, or maintenance, in my life. I disregarded my mental health and it deteriorated. As life's storms blew in, my foundation cracked around the edges and the paint peeled off the exterior. I managed to avoid total destruction, but I was damaged. The structure may not have been totally destroyed, but I needed to remember to keep a balance when I moved to New York.

Perhaps I spent a past life as a palm tree. When the hurricanes in my life hit me—both naturally occurring and self-inflicted—I sway nearly to the point of breaking. My fronds, my heart and happiness, are torn from me, and I am left wounded.

Weak.

In my weakened state, I make terrible decisions.

Eventually, the storms clear, and I find a way to return upright, restart, and look for new opportunities.

## Chapter 9

New York City?!

"You're going to need me!" Thirteen cheered.

I pushed back. "So we're friends now? The last time we had a serious chat, you called me stupid. Said I was trash. Now you want to help me?"

"You know you want me involved. It's dangerous in New York, and you're going to want me around."

"Fine. Keep me safe," I said. I didn't feel like I had much choice.

Another moving day arrived, and all my possessions were loaded onto the truck. I didn't feel particularly sentimental when I left my apartment building for the last time before hopping into a taxi to see Lynda. That all shifted when I got to her office.

"Oh my God, are you okay? It's such an emotional day for you!" my mentor cried out as I walked into her office.

"You know what, you're right. Can I get a hug?" I asked her in an unusually vulnerable moment. Lynda's proclamation and her acknowledgment of the enormous shift brought me into the present, and my feelings finally caught up with me.

"Of course! I also got you a card and some flowers. This is a big deal."

"Thanks. I haven't taken time to feel what it means to leave."

My "other mother" and Pisces soul sister knew me better than I knew myself. Her note and the beautiful flowers reminded me to stop, breathe, celebrate, and feel the change. Lynda, more than anyone else in my life, understood it was no small feat to pack everything hoping to see it again in a new city. And not just any city—New York City.

We spent a few more hours in her office before heading to the airport for a flight to Miami. I was producing a women's health television campaign with her, and we spent ten days shooting and editing before I flew to New York.

My yellow cab pulled up to my new apartment building in Murray Hill about twenty minutes before the moving truck arrived. After unloading several boxes and furniture, I officially became a resident in a one-bedroom apartment, in a doorman building, near the United Nations. The balcony offered an unobstructed view of Tudor City. I was a full-time, albeit unemployed, freelancer and entrepreneur.

For the first few weeks, Thirteen gladly filled me with excessive levels of confidence and cortisol, and I felt invincible. I woke up every morning at 8 a.m., got dressed, and sat in front of my laptop prepared to conquer the NYC freelance producer market. I networked with enthusiasm, certain I would get work.

A month later, with no leads or bookings, the shine wore off my decision to move to New York City. My ego and enthusiasm waned. No one I contacted seemed impressed that I worked for a big agency in a small market. I had to work harder. Failure was not an option. The rent was due, the cosmopolitan martinis called to me, and my savings dwindled.

Today, sending an email, DM, or text is easy compared to the terror of 1997 cold calls to ask people for work. Every day, I rehearsed a script and practiced my delivery. I also prayed my calls would go to voicemail so that I didn't have to actually engage the "maker or breaker" of my future on the phone.

My script sounded something like, "Hi, Mr. or Mrs. Super Important Producer Person. My name is Rebecca Chandler, and I'm a freelance producer with experience with automotive, packaged goods (food), and U.S. Government accounts. Do you have fifteen minutes this week for a quick chat? Please call me. Thank you so much."

I made at least one hundred and fifty cold calls in the first two months. A few people actually called back, but they never offered me any work. Everything miraculously changed when I spoke with Carin.

One of my most favorite humans, she was the one person that returned every phone call and email. After chatting on the phone a few times and meeting me in person, Carin called to offer me my first freelance job. I've never forgotten her kindness.

Carin taught me you can be funny, creative, patient, and a generous leader even in New York City. She understood the nuances of client relationships and creative team peccadillos. She always ensured that everyone working on one of her projects felt respected and included in the process. Carin attracted great people to be part of her team, including Margaret and Lily, who became lifelong friends.

Margaret was a magical blend of humor, an incredible smile, intelligence, and a sense of purpose that never wavered. Not long after we met at the office, it was her birthday. I forgot to get her a gift and felt horrible, knowing Margaret would never forget my birthday.

I dashed into a small grocery store on the corner opposite the office and walked through it, hoping to find something that said, "Happy Birthday!" I was full of dread until I came across the perfect gift–a head of cabbage. Margaret usually ate healthy, save for the occasional cookie dough Sunday blitzes. I knew she would see the head of cabbage, complete with a Happy Birthday post-it, and laugh. Thankfully, I arrived at the office earlier than usual, grateful she wasn't at her desk. I left the cabbage on her chair and waited for her to find me.

"Rebecca!" she called down the hallway through fits of giggles. "Did you really give me a head of cabbage for my birthday?"

"Yes. Yes, I did. You love greens."

"It's the best surprise I've ever gotten," she announced.

We burst into fits of laughter the rest of the day. The managing director, and several other VPs who sat near her, stopped by to congratulate me on giving "the most unremarkable and yet somehow completely appropriate gift" in history.

If you have a friend like Margaret, someone you can give a head of cabbage to and it turns out to be one of the best birthday stories you'll ever share, hang on tight to them.

Lovely Lily was also a beautiful, gentle friend who always managed to laugh no matter the stress levels in the office. She sort of floats when she walks and is one of the more gracious, kind people I've ever known.

She was the one person who knew exactly how to speak to me when I didn't want to listen to myself. Holding nothing back, she somehow managed to deliver the truth, even the painful kind, with a warm smile.

A few times a week Lily peeked over our shared cubicle wall and whispered, "We both need a drink." We would pack up for the night and walk down the street to our usual spot for some cocktails. Our bar chats usually turned into confessionals.

"Rebecca, why are you dating that guy?" she asked.

"The Brain? What about him? It's not like it's a full-on relationship. He's in Boston, I'm in New York. We have fun. Why do you ask?"

"He's an asshole. You shouldn't be dating assholes. You're too beautiful and amazing for that. Stop it," she pushed back.

"Well, it's a little complicated for me," I told her, wary of actually opening up and revealing the truth. I continued to believe I was damaged goods. Intimacy remained elusive.

"Even if it is complicated, you don't need to date an asshole," she admonished.

About a year into my life in New York, my mental health settled down, and I felt good. Not just good, but great. I went to the gym six days a week, and my compulsive eating habits were negligible. My compulsive shopping was an issue, but I ignored it. Still freelancing with Carin and her team, I felt clear and life was pretty fabulous. Save for the disastrously unbalanced relationship with The Brain (a.k.a., "the asshole"), I almost had it all.

I walked, talked, and thought faster, and worked harder. If you ever need to slow down and "figure out life," do not come to New York City. It is a beast. It will chew you up and spit out your bones like a monster if you dare try to stand still too long. The fragments were quiet for large chunks of time. I didn't ask why. I enjoyed the peace and quiet in my head.

Then Buzz, a new addition to my mental menagerie, took over.

Buzz made me feel invincible! I worked crazy hours, ate out, drank sexy cocktails, kept dating The Brain (far too intellectual but good naked), and I felt alive. I was happy to make room for Buzz in my mind and life.

Like most of the characters in A Tale of Early Childhood Trauma, Buzz had a dark side. It liked to encourage my compulsive bits to buy the latest things. Buzz also fed my ego and I began to feel "important" when I spent Sunday mornings in a familiar, expensive boutique and bought clothes.

"Hey, Rebecca," the manager greeted me like we were best friends. "We pulled some really gorgeous pieces for you this morning."

"Great, thanks. Did you get the leather jacket?"

"Yes. It's with the other items. Patricia has a glass of champagne for you in the dressing room."

Buzz and I had a great time. After tucking my worn-out American Express card back into my wallet, I walked out of the boutique toward Central Park to relax in Sheep's Meadow while reading the Sunday *New York Times*. A few hours of sun and fun in the park, and I was ready to make my way over to my favorite eatery, where the chef cooked the world's best pork chop and spinach. Every Sunday cost me about $500. Buzz and I didn't care.

We lived every day in the clouds. I was Buzzing and living in a state of undiagnosed mania.

Having grown accustomed to the wretched despair of Darkness and the tortured chatter of the fragments, Buzz let me feel free. And that was wonderful! Every day, I felt supercharged. Too busy orbiting far away from good judgment and healthy boundaries, Buzz and I ran up enormous debts. All of the credit cards I paid off were once again at their limit.

Here I go, again.

My traumatized, PTSD-infused mind enjoyed running its own sustainability program, recycling the same energy and experiences, over and over.

The first phase started when something new, like a job, friendship, or lover, came my way.

*Oh—bright and shiny! Amazing! I have no balance or boundaries!*

The second phase came when I was surrounded by a combination of trauma, fragments, Buzz, or Darkness ready to make bad choices.

*Buy/eat/screw to ease my anxiety, stress, self-hate, shame, doubt, fear and anger.*

After my energy peaked, I entered the third phase of the program. I was exhausted mentally and physically and headed for the crash.

*I hate myself. I'm a loser. No one loves me. I should end my life.*

The final phase, of course, was when my house fell into ruin. I sat in a heap, wondering what was next, until the cycle began again and I started to rebuild.

*Time to change my life. I need to pay off my debts, leave the loser, shift houses, find a new job, and try a new city.*

I was trapped inside a loop fed by recurring, unhealed traumatized energy deep within. It would take several years before I understood that the ultimate goal was to find a way to permanently expel the energy, stop the cycle and end the program.

Toward the end of my second year in the city, Buzz continued to dominate my life, and I considered what it might mean to make New York City my forever home. I had great friends, dumped The Brain to date a much nicer, albeit dull, boyfriend, and I loved my life. Flight wasn't pulling at me, and I had no intention to leave.

I didn't trust the feeling of calm. It wasn't a vibration that was familiar to me and so I looked for a way to end a good thing. In early 2000, I started to hear about various advertising agencies reducing staff. I reminded myself freelancers were usually the first to go when agencies downsized. I started to panic. Buzz and I had very little in savings to show for the hours I billed for two years. Sure, I had some investments, but they were definitely not at a level equal to my earnings.

As colleagues in other agencies began to lose their jobs, I became convinced I had to leave New York before things collapsed and I couldn't pay my bills. I was irrational. I still had a lot of work as a freelancer. There was no indication I was about to lose my contracts. It didn't matter.

Flight swooped in and said, "We need to get out of here."

Without taking any time to thoughtfully consider my options, I canceled my contracts, packed my things, and drove a U-Haul to Los Angeles.

For the first time since I moved out of my parents' house, I didn't have any actual plans. I was thirty years old and I had no idea where I was going to live or where I would work. It was completely out of character for me but reflected the fact I still lived life with Buzz in the clouds, far and away from reality. I sought refuge with my cousin Sonja once again, and stayed in her home.

"Cousin!" I shouted over my cell phone.

"Hey, Rebecca! How are you? Where are you?" she asked.

"I just moved back to LA. I'm getting things figured out, and I need a place to stay. Just for a few weeks."

"Come on over," she said.

"Can you make the sauce? I'll be there Thursday."

"Yes, I can make the sauce. You're crazy about the sauce," she laughed as we ended the call.

My cousin Sonja is a wondrous mix of heart, intellect, hustle, humor, and beauty. She holds wisdom beyond her years and is always genuine. I love her integrity as much as I love her spaghetti sauce.

"The sauce," as it is known, is the best spaghetti sauce in the entire world. No one will ever convince me I'm wrong. It soothes and nourishes my soul. After staying at her house for about a month, I realized I wasn't going to be able to get a freelance job any time soon. The economy did in fact collapse, and I was in a bind.

I spent weeks searching for any type of advertising agency work in Los Angeles and Orange County. I also searched for and tried to land some international production work. The buzzing part of my brain believed there was nowhere for me to go in America for work, now that I had conquered New York. The natural next step was to work internationally.

Faxing my résumé to ad agencies, NGOs (non-government organizations), and other groups abroad, I hoped the same energy that took me to Washington, D.C., and New York would come through again and help me secure work outside of the United States. Mind you, I had no business thinking that way. Apart from Lynda, I had no connections whatsoever in the international marketing world. It didn't matter. Supremely confident, with Buzz at my side, I was convinced I was going to get work in a far-off land.

To shore up my dwindling savings, I worked part-time for my cousins, answering phones and doing other office work at their small business. I felt like I had reached a dead end but everything changed when my mentor from D.C., Lynda, called me.

"How are you?" I asked excitedly. I was always happy to catch up with my Crunchita.

"Jetlagged. I just got back from a few weeks in Cairo. Some USAID work. How are you doing?" she asked.

"Still trying to get some work. It's so slow right now," I replied, feeling a bit jealous of her international career.

"Well, there's a freelance job for you in Egypt working with USAID on health projects if you want it," she replied.

Buzz and I celebrated. The pay and project didn't really matter. I wanted "international consultant" on my résumé and a trip out of Southern California. Egypt sounded perfect.

Soon after my chat with Lynda, I spoke with Aparna. She was in charge of selecting the right people for the project.

"We need you to produce some television commercials in Arabic with our Cairo team," she explained.

"You all know that I don't speak Arabic, right?" I asked.

"Yeah, that's fine. You'll be working with our local team who can help you. Have you ever done any international work before?"

"Not really," I replied. I was doing a horrible job of selling myself for the role. I wasn't really sure how it was all going to work, but I knew that I could figure it out.

"Hmm. Okay, well, your CV doesn't really have what we're looking for, but Lynda says that you're the best, so I guess it's fine. The contracts office will email you tomorrow, and our travel office will be in touch to plan the logistics."

It was Lynda who first revealed to me that my Pisces-self would always want my world to feel limitless. Flight enthusiastically agreed as I prepared to take off for Cairo.

A few weeks later, on August 4, 2001, I exhaled when the plane took off out of Los Angeles. After reading as much as I could about Egypt online and in travel books, I was eager to see the Nile, gape at the pyramids, and shop in the souks. I was determined to see as much of Egypt as my schedule would allow, reminding myself I might not ever get a chance to return. There was no time to waste!

When I finally walked out of the airplane onto the jetway, the very first blast of summertime Cairo air filled my lungs and hit my skin. It was hot, dusty, and painfully bright in the midday sun. Navigating my way through the throngs of families waiting in the arrivals hall, I managed to find my driver, Mohammed. We walked quickly out of the terminal, past disappointed taxi drivers, and climbed into our van where we were both thankful for the blast of air conditioning filling the cabin.

The frenetic drive from the airport, married with incessant horn honking by my driver and the cars around us, was wonderful. I was almost disappointed when we pulled up to the hotel entrance. The Marriott on Zamalek Island in the heart of Cairo was a grand hotel with beautiful gardens surrounding an enormous pool and several outdoor restaurants. After saying *"shukran"* (thank you) several times to my enthusiastic bellman, I sat down on the bed and blinked a few times. I couldn't quite believe I was actually in Egypt.

It was several hours before sunset, and I wanted to stretch my legs. I decided to take a quick shower before going for a walk through the neighborhood. Adventure awaited!

Like most people traveling to a distant country, I read several traveler's health warnings. The most consistent piece of advice was, "Do not let any tap water into your eyes or mouth."

The warning was fresh in my mind when I stepped into the hot shower with my eyes and mouth closed. Miraculously, I managed to lather up my hair without too much trouble. I panicked when I realized I needed to locate my razor and lather each leg without opening my eyes. After a few minutes of blindly rummaging around in the shower, I had the razor in hand. I bent over to shave my leg and soon discovered that the traveler's warnings forgot to mention that bending over in a hot shower with your eyes closed, particularly after thirty hours of travel-induced dehydration, can lead to good old-fashioned vertigo.

With half of one leg shaved, my brain felt like I just rode the "eggbeater" at a carnival four or five times. Feeling dizzy, I jerked my head up far too quickly and grabbed onto the shower walls, hoping not to collapse. Shampoo ran down my face, and the streaming water hit me square in the mouth like it was at target practice. In some sort of synchronized disaster, I opened my eyes and swallowed a huge gulp of Cairo's finest.

Shower 1 - Consultant 0

I recovered from the shower and stepped outside into the late afternoon heat to take a walk. I loved every minute of it and decided I would stop listening to most of the traveler's advice. The street food, juice bars, markets, and genuine kindness of every Egyptian I met was more than my imagination had conjured before the trip.

I met Mohammed, my driver, Sunday morning (the first day of the work week), and we took a ride down the corniche along the Nile River to the office. Several meetings later, it was clear my days were going to be full. I was being paid a day rate, and I realized that was probably a mistake when it became clear my supervisor expected me to work well beyond an eight- or even ten-hour workday. I had a lot to learn about international consulting.

On the bright side, Aparna, the hiring manager, was in the office, and we started to spend our free time together to see some of the city's nightlife after work. My world became exponentially and forever larger and much more interesting every moment we spent outside of the office. We optimized our Saturdays by going with my new driver, Gamel, to visit the Giza Pyramids, Sphinx, and Egyptian Museum. Aparna had a lot more experience traveling in different cultures, and I admired the way she never seemed surprised or vexed by anything we saw in Cairo. Her parents were also staying in Egypt at the time, and she invited me to their house for lunch.

I really wanted to make a good impression. Her parents were wonderful, and it was important to me that I didn't do anything foolish while having a meal in their house. We sat down at a massive dining table to eat. After all the dishes were laid on the table, my plate was loaded with amazing Indian food. I ate every dish with my right hand, hoping I was respecting all of the cultural nuances. About halfway through the meal, I noticed Aparna was using a fork.

"Hey, you're not eating with your hands," I whispered when her mom went to the kitchen.

"Yeah, I just wasn't in the mood today."

"Thanks a lot. I've been trying to act all casual like I know what I'm doing, and you're using a damn fork."

"Relax," she said, laughing. "Some of that stuff is impossible to eat with your hands."

"No kidding!" I said laughing with her.

Aparna is someone I hope I am always able to call my friend. She's beautiful, funny, smart, kind, and one of the very best travel buddies I've ever known. If you can survive Cairo summer in the heat among ruins and enjoy it with your friend, never let them go.

After a few weeks of prep, I started shooting with a local film company, and I didn't have a day off for quite some time. I stopped seeing Aparna after work as my hours grew longer, and we shot and edited well into the night outside of the office. As the Labor Day holiday approached, Aparna called me to remind me I didn't have to work.

"You get the weekend off. Our office is closed for the American holiday," she told me.

"Good. I need a break."

"Yeah, I think we should go to Luxor and tour the Valley of Kings and Queens. We'll get a local guide for two days and see it all."

Aparna's planning skills surpassed my own. Two weeks later, we checked into our grand hotel in Luxor with a wondrous view of the Nile River. It was only 7 a.m. when we met our guide, Miriam, and took off to see the tombs. After a few hours of learning about the female emperor Hatshepsut, creeping down into King Tut's tomb, and studying hieroglyphics in the Valley of Kings and Queens, it became clear why our day started so early. The heat became impossible. We ended the trek around 12 p.m. and returned to the hotel for a swim before venturing out to Miriam's house for dinner with her family.

The trip to Luxor was a cherished break, and I returned to Cairo eager to deliver the documentaries and commercials for USAID before I flew back to America. Sadly, time stood still for all of us on September 11, 2001, and my flight to America, like all others, was canceled.

The world turned upside down.

I checked out of the Marriott Hotel, grateful to stay with Aparna's family until flights resumed several days later. I was heartbroken by the attacks and the loss of friends and colleagues in New York and D.C. But I was also deeply saddened by the knowledge I would probably never be able to convince anyone at home that Egyptians, Arabs, were incredibly kind, generous, funny, good people. I loved Egypt and hated to see it become the target of so much hatred in the West.

Flights eventually resumed and my departure date was set. Before hopping on the plane, I met with a few Egyptian film company owners and mentioned I'd like to return on a contract for a full-time job as an executive producer. One company was keen and they reached out to me about a week after I returned home and offered me a job. I was moving to Egypt.

Flight was ecstatic.

Buzz was thrilled.

All other fragmented opinions were irrelevant.

I relocated to Cairo in December 2001, and life was immediately challenging. No longer living a tourist's life in the Marriot, things got a lot more real when I had to negotiate an apartment with my *"simsar"* (apartment broker), buy groceries, contact a plumber, and meld with my friends and neighbors.

Culture Shock 101.

A hundred guidebooks could never have prepared me for a full-time life in Cairo. Although my affection for the people grew each day—I have never felt more welcome anywhere in the world—living in Cairo was difficult. I tried to navigate complicated lessons about multicultural work environments, diplomacy, and expat politics. Unfortunately, I wasn't prepared, or properly supported, and I grew frustrated with management. Being an expat is full of twists and turns and requires an enormous amount of patience—which I didn't have.

I really just needed to take a break and breathe so that I could reset in Egypt but I didn't really understand how to relax and slow down. Instead, I stood fast to the American belief that a seventy-hour work week belonged to everyone.

It clearly did not.

My culture shock coupled with office dynamics created rifts that could not be reconciled. When I started to feel like my boss was deliberately sabotaging my work, I let Thirteen push in and fight. My attitude was horrible. I was too immature, impatient, and immersed in my own issues to correct my mistakes and my contract ended sooner than expected.

As I packed my bags for yet another move back to L.A., I reassured myself Egypt was just the beginning of my overseas adventures. The one true consolation was that I made incredible, lifelong friends. Riding in an old black and white taxi on my way to the airport, I cried. My lovely driver, Gamel, who ferried me all over the city for over a year, asked me what was wrong.

"Mama, why are you crying?" he asked in the simple, "child's Arabic" he helped me learn.

"I don't want to leave," I replied.

"But you are going to America. It's freedom," he told me. He couldn't imagine anyone being sad about living in America. America, at the time, was the ultimate dream destination.

"I know. But I also really love Egypt."

"You'll come back, inshallah," he said with a smile.

"Inshallah."

I didn't have enough Arabic to explain to Gamel I wasn't ready to go home. Home didn't feel free. Home made me uncomfortable. The fragmented chatter, compulsive behaviors, Darkness, and Buzz had all but vanished when I was in Egypt. It scared me to think about what would happen to my mental health when I went back home and had to rise from the ashes one more time.

In Tarot, "the Tower" card signifies the end of something significant and the beginning of something new. As a traumatized survivor with complex PTSD, I constantly built houses with towers, and they eventually toppled. I felt a crash coming, and within weeks of returning to Southern California, my mental health dipped, once again, into Darkness.

"*What are you going to do now? You blew it in Egypt,*" Darkness hissed. It slithered out from under its dwelling place in the dark, eager to wrap itself around me once more.

"*I didn't blow it. I did my best. I had zero support at the office, and it didn't work out.*"

"*Well, now what are you going to do?*" Thirteen asked, impatiently.

"*I'll figure it out. I always do.*"

"*When can we leave again?*" Five asked. "*It's not safe here. I don't like Los Angeles.*"

"*I don't know.*"

"*I wish we could go back,*" Seven added.

Unfortunately, being kind to myself while the tower was rebuilding didn't come naturally. I was impatient and ignored the need to for time and space to heal. My cousin Sonja helped me get an apartment near her house and I started working in the financial industry. The job, and my new life, was a million miles away from marketing, filmmaking, and storytelling.

The fragments were not amused.

"*This apartment and job are new. I'm afraid,*" Five said to me more than once.

"*Stop. There's nothing scary. We're back in America. Relax.*"

Thirteen chimed in. "*Yeah, there's no time for us to be scared. I don't care where we've been or what we've been doing. We're fine. Get your ass to work. There's no time for feelings.*"

The Darkness that returned once I was back in America became stronger and more deeply embedded. I felt terribly unhappy. The fragments persisted, and I began to "rapid-cycle" between them. I could wake up feeling pretty good only to spiral into a Thirteen-inspired angry outburst at my assistant over being late. Thirty minutes later, I felt guilty about blowing up at my assistant and became overwhelmed by Seven's sadness. I spent the afternoon fearing I would be reprimanded and Five's whimpers filled my head.

It was time for a mental health tune-up. I was depressed, lonely, angry, sad, and afraid. I went back to Dr. D.

"So what have you been up to?"

"Well. I moved from L.A. to D.C., then to New York, back to L.A., and then to Cairo. And now I'm back."

"Wow. That's a lot. When we last spoke, you were feeling pretty good about the family dynamics and we were exploring some issues around intimacy."

"Yeah. I'm still a mess with intimacy, and I still have a lot to say about my parents. More importantly, there's a growing weird tension within myself. It feels like I'm at war with myself," I said, not directly referring to the fragments.

Dr. D recommended I see a psychiatrist for a bipolar disorder assessment. Always keen to learn, I consulted the internet when I went home to try and understand the nature of bipolar disorder before my psychiatric evaluation the following day.

After twenty minutes of fairly generic conversation with Dr. Pill Pusher, she determined I was, officially, bipolar. As usual, I stopped listening to the scientific gobbledygook coming out of her mouth and silently interpreted her words into a language I understood.

"So, Rebecca, we need to stabilize your mood. I'm going to prescribe four medications. The blue pill will lift you out of depression. The great big white pill will make sure you don't go into mania. The super-duper pill will round out the bipolar edges and help with sleep. The fourth magic pill will help with any remaining issues. The medications work together, and we call it combination therapy."

It sounded like a lot of medicine, but I didn't have the energy to challenge the treatment plan. I wanted relief. I found out much later that Dr. Pill Pusher forgot to tell me that combination therapy wasn't actually tested. She pretty much had no idea how taking four different, powerful medications would impact my body long term. She also didn't mention that trauma and bipolar disorder shared a lot of the same symptoms. At the time, trauma was regularly misdiagnosed and bipolar disorder was one of many "diagnostic labels" used to treat people.

I worked with Dr. D and checked in with the Pill Pusher for several months. During my therapy sessions, I talked about my self-esteem, body image, compulsive eating, and a general sense of unworthiness. Oddly, the concept of shame never directly came up. We spent several sessions focused on family dynamics.

"My parents have never apologized to me for failing to protect me." The absence of an apology still sat like a cold stone in my gut.

"Wow. You've never had a conversation about accountability?" he asked, looking up from his notes.

"Never. They've never asked how I was doing with my healing. I was never brave enough to push for the conversation. It simply isn't discussed. Like it doesn't exist. I get the sense that everyone would just prefer it if I shut up and move on."

He raised his eyebrows. "Do you want to shut up and move on?"

"I'll never shut up," I told him. "I was silent from age five to nineteen. That's all the silence they're going to get from me. Moving on sounds great, but this shit just keeps coming back."

"Yes. Trauma recycles itself. It will get better with time, and therapy, but it will never just stop."

His words cut into me. My trauma was attached to me forever like a ravenous parasite. My parents didn't protect me. My maternal grandfather raped me. And yet, I was the one serving a life sentence for other people's crimes.

"Have you ever given yourself permission to be angry with your parents? I mean really pissed off?" he asked me. I knew he was trying to help me feel my anger, but I couldn't. I couldn't tap into it when it came to my parents.

"No. Parents are always right in my family. I don't know how to feel pissed off at them without worrying about their feelings. It's like I make sure that my feelings don't even matter."

My parents were masterful at turning any conversation about something uncomfortable into a conversation about their own unresolved experiences that laid a foundation for my trauma.

"'Kids don't come with an instruction manual,' they love to say in my family. It basically gives parents a free pass to be negligent without ever having to experience any real repercussions," I said matter-of-factly during our session.

"Well, you may not have come with an instruction manual, but the basic, natural instinct to protect you was certainly fair to expect. It's your parents' duty to process their own trauma and issues so that they are free to provide you with all your basic needs. Their trauma, their issues, should never bleed into your life."

"Well, we know that didn't happen. It bled all over me," I told Dr. D growing more angry. I never had a problem feeling pissed off at my parents. I had a problem expressing it to them directly.

"It's hard because we're taught to love our parents no matter what—even when they harm us. 'Honor thy father and mother' and all of that. It's a disastrous concept," Dr. D said.

He was right, of course. Unfortunately, I didn't know how to turn his words into a reality check with my parents. I could have asked them to come to therapy with me. I could have sat down with them and told them all my feelings and asked for an apology. I wasn't as brave in my thirties as I was when I was just twenty. I don't know why things changed.

If given the chance, I would rewrite this part of my healing journey. Things may have shifted earlier for me had I trusted Dr. D, and myself, to speak to my parents, openly discuss the fragments with Dr. D, and explore more detailed accounts of the abuse. My bipolar diagnosis would have, perhaps, been replaced with a more accurate diagnosis of D.I.D. I feel like my life could have been quite different. The painful fact is I'll never know.

Every type of therapy that a survivor tries serves a purpose in their healing journey. Given all that I know now, I would not personally recommend talk therapy as a single, healing approach for sexual trauma. It feels too event based. I think I should have mixed things up a bit earlier in my pursuit of healing.

After another year with Dr. D, I pushed Darkness back into the depths of the root cellar, filed away more layers of understanding about myself and my family, and I finally felt like my house, my tower, was on track to rebuild. I knew I would need more healing down the road. It was inevitable, but it could wait. It was time to expand the boundaries of my world once more and shake loose from Southern California.

At age thirty-six, I was about to send myself on a trip I had dreamed about my entire life, when I booked a five-star safari to Kenya.

# Transformation

*"Try not to resist the changes that come your way. Instead, let life live through you. And do not worry that your life is turning upside down. How do you know that the side you are used to is better than the one to come?" (Rumi)*

# Chapter 10

When I set out to rebuild my life and a new tower, I never included plans for a family. I had no drive to marry or have children. The only babies on my mind were the furry ones I would see while on safari.

Just a few months prior to my departure to Kenya, I caught up with my amazing friend Shawna. We hadn't spoken in a few years and agreed to meet in New Orleans for some hurricane cocktails and a bit of business. I flew in from a TV shoot in Chicago. By the time I met Shawna at our hotel, she was heading into a "Category 3" cocktail storm of her own choosing.

Always a willing accomplice, I did my best to catch up. We lounged at the glorious hotel bar chatting until the music of the French Quarter lured us outside. Drifting leisurely from one bar to another along crowded Bourbon Street, we proudly earned several strands of Mardi Gras beads from new admirers.

Shawna and I have been friends since the first grade. We played AYSO soccer together and followed each other through high school graduation. Even when our lives sent us in opposite directions, we stayed in touch, sharing a passion for travel, and shenanigans. A mythical creature, Shawna is a striking blend of beauty, creativity, kindness, and entrepreneurship.

As we recovered from Friday night's total debauchery, making even Bacchus himself blush, we sat quietly on the hotel veranda, and I mentioned the trip to Kenya.

"I'm going in November. My dream trip. I've been researching and planning it for two years."

Her eyes sparkled. I could see the hangover lift as wheels turned in her mind.

"Kenya? Sounds incredible. Can I come?"

"Sure," I replied nonchalantly. A lot of people said they wanted to join me but never actually committed. But then I remembered Shawna is an entirely different kind of person. When a great adventure approaches, she gets serious.

"No, really, is there time for me to tag along?" she pressed.

"Yeah, I think so. Be warned, you're gonna have to get some shots. And it's a five-star tour, so it will break the bank a little. I'm talking about a luxury safari, hot-air balloon rides, and bush treks. I've even managed to book a few nights at Giraffe Manor. Trip of a lifetime."

"I'm in," she said with a smile before we went back to nursing our headaches with Bloody Marys.

Just like that, I gained a travel buddy. I couldn't stop smiling. A dream solo trip was now made even better because I was going to see Africa with one of my best friends.

We landed in Kenya two months later and savored the luxury and beauty at some of the most exclusive safari camps in the world. Every day in Kenya felt and looked like a rich and wondrous film. We needed only to open our safari tent flaps to capture mesmerizing beauty. Kenya is home to the cradle of man, where every human story begins, and my body felt unusually at ease the moment we landed. Nothing quite compares to sitting in front of an enormous pride of lions under the endless, equatorial sky.

Gorgeous people, the Kenyans shared warm, genuine smiles and incredible hospitality. Their generosity of spirit reminded me of the Egyptians I had met many years earlier when I first worked in Cairo.

The final stop during our safari before returning to Nairobi was a three-night stay at a particularly posh camp where I contracted "khaki fever." The symptoms included a somewhat lonely, hormonally charged, single female pulled by supernatural forces toward a tall, dark, handsome, intelligent, and charming Kenyan male. I also suffered from a secondary infection of cliché.

When I met The Guide, my biological clock, or "BC," started ticking so loudly I couldn't hear a single fragment. The script about never wanting to be married or have babies was bound for the shredder. As the khaki fever escalated, BC dusted off my bored ovaries and shouted, "Make a baby now!"

"What's up between The Guide and you?" Shawna asked during our second night at camp. We climbed into our individual, four-poster beds in our shared, palatial tent. We both shuffled under the covers, eager to enjoy the hot water bottles tucked between the sheets at the foot of our beds to stave off the chilly night.

"I have no idea. All of a sudden my body is telling me I need to have a baby with that man."

"A baby? You don't want any babies," she said, surprised.

"Well, I didn't until I met him. Now all I can do is think about shagging him rotten."

Grateful to have Shawna with me, we burst into girlish laughter for several minutes. When we finally stopped, she got a curiously stern look on her face.

"There's definitely something between the two of you. I mean, he makes sure you sit in the front seat every time we head out on a game drive. There's some sparks there."

"Yes. I know. My ovaries and I are aware."

The Guide and I spent sunrise to sunset witnessing the great migration and talking about our lives. The energy between us was, admittedly, electric. I could feel the Khaki Fever rising as he explained the wildlife and natural beauty all around us. We never spoke about the fireworks between us, but The Guide and I exchanged contact details just before our departure from camp. I was unsure if I would ever see him, or Kenya, again.

We began texting a week after I had arrived back in California. As our transatlantic chats continued, we began to flirt.

"Hello, beautiful, how's your morning?" he asked.

"I'm great. Just getting ready for work. How was your day, handsome?"

"It was fantastic. We spotted a rhino today. The guests were really chuffed."

"Sounds amazing. Sadly, there are no rhinos here in Orange County—just traffic. Have a great night!" I texted just before leaving the house.

After exchanging missives for several months via text and email, The Guide wrote an email to me in early 2007 and said, "I want you to come and visit. Come back to Kenya."

*"He wants us. He's in love with us,"* I announced.

*"It's not love. He doesn't know you're broken,"* Thirteen snarled. *"This feels reckless."*

"Why is it reckless to fall in love?" I retorted.

"You don't know each other. You can't know anyone by texting," she spat back at me.

"What if he finds out about us and doesn't like us?" Five asked.

"Can I just be happy?" I asked in exasperation. "Is it so hard to believe I might have actually met the man of my dreams?"

Just a year after we first met, I flew east again to soothe BC's insatiable desire to be with The Guide. I thought I was in love. After landing in Nairobi, I hopped into a small, bumpy bush plane, and I took off to the Maasai Mara. Once I disembarked, I saw The Guide standing in the equatorial sun, handsome as ever, and my heart beat faster. His hug felt like home, and we took off, ready for four days of safari and courtship.

"He is hot," I said to the fragments.

"Yes, he's hot, but does he know you're broken yet?" Thirteen asked. The most monstrous version of herself surfaced whenever I came close to even thinking about intimacy.

"Why does he need to know?" I asked.

"You have to tell him. If he still loves you after you tell him, then it's real," Seven explained.

"I'm here for four days. I'm not going to sit by the campfire and tell him I was raped for eight years. No way. I'm just going to be in the moment."

"It's a lie," Thirteen snarled.

"It's a life. Shut up!" I yelled at her.

Handsome and incredibly charming, The Guide felt like my soulmate. Our final night together culminated in wine and incredible sex. It was glorious. The next day, we stood at the dirt airstrip once again, and I did my best to be brave. I didn't want to leave. BC didn't want me to leave. Kenya, and The Guide, felt like a salve to a lifetime's worth of pain. Just before I boarded the plane, he pulled me aside, and we professed love for one another.

"I love you. I want you to move to Kenya," he said.

My ears, and other body parts, interpreted every word of his invitation as a bona fide proposal. No man had ever told me he loved me, much less asked me to move and be with him. All the pieces of me craving love and affection lit up, and I felt truly alive.

Biological Clock drowned out all reason and responded from deep within my womb.

"Yeah, I should move to Kenya," I said to him. We embraced for a long time and agreed to talk about the future once I returned home. A few days later, back in America, I announced my love and intentions to move to Nairobi.

It was an absurd declaration to be sure, but the only real objection came from my sister: Moving to Kenya to be with someone I didn't know was erratic. And while that was a fair assessment of the situation, I didn't listen. Flight was in the driver's seat while BC overruled all common sense and the fragments.

In May 2008, I boarded a plane to Kenya to start a new life. The Guide managed to get a few days off from work and was in Nairobi and we agreed he would join me at an exclusive hotel. After two long flights, I pushed nine enormous duffel bags past distracted customs officers into the fresh evening air. Kenya was officially my new home.

*"Right after we get to the hotel, let's order room service and shag for seventy-two hours," BC sang.*

*"Agreed," I replied.*

*"And then what?" Thirteen asked.*

*"Yeah, what's next? We don't have a job. We only know one other person besides The Guide. How are you going to pay for the apartment you just leased without any work?" the fragments asked.*

*"I have no idea. For now, I'm just going to enjoy the fact I'm in Kenya and in love."*

Two hours later, The Guide had yet to arrive at the hotel. I tried to call and text him but never got a reply. I didn't quite know what to do. I sat alone in "our" hotel suite and interrogated myself.

*Did I completely misread the intention of every text and email? Were my feelings genuine or fantasy? Or both? How could I explain to anyone the love of my life never showed up? Was I an idiot?* Paralyzed with embarrassment, confusion, and blossoming heartbreak, I refused to leave the hotel.

After three days, I had to check out of the hotel and move into *our* apartment. When I showed up alone, the manager asked about The Guide. The lease listed both our names. Her queries hit me like a gut punch. I swallowed my feelings and told her his plans had changed and asked for a new lease only in my name. After unloading my bags into the apartment, I shut the blinds and went to bed crying.

A few days later, The Guide finally sent me a text.

"Sorry! I was called back to camp earlier than expected. We are really busy, and I haven't had any free time. The mobile signal at camp is terrible. How's your new apartment?"

"*How's your new apartment?*" snapped Thirteen. "*What the hell is that? When did he decide it wasn't our new apartment?*"

"*I agree. Am I just supposed to ignore the fact he never showed up after I moved 10,000 miles away to a new country to be with him?*"

"*He doesn't love us,*" Seven whimpered.

"*What are we going to do?*" Five asked.

I didn't have any answers. I was in shock. When The Guide offered all manner of explanations, my confused, lovesick mind and body believed every word. I spent the next few weeks doing my best to get to know my neighborhood. I was treating myself to lunch out of the house when I met two women in a nearby café. When I told them I was new to Kenya, they invited me to join them for some tea and cake. Eventually, they asked me why I came to Kenya.

"I came to Kenya to be with my boyfriend. He's a guide in the Mara. Things have gotten really weird. I haven't seen him since I arrived," I explained.

"Are you sure he's not married?" they both asked. Neither of them seemed particularly surprised by my story.

"No, no way," I rebuffed. "Why would he tell me to move here if he's married?" I couldn't imagine a man would profess love as some sort of casual lark.

"Okay, well, sometimes Kenyans just go quiet," they said. "We stop answering messages until we figure out a problem. Maybe he's just gone quiet for a while." Kenyans have an uncanny ability to avoid saying the hard things out loud. There is no limit as to how far they will go to protect a person's feelings. It's an endearing and frustrating part of the culture.

When another new friend who was living in my apartment building invited me to tea a few days later, she finally set me straight. "Aya, please," she said as she whistled through her teeth. "Rebecca, that man hasn't gone quiet. That man is married and has children. You, you are his *mzungu* (foreign) *chips funga*."

"*Chips funga?*" I asked. I had no idea what she was saying.

"In Kiswahili, it means *chips* (French fries) *funga* (on the side). Many women move to Kenya and become someone's *chips funga* and have no idea it happened," she explained. "He probably never expected you to actually move here. He has no idea what to do with you. You need to forget about that man."

It took a few more days before the reality of her words finally took over, leaving my heart and fantasies about love in ruin. I was his *chips funga*, a mere side dish. Humiliated and heartbroken, I lashed out at BC.

"It's all your fault! I was content to never even consider having a baby much less marriage. I was content not being in love. And now, here I am, away from home, no job, and no babymaker," I shouted into the abyss. BC was silent. She had learned from my Kenyan friends and gone quiet.

The fragments had a lot to say about the situation.

"Did you really think he loved you? How could you be so stupid? What are we going to do now? We don't know anyone. We don't have a lot of money. We can't just hang out. What in the hell have you done?" they screamed.

Seven added another layer of pain. "He doesn't love us. He never loved us. No one is going to love us. What are we going to do? How are we going to stay safe? We don't know this place."

A decision loomed: Did I move back home and try to rebuild yet again? Or should I pull up my socks, stand up straight, and get to living? I was completely out of my depth when it came to making a new life in East Africa, but Flight and I weren't quite ready to surrender.

I told Seven to relax and Thirteen to shut up. The only thing that ever helped me feel settled was work. The time had come to start networking locally and internationally to try to find an opportunity.

I boldly, and naively, chose a new life in Kenya.

Starting over doesn't typically frighten or deter me. It's part of who I am: the feeling that no matter how difficult life may become, I can make it work. After all, I've already survived the worst life can throw at me. Choosing to stay in Nairobi was an opportunity to show myself, and everyone else, I could not be defeated. I would not give up.

If I was going to build a new life, it meant saying goodbye to The Guide. We would never speak again. My heart hurt. I didn't know if I would ever fall in love again or if my lingering desire for a family after The Guide would come true. In the first few months after I cut him off, I felt tempted to send a text or call. But I stopped myself short each time. Life on the equator in a new culture was complicated enough without making room to be his *chips funga* ever again.

When I reached out to my mentor Lynda in Washington, D.C., for any helpful contacts, she said, "You should meet Wangari. She worked in our office. She's brilliant and moved back to Nairobi about a year ago. When you get in touch with her, use my name."

Wangari and I met for lunch a few days later. After enjoying a plate full of delicious, freshly fried chips (French fries), we hit it off right away. I appreciated her creative, warm soul and infectious smile.

"Reach out to my friend Wanuri," Wangari told me. "She recently graduated from film school in the U.S., and now she's directing her first feature film back in Kenya."

I emailed Wanuri, wondering if I would ever get a reply. She didn't know me and was busy shooting a feature film. Much to my surprise, she answered my email just two days later. We agreed to find time after her film shoot wrapped.

About a week later, we met at Moniko's cafe in Lavington Green, which, thankfully, was a short number forty-eight bus ride away from my apartment. Within a few minutes of chatting, we just clicked as we talked about filmmaking and storytelling. A few hours later, Wanuri completely changed my life when she asked, "Do you want to produce a documentary with me?"

I had never produced a single bit of content in Kenya but knew it was time to start. "Absolutely," I replied, trying to control my excitement.

"Great", she replied. "Let's meet at my house next week and go through the script and talk about it."

A week later, I hopped on the forty-eight bus once again for another meeting with Wanuri at her home. I arrived to find the house quiet. Too quiet for a 9 a.m. meeting. After calling Wanuri's line a few times and knocking on the door, she greeted me and invited me inside. (Note to self, 9 a.m. meetings in Kenya were likely 10 a.m. meetings.)

"I'm directing a documentary about a famous Kenyan environmentalist," she explained as she brewed a fresh pot of tea. Her kitchen was wonderful. Fresh vegetables lay on the counter, ginger and other roots dangled from a basket, and beans soaked in a pot on the stove. Wanuri, I would learn, was a terrific cook.

"Our client is in South Africa. I need you to line produce. You know, create the budget, control the costs, keep us on schedule, and do all the paperwork."

"Got it. No problem. You know I haven't done this in Kenya before, right?" I asked her from behind my mug of tea. I was reminded of my conversation with

Aparna years earlier. I always felt compelled to admit my shortcomings. I needed to say it out loud.

"Yeah. It's fine. I can tell you who to call for crew and equipment. We'll figure it out. It's a pretty low budget, so we need to keep things simple."

Wanuri attracts equal amounts of love and excellence as she shares her enormous, gentle heart. It's humbling and nourishing to spend time with her. After welcoming me into her life, beyond our first project, we became business partners, and I met her friends and Mummee and Daddee, as well as the rest of her family.

With some work coming my way and new friendships taking root, life in Kenya started to settle down. After posting a "Hey, I'm new here; want to get a drink?" message on Internations.org, I expanded my social circle even further. Not long after my post went live, I heard from and made plans to meet Breanne. An American who was back in Nairobi for a second tour, she consulted for humanitarian agencies as a lawyer. We met around 6 p.m. at a local nightclub several hours before the band and crowds filled the Moroccan-themed space for a night of partying.

"That's pretty fucked up," she said to me after I told her why I was in Kenya. "You actually moved here to be with someone who never showed up. How horrible."

"Yeah, it was horrible, but it's over now, and I'm trying to figure out a new apartment, work permit, and a job."

Just as the throngs began to arrive at the club, we walked home, and Breanne became my closest friend in Kenya. A few months later, we decided to rent an apartment and share the costs of a monthly rental car. The forty-eight bus was replaced by a gold Honda Civic, and we both adjusted to driving on the right-hand side of the car on the left-hand side of the road.

To celebrate our move, and the new wheels, we went out about a month later on Saturday night, and Breanne was the evening's designated driver.

Nairobi nightlife starts around midnight and DJs play a fantastic mix of local and western music to keep people dancing. At 6 a.m., drunk, tired bodies pour out of the clubs, eager to make their way to the closest fried chicken and chips restaurant where the grease, salt, and Fanta Orange push back against an ungodly hangover.

Not serious club hoppers, Breanne and I still managed to stay out until about 3 a.m. After several cocktails and far too much dancing in heels, I piled into the back seat of our car along with our friend, Ahmed, who was going to crash on our sofa for the night.

Sixty seconds after leaving the parking lot, Celine Dion boomed from the car speakers. My buzz evaporated. The music was far too cheesy for me. I was about to yell at Breanne to change the station when I realized she was singing her heart out to a classic ballad.

She knew every word. Hit every note.

"Are you actually singing along to this?" I shouted at her, not quite understanding what was happening. I'd never met anyone who knew a single lyric to a Celine song, much less a person who proudly shouted them out at the top of their lungs at 3 a.m.

"Don't say a damn word about Celine. Not a word," she barked from the front seat as we headed home. Breanne was a hard-charging human rights lawyer who fought bravely for refugees every day. I knew from her tone she had very little accommodation for our backseat, drunken whimsy. Her robust defense of humanity extended all the way to the right to enjoy cheesy love songs.

Ahmed and I laughed uncontrollably while Celine, and Breanne, proudly sang about love all the way home. "Breezy" remains one of my closest friends and confidants, and she is one of the most intelligent, caring, and wittiest people I have ever known. My friends helped me build a wonderful new foundation and I loved the camaraderie, laughter, and sense of family blooming in Kenya.

Life had balance. I had a great flat with an awesome roommate and freelance work bubbled. Collaborating with Wanuri on the documentary project opened doors into the local Kenyan film industry. I made scores of contacts, including Guy and Ginger, who owned a local film company. They were patient, generous, and particularly forgiving as I made endless mistakes trying to forge a life and career in Kenya. Their office was a fantastically chaotic blend of creative professionals, rescued dogs and cats, cheeky kids, and Guy's signature brewed tea. Life in Nairobi made sense.

At the end of 2008, some six months after I first landed in Nairobi, I had fairly steady freelance work, an amazing roommate, and wonderful friends. My life was surprisingly full. Navigating a new country, culture, language, and becoming part of a complicated local film industry didn't leave a lot of room for fragmented chatter. It suited me. I didn't miss any of them.

I put off dating entirely for about a year, and then I met The Geek in early 2010.

What can I say? I'm a Pisces and he was a tall, dark, handsome, funny, and smart Taurus. We met one day on a film set while shooting a commercial. I didn't have a lot of time to chitchat, so I asked Fatuoh, my Kenyan-Somali sister and makeup artist, to talk to him.

"Ask him if he's single," I told her between takes.

"Eh, all men in Kenya are single if they want to be," she replied. I certainly knew it was true. Memories of The Guide came forward, and I felt a twinge in my stomach. I still wasn't entirely over him.

"Okay, well, ask him some questions and find out about his life," I told her.

"Boss, let me do what I do," Fatuoh said.

Every person should live in such a way that they actually deserve a Fatuoh. She is a fiery, hilarious, incredibly talented sister. She came back to me later in the day with a full report. "He's single, like, 'single, single,'" (for my expat friends, if you know, you know), "does something with computers, is kind of shy, and he seems pretty nice," she reported.

"Here—give him my business card," I said.

When the shoot wrapped, I took off for home. The Geek called me twenty minutes later and we made plans to meet at The Pub near my house.

Biological Clock suddenly stopped being quiet. Rising out of self-imposed exile, she heard his voice and yelled, "He is hot! It's time to feel the tingles!"

Breanne and Fatuoh agreed to join me, and we walked into The Pub around ten. Not long after we arrived, The Geek came in with a few of his friends, and we all enjoyed some drinks. Besides being quite handsome, he was also cheeky, and he made me laugh. After a quick make-out session in the car park, he took off with his friends, and I headed home excited to see him again.

We texted each other over the next few days and managed to go on some dates. A month later, it was clear we liked each other. Practical conversations around safe sex, HIV testing, and our results became necessary. It was time for serious tingles.

"Hey, gorgeous, what are you up to?" The Geek texted me late at night.

"I'm at home. It was a long day on set. Where are you?" I asked. "Do you want to come for dinner tomorrow night?" It was the first time I had offered to cook a meal in my house for anyone. BC couldn't have been more pleased.

"Cool. Have you gotten your test yet?" he asked.

"No. I will tomorrow. We're actually filming at a family health clinic, so I'll just get it done there. What about you?"

"I got mine today. I'll come over for dinner, and we can share our results," he texted back.

The next evening, The Geek came over to my house. The dutiful conversation around test results ended and gave way to a really wonderful make-out session on the couch. A few hours later, BC and I relaxed in bliss after tingle-inducing sex in my bedroom.

"So what is this?" The Geek asked somewhat seriously, lying beside me in bed.

"What is what?" I answered, confused. I was in a post-coital haze and clear thinking wasn't part of the experience.

"Is this just some sort of one-night-stand, casual thing or are we dating?" he asked.

Unprepared for the question, I stared at him in stunned silence for a few seconds.

"Well, I'm not interested in having a casual thing. It's not really me," I answered, completely ignoring the fact I just had sex with a man I had known for a total of one month. I also managed to forget my first date with Surfer Dude and the affair in D.C. My track record didn't reflect a long history of quality, monogamous relationships.

"Okay, well then, if it's not a casual thing," he said rolling onto his side to face me, "then we should make a pinkie promise with each other."

A pinkie promise! I was smitten. BC danced.

We interlocked our pinkies and committed to each other that we were in an exclusive relationship. We agreed if either of us had sex with anyone else, we would talk about it. The rules were clear and our health hinged on being honest with one another.

One of the things I enjoyed most about The Geek was his particularly ridiculous sense of humor. Absurd, childish things, like farts, cracked both of us up. I still think fart jokes are funny. Our shared laughter at nonsensical things made the early months of our relationship a lot of fun.

Great sex and laughter made it easier for me to ignore his need to get absolutely blind drunk three nights a week. I also made excuses for the fact he never invited me to join him when he went clubbing or when he introduced me to no more than just a few friends. I wasn't welcome into his inner circle or even taken out for a meal. The broken part of me was happy "just to be in the room" and much stronger than my self-respect. I accepted the terms of the relationship, but the fragments complained.

*"He doesn't love you,"* Thirteen shouted. *"He's hiding something."*
*"He's private,"* I explained, ignoring the pieces of me that knew Thirteen was right.
*"If you make a fuss, he won't want us,"* Seven cried out. *"We can't be alone again."*
*"It's fine the way it is,"* I argued. *"I'm way too busy to dig into this right now."*

In 2011, three months after meeting The Geek, I took on contract work as an executive producer for a global advertising agency group in Nairobi. My time was split between several different countries in Africa, as well as in India and Europe.

The Geek's behavior, and the dynamics of our relationship, didn't improve. My considerations, wants, and needs were largely ignored. I was unhappy but unclear about what to do. I sat in a Gabon hotel room one night debating with the fragments about whether the relationship with The Geek should continue.

*"If I break up with The Geek, I will be alone, again,"* I told the fragments. *"I am barely home for more than two or three days at a time. How and where am I going to meet someone else?"*

*"Is that what this is all about? You don't want to be alone? You're pathetic,"* they threw back.

*"Fuck you. First you were afraid of being alone and now I'm pathetic? It's not pathetic to come home after five weeks of travel and want and need to connect with someone while I watch a movie."*

*"So he gets to do whatever he wants, no matter how hurtful, because you don't want to make an effort to connect with someone who's actually nice. Got it. Stay with him, then. He's going to screw you over, but you'll find out in your own time,"* Thirteen snapped. The others went quiet.

The Geek offered me an unfulfilling form of love, but it gave my life a predictable rhythm. We did manage to have some fantastic adventures. A trip we made often was to northwest Kenya, to Kisumu, which sits on the edge of Lake Victoria in the heart of Luoland.

I loved the quaint, small town and easygoing nature of its residents. The best part of the trip was walking down to eat dinner at one of the many fried fish stalls on the shore. Nile Tilapia, caught fresh early in the morning, was tossed into an enormous cast iron wok to deep fry, along with fresh chips. The pop and hiss from the grease released a mouth-watering aroma wafting over our table as we cracked open Tusker beers and watched hippos in the lake during a beautiful East Africa sunset. Those moments were charming, but not enough.

When I wasn't spending time with The Geek, I shared bottles of wine during drunken mani/pedis with Breanne and another good friend Kelsi, took weekend safari trips, and enjoyed a steady stream of dinner parties with my girlfriends. A year later, in 2011, I turned forty-one, and I finally admitted to BC and myself I wanted a child. I wasn't sure The Geek was the ideal candidate; he certainly had his faults. But he was funny, highly intelligent, inquisitive, and caring. Those qualities may not have always been reflected in our relationship, but he had his own burdens, and I loved him. He was also available and BC's clock was ticking.

"I think I should go off of birth control," I told The Geek after a particularly long business trip to Cape Town, South Africa.

"Good. Go off it," The Geek replied a little too quickly. We were lying in bed and I was sure he was distracted.

"You're okay if I get pregnant?" I asked, somewhat surprised. Didn't most men need days and weeks to consider this sort of life change?

"Why not? You should get a baby," he said in a classic Kenyan phrase. Women didn't get pregnant. They "got" babies.

"Okay," I said, staring into his eyes. "We're going to officially start trying to make a baby," I said, almost in shock at how simple the moment felt.

"Yes!" he proclaimed as he smiled before things heated up, once again. "We are making a baby!"

The Geek took my announcement seriously. Baby making became the top priority. I continued to ignore the fact we lived separate lives and he spent three nights a week partying. I shoved all the red flags into the Denial cupboard in my mind and focused on having a baby.

He tried to "give me a baby" often, and it was a lot of fun until my period kept coming month after month. Eventually, I started to get worried. In late 2011, The Geek joined me in Johannesburg for a quick visit with a fertility specialist. He left a sperm sample, and I was examined for other potential challenges. We met with the fertility doctor a few days later.

A soft-spoken, holistic fertility practitioner, she spent as much time analyzing my love of thunderstorms as she did my ovulation patterns.

"So, Geek, I reviewed your results. Tell me, do you drink often?" she asked after lighting a candle at the start of our consultation.

"I mean, I go out every Thursday, Friday, and Saturday," he answered.

"Okay, well, that's actually quite a lot, especially when you're trying for a healthy pregnancy." I was embarrassed. The Geek's lifestyle I had done my best to ignore was now part of my medical file. "Do you smoke a lot of marijuana?" she asked.

My head turned on a swivel to look at him. Pot?

"Yeah," he said casually, "I smoke it during the week some days and on the weekends. Is it a problem? I mean, I didn't have any issues leaving a sample a few days ago."

"The amount of time you needed and the quantity of your sample was fine. Unfortunately, the sperms themselves show signs of laziness. They're slow and confused. They're essentially stoned," she explained. "If you really want to focus on getting Rebecca pregnant, you need to stop drinking and smoking for several months."

"Okay," he said as if we were talking about choosing a pair of shoes.

*What does "okay" mean? I asked myself. Okay, I hear you and I'll do it, or okay, fascinating, I don't believe you?* The Geek had a habit of giving one-word replies when he felt uncomfortable or, more often, when he didn't believe the conversation merited his attention.

When she started to explain my low ovarian reserve, age, and other challenges I faced to get pregnant, I became restless. It was the first time I understood getting pregnant might be a problem. All the talk about my body and my fertility triggered me from deep in my core.

So I detached.

I watched from the corner of the doctor's office as The Geek and I listened to her diagnosis. I wasn't prepared for problems. I had to get pregnant. Infertility wasn't even part of my vocabulary. *If we couldn't get pregnant, did we even exist? I asked myself in a panic.*

Admittedly, our relationship had dissolved into a largely one-sided effort led by me. I was alone most of the time inside of our relationship. If the baby-making effort failed and no longer took center stage in our lives, not much left existed to celebrate. The thought of being single and living life without a child was almost too painful to consider.

We left the clinic in silence. The news was grim. Low ovarian reserve. I essentially had very few eggs left, and they were fragile. Low quality. My eggs and The Geek's stoned sperm did not speak kindly to getting pregnant. It was a lot to absorb. We flew back to Nairobi the next day and got into a terrible fight at my house.

"What are you doing? Are you actually getting ready to go out tonight?" I barked at him, noticing he'd changed into his "club" look.

"Yeah. It's Thursday night," he replied, buckling his belt. "Why wouldn't I go out?"

"For real?" I asked with my hands on my hips. "We literally just sat in a doctor's office and you were told not to party so I might actually have a chance to get pregnant. Why the fuck did we do the testing and see her if you're going to ignore all of her advice?"

"Whatever," he said, never once meeting my gaze. It was not lost on me in the moment that he never even skipped a beat during the conversation. Feelings were his kryptonite. He just kept picking up the things he needed to have a good time.

"If you can't get pregnant, it isn't about me," he said.

His words stabbed my heart. He knew about my abuse and used my brokenness against me. It should have been the end, but it wasn't. I was emotionally color-blind and continued to ignore every red flag. I couldn't give up on The Geek. More importantly, I couldn't give up on my urge to have a baby. We kept trying.

The Geek refused to change any part of his lifestyle, and I had to own a terrible bit of truth. When he said he wanted to "give me a baby," he meant it in the same way as when he said he wanted to take me on a grand vacation. It would be nice, but it wasn't really a priority. We were not a priority. And if I'm honest, we never really existed.

Another year passed, and I still worked and traveled all the time. I still wasn't pregnant. Rather than stop the madness and end the relationship, I raised the stakes and waged a last-ditch effort to make it work. The desire to not be alone and have a baby was still so strong I believed that letting him move into my house was the answer to our problems. I convinced just enough of myself that if I could just have a baby, he would change. I would never be alone again.

The problem with Denial is, of course, that it never works.

The Geek moved into my apartment on Friday night. On Saturday morning, he headed out to run errands and left his laptop open. When I heard the Skype notifications coming from his computer, a moment of sanity took over. I shoved Denial out of the way and finally listened to the instincts that had nagged at me for most of our time together. The fragments' dire warnings about the miserable state of my relationship with The Geek echoed in my head as I read his messages.

The ugly truth was in writing.

The Geek was in a long-term relationship with another woman. They freely chatted about the sex they had Friday morning when he showed up late to move his things into my house. A bit of remorse about the D.C. affair rekindled in my heart as I felt the first stabs of his deception.

I was a childless, forty-two-year-old fool. We would never have a baby. I wasted years ignoring all my wants and needs, throwing away my chance at a family with a liar, drunk, and a cheat. When he came home later, things kicked off.

"So who's Irene?" I asked calmly, standing in the kitchen. I leaned my arms on the counter as my legs shook. "You know, the other woman you're fucking," I said coldly.

"How did you find out about her?" he asked wide-eyed. I was immediately pissed off. His concern with how I knew outweighed his concern for betraying me.

"How doesn't matter," I said. "You're fucking someone else. You're a liar! What the fuck have you been doing this whole time? What happened to your pinkie promise? After all the shit I've done for you. Flying you around, taking care of everything, and all you can do is fuck somebody else?"

"I never asked you to do anything for me. I knew you wanted a baby, so I didn't tell you about her. I didn't want to hurt your feelings," he offered pathetically.

"So you were doing me a favor while you fucked me and someone else? Did you ever consider the fact that you've been playing with my life? You're so fucking selfish."

I walked away and texted my girlfriend. I didn't know what to do.

"I'm coming over," she immediately texted back. "We have to make sure he gets out of the house *tonight*." In shock, I walked to the living room sure he would be packing. I heard the voice of my early Kenyan friend in my head. *Silly woman. That man is sitting on the couch watching television. He thinks you're going to behave like a good chips funga and stay quiet.*

"What in the hell are you doing? You have to leave," I shouted from the stairs. I hung onto the banister so tight my knuckles turned white.

"What?" he asked, completely unaware he couldn't betray me and live with me.

"You can't stay here. You can't fuck another woman and stay in my house," I shouted. The obtuseness of the moment was too much.

"Where am I supposed to go?" he asked pathetically.

"I don't give a shit where you go. Go to her house! Go to some other whore's house. But you need to leave right now," I said just before the tears started flowing.

Standing in the kitchen, I cried as I watched him silently pack his essentials. We avoided looking at each other as he walked by me to go upstairs and collect a few clothes. When my friend showed up, she stood with me. After what felt like an hour, he came downstairs and headed for the front door.

"The keys," I whispered to my friend. "He has keys to my house."

"Geek, we need the keys," she said, extending her hand before he could leave.

I heard them jangle into her hand as she closed the door behind him.

Shattered by the betrayal, I was completely humiliated. My girlfriends had all told me he was bad news. I told myself he was bad news. Even the fragments thought he was rubbish. It didn't matter. Broken love was somehow better than no love.

My friend sat in silence while I cried it out before putting a plan into action.

"Right," she said, reaching for my hand to help me off the floor. "Let's get his crap out of here. We need to pack all his stuff right now. Text him and tell him he can collect it tomorrow," she said.

"Right," I said, and the tears stopped. I could cry later. It was time to sort out my house.

Thirteen exploded.

*"I can't believe you put up with his bullshit for two years,"* she raged in my head. *"He never took you out. He never wanted anyone to see you. He probably took her out,"* Thirteen snarled.

*"I am aware,"* I answered meekly.

*"And now we have to pack his shit? You're an idiot,"* she screamed.

*"Shut up!"* I shouted back in my head.

*"What's going to happen to us? Are we going to have a baby?"* Seven asked.

*"I have no idea. Please, just leave me alone!"*

All the clothes, shoes, electronics, and other personal items The Geek and I unpacked thirty-six hours earlier were shoved back into the very same bags and readied for removal.

"Should we cut all the buttons off his work shirts?" my friend asked with a serious tone.

*"Yes!"* Thirteen shouted. *"Exactly!"*

"I can't. I don't have it in me, but it's nice to think about," I replied to my friend.

*"God you're so pathetic,"* said Thirteen.

"So we won't be burning any holes into his shirts then," my friend asked with a straight face. "You know, we should at least burn some things in the driveway. That's how women handle these things around here."

"*Yes! Burn all of his shit!*" Thirteen chimed in.

"No," I said to my friend and Thirteen, "but I will keep every one of his hangers." Hangers were sold in sets of three, and they were oddly expensive. It was going to cost him a small fortune to buy enough hangers for his wardrobe.

"*Hangers? You're going to keep his hangers. You are so fucking pitiful,*" Thirteen muttered.

I was crushed.

I sent a text to Wanuri later that night, and she volunteered to be in my house the next morning while The Geek removed all his things. I had to go to work and prepare for another big shoot in India. Thirteen lectured me the entire day.

"*You know, the incessant drinking. The weird way he always kept his life separate from yours. He had at least two lives. At least two lovers. You gave everything, and he gave as little as possible. He never loved you. Never deserved you. It was toxic.*" Thirteen was predictable. She was either my friend and protector or my hater. I always felt powerless no matter which way her mood was swinging.

In this instance, I had to admit she was right. Our relationship never had any healthy balance. For every bright and shiny moment, ten more left me feeling lonely, ignored, and taken for granted. I did all of it for the sake of my eager womb.

Alone at home later that night, I took a moment to really consider my definition of love. Did I even have one? Did I just forget or deny it in my desperation for a child? A few weeks later, I stayed in yet another hotel in Mumbai, and I asked myself to define Love.

"*The Love I want is fanciful and romantic. It makes me feel safe. Love is my Champion. Love listens to me when I am triggered. Love hears me when I need to be hugged every single day. Love stands with me as I stand in my truth. Love wraps its strong arms around me and holds me tight in the morning and in the evening. Love releases every knot I've tied one frayed fiber at a time. Love reassures me in my career. Love is strong and ferocious and defends me. Love is tender. Love makes me laugh, rarely makes me cry, and wants me to soar. Love makes love to me and loves every single curve and dimple in my body. Love makes space for me to love myself. In return, I let down all my walls and let Love in.*"

I had made space in my heart, and tower, for a partner and child and it all crumbled. The rubble crushed me, once again.

The Geek betrayed me, but so did my body. It was the first time I ever felt totally out of sync with my physical self. What was the point of even sounding the

Biological Clock alarm bells if the net result was I couldn't conceive a child? I turned my sadness into determination.

I booked appointments with fertility specialists during future business trips in Europe, India, and South Africa. Every consultation ended with reassurances that I was fit to get pregnant despite my ovarian reserve. All I had to do was find a suitable partner.

"What are we going to do?" the fragments asked. "Is it too late to get pregnant? The year is nearly over."

"No. All of the doctors say I'm fine. The Geek was the problem. Women much older than me get pregnant. It will all work out," I told the fragments confidently. "It's going to happen."

In 2012, my career took off, and I produced social media and television commercials, TV shows, and other content. Storytelling was my world, and I genuinely loved all of it. My global family in Nairobi, Dubai, South Africa, Mumbai, and London was strong, but I continued to feel unsettled.

Four years after I first moved to Kenya, I couldn't ignore the jittery feelings in my bones. Flight tried to convince me to move away from my pain, but I assured myself all would be well if I just got a baby.

## Chapter 11

It was time to innovate. Science and some donated sperm seemed like a good option. I didn't have the energy, or time, to meet someone new, much less build a relationship to get a baby. In 2013, I booked an IVF (in vitro fertilization) consultation with a clinic in Nairobi.

As part of their preliminary review, they ordered lab work. In parallel, I found a fertility expert in India and sent her my results for a second opinion. I was anxious when the doctor from India called me to discuss the results.

"Rebecca," she said, "I've looked at all the labs you sent from the past two years. Your ovarian count is practically nonexistent. It's one of the lowest readings I've ever seen for a woman your age. I'm sorry, but you're not going to conceive."

"How is that possible?" I asked. Her words lingered in the air all around me. My body and mind refused to accept the news. "All the other doctors told me I shouldn't have a problem getting pregnant. They prescribed medication to improve ovulation."

"I'm sorry. They're not being honest with you," she said. I could hear her sadness for me grow as she delivered the worst possible news. "There's no way you're going to get pregnant."

"Not even with IVF?" I asked, still unable to believe all my options were dead. I felt completely numb.

"IVF only works 25 percent of the time in women who are 100 percent healthy," she explained. "Your ovarian reserve is in the lowest one percentile. You have very few eggs left, and the quality of those eggs isn't hopeful. IVF will never work. I am so sorry. You've been misled all this time."

I told myself to breathe. I felt small.

Nonexistent.

Barren.

Seven's sadness washed over me, making us both inconsolable. I saw my life, alone, full of darkness. The truth smacked of treachery. I could no longer trust my body. Our partnership disintegrated. I felt cheated. It was a level of anguish I think can only be appreciated by others who come out of their own infertility journey without a child.

I reached out to some close friends. I needed to talk. But it felt like no one wanted to talk to me about it. Even some of my closest friends felt distant as I tried to find the words to share my pain. Most of my friends had children. Some were even pregnant. What do you say to someone who can't get pregnant when you're celebrating the birth of your own child?

In 2013, I was still recovering from a bad breakup with The Geek, turning forty-three, surviving a relentless work and travel schedule, and now choking on infertility. I leapfrogged over all my feelings and decided to produce motherhood.

I would adopt a child.

After completing some preliminary documents in the spring, I received a formal rejection. The notification declared I was "unfit as a single parent" as a result of admitting to past treatment for depression.

Infertile.

Unfit.

Thirteen's cruelty scaled new heights as I sat in the corner of my bedroom one dark afternoon. *"Your mind and body are unfit. The universe knows you'd be a horrible parent. It won't let you have a child. It doesn't trust you. Stop with all the baby bullshit. You're obviously not mother material."*

My mind spun out of control and I started to ask myself some difficult questions. *Did the Universe, God, declare me "unfit" and destroy my uterus in some sort of destiny-planning workshop? Or did the Universe not trust something about me? Was my karma so foul I deserved eternal loneliness? Was I incapable of loving a child? Was this all happening so I could never harm my own baby? Was I a monster just like my grandpa?*

I cried for weeks. When my tears finally stopped, I sat in the corner of my bedroom alone and in the dark. I couldn't run from the most fundamental question of all.

Did my grandpa's rabid desire for my flesh destroy my womb? Did he rape away my chances of being a mother?

When I finally let myself ask the question, I detached from my life. My body. My womb. From the world. I decided that if God, in all of his/her wisdom, chose to punish me even after surviving horrific abuse, then we were never truly friends. It felt like my faith was mocking me. It sounded less like love and more like a bad joke. My conversations with God became one-sided and rich with venom as I wrote in my journal.

*"You tossed me into the flames as a child, and you're still tossing me around! I'm like a kite caught in a windstorm with no real direction or purpose. I'm not allowed to just be happy. To be normal. You made me my grandpa's toy when I was a child. He played with me, and now you're playing with me,"* I wrote. *"How are the two of you any different? You're both sick and twisted."*

Angry at God and disgusted by my new truth, I became a recluse outside of work. My world lost all its color, and conversations sounded like static. A few months after I disappeared inside myself, Fatuoh called me, worried because she hadn't heard from me.

"It's all hopeless, Fatuoh. The doctor said I'll never be a mother. I don't even know what to do."

"Hey, take it easy, mama. We need cake and *dawa*. I'm coming to get you."

She picked me up from my house, and we went to our favorite café. In Swahili, *dawa* means medicine. The best drink to have when you're under the weather is a hot *dawa*, which consists of boiling water, honey, lemon juice, and fresh ginger.

The waiter lit the outdoor heat lamps to push back the chilly, Nairobi winter air and Fatuoh and I shared a piece of tricolade cake. I couldn't tell her my whole story, but that was okay. Even sharing a little bit of the journey felt therapeutic. We talked for hours until I laughed more than I wanted to cry.

"I am done with these pathetic men of yours," I announced to Fatuoh just before enjoying yet another mouthful of the decadent chocolate cake.

"RC. The women in the village say there are three types of Kenyan men," she explained.

"*Sawa*. Tell me."

"The first one treats you so well you make him breakfast in the morning. You make it fresh and take your time while he takes a long shower."

"Okay, the second?" I asked, sipping hot *dawa* and trying not to laugh.

"The second man comes out of the bedroom and you order him a taxi. No shower. You offer him coffee or tea but no food."

"Good. Yes. And the third?" I prompted. I loved her advice from the village.

"Aya, the third! He did not do his job well at all. You only offer him hot water or cold water while you tell him to wait outside because the tuktuk taxi is on its way."

"That's it. That's as good as it gets?" I asked her.

"That's it. The problem with you is that you'll cook breakfast for anyone."

We laughed so hard my stomach hurt the rest of the evening. She spoke the truth, and I never forgot it.

My daily life and struggles in Kenya didn't necessarily reach America. I shared a bit of my life abroad via email and some phone calls, but the darkest days I faced were kept mostly to myself and my overseas friends like Breanne, Fatuoh and Wanuri.

I converted my sadness into a "tenacity disorder," logging eighty hours a week at work while traveling constantly. I spent the rest of 2013 ignoring my pain, giving space for loneliness and infertility to intertwine like lovers. They gave birth to resentment, and I ended the year exhausted, bitter, and ready for a shift.

Richard, the executive creative director and my manager, retired from the advertising agency where I worked in early 2014. He reached out to ask if I wanted to partner with him to build a creative hub. It felt like the sort of business opportunity, and distraction, I needed to push beyond the scars of 2013.

Six months later, Richard and I owned two film companies, an edit house, sound studio, casting agency, and a holding company to manage the operations. Richard's job was to bring clients to us through his vast connections. I had experience running an independent business in Kenya after running a film company with Wanuri for a few years. I understood the tax code and financial requirements, immigration rules, and business structures. We complemented each other well, on paper.

We established the hub in a large villa and housed all the companies in the various buildings to keep things as simple as possible. Richard and I shared an executive office in the front sitting room.

The responsibility of employees, contracts, HR, legal, bottom lines, and clients proved exceptionally demanding. Still tending to my wounds and processing my infertility and the rejection to adopt, I was far too busy to notice Richard was a bully. A very clever bully.

"Rebecca, you know the crew don't like you very much. That's what I'm hearing," he would lob at me as we sat in our office discussing the next film shoot.

"Really? I know all of them. We've never had any issues with each other. That's really odd."

"I hear that no one wants you on set. You should stay in the office during the shoots. Let the line producers manage things and give everyone a break."

"Well I don't want to cause any problems. I'll hang back and just take care of things here," I offered, never once considering that Richard was just an asshole.

He dropped little bombs like "no one wants you on set," and over time, I started to listen, and believe, every word. I think the heavy emotional bruising I took in 2013 left my ego, and typical defenses, weakened. The fragments were quiet and self-doubt took over.

I stopped going to shoots and did my best to manage all the financial, legal, and human resources issues. Richard continued with his manipulative tactics.

"Rebecca, the girls over in casting don't want to speak to you about the monthly P&L."

"Really? Why? We had no issues last month," I asked, worried that I had upset someone. It didn't seem to matter that I owned part of the company we were discussing.

"Yeah, well, they just feel like you don't really understand the business. You need to back off," he pushed back, and my self-esteem withered like an old balloon.

In just six months, Richard convinced me no one liked me. I was stupid. He alone was in control and I believed him. Bullies like victims. They get off on how it feels to hurt others. To feel in control. I think Richard enjoyed every day knowing he could demean me over and over and brag about it to his friends.

"*He is an asshole,*" Thirteen snarled as Richard left the office for the day.

"He's just telling me what I need to hear. I can be demanding-especially on set."

"*He's full of shit. There's nothing wrong with you. Why do you listen to him so much? What's happened to you?*" she clapped back.

"If I leave all of this, what in the hell am I supposed to do? His connections run deep. He's going to tell everyone I approach for work that I'm stupid, nasty, and incapable. Where do I go? No one will want me," I said, discouraged and weak.

I was the official CEO of Headaches. Richard never appreciated what it took to keep several companies afloat and compliant in Kenya. The relentless needs of our clients, suppliers, regulatory bodies, employees, and freelancers were taxing. I started to loathe going to the office. Stressed out, lonely, and tired, I turned sour.

"What's happening with you?" Wanuri asked. "You're really unhappy. Everyone can feel it." I always appreciated her ability to express concern while also calling me out on my bullshit. I wasn't just sour. I was salty and sharing my unhappiness with everyone. We'd known each other for six years, and there was no point in pretending she wasn't right.

"Yeah. I know. I hate my business partner. The hub is just too many people and too many problems," I told her while sitting in our favorite café.

"Then quit. Stop doing it and do something else," she said matter-of-factly.

"I can't imagine leaving. Richard would be furious," I explained nervously.

"Who cares about Richard?" she asked. "You sound like you're afraid of him. Why are you more concerned about him than yourself?" she asked, looking annoyed.

"I guess I feel like he decides what I do," I admitted. "He's unpredictable and powerful. I have no idea what he'll say or do if I tell him I'm out."

"Well, that's just nonsense. It sounds like an abusive relationship. Except, he's not your spouse. You're business partners. Don't let him drag you down."

Wanuri's words broke through my broken self. It felt like I was waking up from a long, confused sleep.

"Yeah, you're right. I need to find a way to get a divorce."

Could I walk away? Was I strong enough to leave and survive on my own? Something had to give.

A week after my chat with Wanuri, the office was unusually quiet in the afternoon. We'd just wrapped another massive shoot and our team left early for a much-needed break. The month-end reports sat in front of us. As usual, I was the only one reviewing the information and paying attention to the business. The numbers, on paper, looked great. But when I looked a bit closer, I recognized a trend dangerous for us as foreigners.

"Hey, Richard, I was just looking at our business plan last night. We intended to lock in about forty-five percent of the local business the first two years."

"Yeah, that sounds about right."

"Well, according to this month's reports, we've exceeded our goal. We're at seventy-eight percent as of this month," I explained with a bit of trepidation in my voice. "We need to cool off and slow down. We're going to attract unwanted attention. It's not smart to monopolize the market. We're going to attract trouble," I explained.

"Fuck 'em. We're not going to stop," he replied.

He didn't get it. He'd spent so many years at the top of the industry that he'd never built up any real street smarts. I spent the first few years in Kenya as a freelance producer. I knew the industry would never tolerate us if we bashed our competitors on the head.

Just a few weeks later, I spent a lovely Christmas and New Year's break in Dubai. I had enough time and space away from all of it to recognize it was truly time to part ways. Richard and I weren't partners. He treated me like a secretary and didn't respect me. I couldn't spend another year, month, or week attached to his miserable business philosophies and corrosive nature.

The first few months of any new year were always quiet while clients sorted out their new budgets. I took an extended break from the office to reflect on my time in Kenya. What was next? I prayed and meditated, hoping for answers. I realized I wanted to stay in Kenya to build a new life—a new version of myself in 2015.

Part of my renaissance would mean I had to officially let go of any hope to have a baby. At forty-five, it was simply never going to happen. No pregnancy. No adoption. It took a few months and a lot of sorrow, meditation, and practicing gratitude for what I actually had in my life to feel free of my body's yearning for a child. Once I turned the corner away from that journey, I felt ready to start a completely new chapter.

As part of creating a new version of myself, I felt I needed to take time to apologize to Kenya. I sat in my house and took responsibility for the miserable person I had become over the years. I shared most of my PTSD with Kenya. Pain, anger, fear, and frustration flowed out of me to most of the people in my life. I never truly appreciated the privilege of living in one of the world's most amazing places. I committed to being a different person if Kenya would give me a second chance.

I promised to stop using Thirteen's anger as a tool. I would not get angry at Richard, or anyone else, as I started over. Getting defensive or going on the attack wasn't going to be useful while threading this particular needle. Nuance was required, not grit.

"*So you're not going to use me to get through this mess with Richard, is that what you've*

## It Won't Hurt None

decided?" Thirteen asked.

"That's right."

"Well, when he comes for you, or stops you from getting work, don't expect to find me. You can't just flip me on and off like a switch," she huffed.

"I'll keep that in mind," I said coolly. Thirteen was so damn annoying.

As the new year pushed forward, I went quiet and slowly distanced myself from the businesses. In late March, Richard and I met at a pub near our office for a chat.

"What's going on with you?" he asked. "You're not checking in or coming to the office. We can't keep paying you a salary if you're not going to work," he decreed. Apparently time and distance reinforced his fantasy that the shares I owned in our thriving companies were meaningless. He truly believed that he'd successfully convinced me that my contributions to the businesses didn't add any value.

"You actually don't decide if I get a salary. Remember, I own fifty percent. But let's keep things simple. I want out. I want out of all of it," I said boldly. *Try to bully me now motherfucker,* I said to myself while staring straight at him.

"Fine. I can get James to fly in and take over your work," he jabbed.

"So be it. But remember, until I sell my shares, I still have the right to my salary. I'm still going to review bank statements, P&Ls, and reconciliations." I stood up, ready to leave, but decided to drop a little truth bomb of my own. "How much do you think all the financial, legal, human resource, and business processes are worth? How do you calculate my contribution? How much do you think I'm worth given that every company just passed its first audit? Think long and hard about that and come back to me with a number."

I felt uncaged. Set free. The strong-arm tactics and endless issues with all the companies were at an end. I glided away from his look of astonishment and got into my car for a joyful ride home. I wasn't sure what was next. At first it felt like life turned upside down. But the more time and distance I gained away from Richard and the old version of me, I realized I was, in fact, righting myself after being off course for a long time.

The Universe is a cheeky beast. Within days of slamming the door shut on Richard, all the companies, and a far-too-miserable version of myself, a new door swung wide open.

Monali, a former coworker and friend from my days at the Nairobi advertising agency, called me just a few days after I met with Richard. Beautiful and charming, Monali has a razor-sharp intellect and can wow a crowd with her mad DJ and dance skills. I love her wonderfully bright laugh.

"Hey," Monali said, "what are you up to?"

"Not much," I replied, not wanting to share the recent drama with Richard. "What's happening?"

"We have a big project, and I want to get your opinion about a few things. Can you come to my office this week?" she asked.

"Sure," I said, "how's tomorrow afternoon?"

"That works. Come by around three."

I was intrigued. I hadn't spoken to Monali in about a year since she moved over to the client side to work for a global brand. The next day we met in her office and talked about the project. It was clear she needed a full financial and technical review for work being produced in Africa.

"Is it something you could consult on?" she asked.

"Of course. I'd love to," I told her. "I'll work with you any time, Mo. You're the best."

"Great," she said. "Let's work on a consulting agreement."

I began to experience Kenya through a more grateful lens. Relieved of the pain of infertility and the acrimony with Richard, Flight and the fragments went silent. I started visualizing a better, brighter version of myself and my life.

## Chapter 12

What does a bully do when you stop being their punching bag? They swing wildly hoping to leave a mark. I refused to get into the ring and engage with Richard's abusive emails while I waited patiently for my contract with Monali to finalize. I had more time for fun than I had enjoyed in years. It was a welcome break after working hard and charging through seven years in East Africa.

I went zip lining, spent endless hours in the Nairobi National Park, and lazed on a dhow at Kenya's famous beach destination called Lamu. A long-overdue gorilla trek in Rwanda extended my period of relaxation. I spent a lot of time meditating.

My new calm struggled as negotiations with Richard dragged on. My nerves frayed and I needed to talk to my good friend Shawna. It had been some years since our safari, but she remained a close friend and confidant. She was a successful entrepreneur and I knew that she would understand my frustration with Richard. After forwarding some nasty emails from him, I called her to talk about the poisonous negotiations.

"The whole thing with Richard is just toxic. I mean, the emails you forwarded me are so angry."

"Yeah, I'm triggered every time I see his name in my inbox." I said, "I think he actually believes I'm going to walk away from the businesses free of charge."

"Screw him," Shawna said. "Step away from it. The companies aren't going anywhere. Ignore him. What's he going to do?" she asked.

I took Shawna's advice and went quiet like a good Kenyan, ignoring Richard's acidic emails. I stuck to my commitment from months earlier and stayed positive. My silence worked. For a bully like Richard, a one-sided fight wasn't much fun at all. After a few more weeks of wrangling, and a soft threat to return to the office and continue our partnership, Richard and I finally agreed on terms and the matter was closed.

My contract with Monali finalized around the same time and I began working as a global content consultant. The scope of my agreement expanded beyond the original plan, and I supported projects across Africa, the Middle East, and Asia. It was exactly the opportunity I craved--a dream come true.

My tension lifted, and I felt free and easy. I was ready for a move and shifted into a new house in Karen, a suburb of Nairobi, away from the noise and hustle of the city.

"Nana's cottage sits in one corner of the lot. The big family house sits just opposite," my real estate agent explained as we cruised down a tree-lined dirt road, the car slipping sideways in the dark red Kenyan mud. The long rains had arrived. "It's on about four acres, so there's plenty of space. I hope you don't mind big dogs because their hounds are enormous."

Before I even opened the door to get out of the car, I was greeted by Remus and Romulus. A mixture of Great Dane and Rhodesian Ridgeback lines, they were about six feet tall on their hind legs and each weighed about 150 pounds. They were glorious. I soon called them The Double Dingus.

Surrounded by a lush forest, the cottage was a gift from the universe. Deciding to rent from Nana was one of the best decisions I made during my entire stay in Kenya. I was grateful to live next to Nana, her daughter and son-in-law and their two kids. They soon became my close friends and generously welcomed me into their lives for parties and holiday gatherings. For the first time since moving to Kenya, I felt like I was home. I belonged.

When I wasn't traveling for work, I spent time with Nana. She used to sit in the garden surrounded by her four small dogs, as well as Remus and Romulus, and her African Gray parrot Winnie. Nana was a gorgeous world-traveler, full of love, sass, and kindness. About two months after I moved into her cottage, I saw Nana sitting in the garden. I walked over to say hello and noticed she was a bit melancholy.

"Hey, Nana, how are you today?" I asked. She didn't greet me with her usual smile, making me worried.

"I'm okay," she said as I sat down beside her. "Sometimes, it's really hard to admit I'm growing old," she said with a tremble in her voice.

I reached out and grabbed her hand, and we sat together for a few minutes. My heart hurt for her.

"I'm sorry today is a rough day. How about I go make some guacamole and we eat chips and dip and a piece of dark chocolate?"

"Sounds perfect," she said. A little while later, we had an unusual picnic out on the lawn, and she started telling me some of her racier stories. Nana had indeed lived a full life.

"My God, you are saucy!" I said to her between dark chocolate bites. The afternoon turned out pretty good for both of us. It was an unexpected and extraordinary gift to gain another granny at that time in my life.

In 2016, I loved "Rebecca in Kenya, Part 2".

In spring, a good friend called to ask me if I wanted to book a tarot card reading.

"Welcome home. You've been gone for five weeks. How long do you get to stay this time?" she asked. My travel schedule was indeed relentless.

"I'm home for ten days! What are we going to do to celebrate?" I asked. I loved being back home in the cottage.

"So, there's a French woman who is an empath. My friend just went and said her session was amazing. I'm booking you a session, as well as one for myself," she said.

"Perfect," I said. "I'm so excited!"

I wasn't quite sure what my session would uncover, but I felt open to all possibilities. When I got to my appointment a few days later, Amelie greeted me.

A lovely, beautiful, kind soul, she was funny, a bit cheeky, and surrounded by calm energy. I walked into her house, and we sat down on a comfortable sofa, the kind designated for watching a romcom on lazy Sundays. For the next ninety minutes, she used various decks of tarot, spiritual, and arcana cards to explore my life. The first card she pulled spoke to childbirth.

"Are you pregnant?" she asked.

"No," I answered, surprised by the question. I was two years past the end of my infertility journey. It was well and truly behind me. I almost giggled, given the absence of sex in my life.

She closed her eyes, took a deep breath, and said, "Are you sure? I'm feeling something very strong with you about birth."

"I am absolutely not pregnant," I said. "Could it also mean a rebirth of sorts?"

"Yes! That's it," she exclaimed and continued to pull more cards. "Look, there are two identical cards. One is facing your past and the other is looking at your future. Have you recently turned away from the negative and focused on the positive?" she asked.

"Yes," I said, thinking of the recently closed negotiations with Richard. "Exactly. I'm focused on the future," I said.

"It's working. You have a new opportunity, and it's going to be successful. You're going to travel all over the world for a few years," she explained. She offered multiple insights into my new life and left me feeling positive. Elated.

"Miserable Rebecca" was gone. "Bright, Shiny, Global Consultant Rebecca" thrived.

After my first meeting with Amelie, I wanted to speak with her more about my life in general. I found it easy to talk to her and thought it might be worthwhile to dive into my head a little bit for a tune-up.

When we met a few weeks later, Amelie asked me what I wanted to focus on during the session. I paused for a moment and held my breath. When I finally exhaled, I told her about the fragments and the all-too-familiar story of abuse, courage, and survival. Amelie became a good friend, mentor, and healing guide. We spent a few months working on my meditation practice before I had to take a break as my travel schedule became more demanding.

In 2017, a year after our last session, I sought her help after my partial hysterectomy and she helped me get through the immediate effects of the post-surgical trauma. Unfortunately, my work schedule couldn't accommodate the sort of time we needed to deal with the actual fragments. That work was going to have to wait.

In 2018, I was waiting for my consulting agreement to be renewed and my travel schedule eased. I took advantage of the break and reached out to Amelie. Although we hadn't seen each other in about a year, we picked up our conversation about the fragments exactly where we'd left them in 2017.

"I want to integrate the fragments," I told her when I visited her new office.

"So, you're ready?" she asked. "You have the time now? You're not traveling?"

"I'm ready. I'm exhausted by all the chatter in my mind and the fragmented energy. My travel schedule has stopped for a few months. I really want to take advantage of the break and end this cycle," I told her, not understanding the complexity of the work I was describing.

"You know, in a way, they've been a strange sort of gift. Dissociation is a complicated defense mechanism. I know that they've been difficult to live with but they shielded you from a lot of suffering when you were young," she explained.

"I get that. They served a purpose for a long time. But not anymore," I replied. "You mentioned once that you felt they were stuck in time and said it was possible that they didn't know the trauma was over. Do you still think that's true?"

"Yes, I do. If you want to integrate them and extinguish their energy, you first need to reconcile with them. You have to become friends, gain their trust, and find out why they're still with you. Ask them what they need to heal."

"If I can do all of that, will it all finally stop? After we reconcile and integrate, can they be released?"

"If you can really convince them they can trust you and you'll keep them safe, then yes, I think they can be released. It's going to take time and patience. Let's schedule a session and meet one of them next week."

"Okay. Let's start with Seven. She's sad but she's also young. I think she'll be easier to get to know than Thirteen who's just busy being an obstinate, angry teenager."

"Sounds like a good plan. Set an intention in your meditation this week to meet Seven in our next session," Amelie said as I left her office.

Amelie was the first healer who discussed my fragments in practical terms. A week later, we stepped into her cozy office and sat on the comfortable sofa; we took some deep, cleansing breaths together. Releasing all tension, I shut my eyes. Amelie asked me to describe what I saw, heard, and felt as I maintained a deep state of relaxation.

During each session, I transmitted information from my body and mind and converted it into rich, full-color vignettes. I relayed the scenes to Amelie, who guided me so I could connect with an individual fragment. Eventually, I learned how to meet with all of them on their own and as a group.

My role during each interaction was to listen and slowly create a new dynamic. I needed the fragments to lower their defenses, trust me, and allow me to take charge and live more fully in the present, free from their influence. Once we reconciled, they could integrate back into my body. Ultimately, I would release them and be whole.

Our work together would lay the foundation for future sessions with other somatic healers. Some interactions with the fragments became self-guided once I grew more comfortable and confident in my own meditation practice.

# Reconciliation

*"These pains you feel are messengers. Listen to them."*
*(Rumi)*

*Seven*

## Chapter 13

AT SEVEN YEARS old, I had strawberry-blonde hair. Freckles dotted my nose and cheeks, and I was missing my two front teeth. Called a tomboy, I wore out the knees in my hand-me-down jeans sliding on the grass at school. I loved playing in the dirt.

There were endless possibilities for adventure in the woods where we lived. When the streetlights came on in our neighborhood, it was a cue to come inside for dinner.

I preferred stuffed animals to dolls and talked to them as if they were real. Each had a name, and they were my friends. Every morning before heading out for the day, I lined them all up in their own spot on my bed. Playing goalie in AYSO soccer was the best part of my life, except for time with my best friend and cat, Snowy. I loved learning and particularly enjoyed reading and writing.

In first grade, my teacher, Mrs. Dickson, made me feel secure, and I loved her hugs and bright smile. Mrs. Dickson and other teachers nourished me with their love at a time when life at home was tumultuous. Our house broke in two when my parents bitterly divorced. My dad gained custody, and we lived with him and my stepmom during the week. Every weekend, we saw my mom and stepdad. Life split between two distinctly different houses, and it was confusing.

My dad and his new wife became incredibly devoted to their faith, leaving less space for me to enjoy the father I knew before he remarried. They had a son, my younger brother, who I thought was a fantastic addition to my life and still do. My mom and her husband had no faith-based distractions. My mom found her guiding principles within her family. My stepdad was a kind, funny, and loving man. He was an incredible person and I am grateful that he was a part of our lives for many years.

The acrimony between my parents meant we did not share holidays. They did not peacefully co-parent. The divorce permanently broke the foundation of our world, and I fell through the cracks.

Physically imposing, my maternal grandfather loomed over my mother's entire family. A gruff man with little education, he was a welder by trade. I was taught to hold a cult-like devotion to him, never questioning or challenging him. My mother and aunts used to call him "Daddy."

He was disgusting, rude, ignorant, and belligerent: a monster. People in the family saw him grab at me.

Grab. Grab. Grab.

They saw him touch my bottom and listened to him make lewd comments to me. No one ever said a word or came to my defense.

We used to drive up to my grandparents' house at least twice a month on the weekends to work in their garden or just to spend time. I have fond memories of eating warm garlic right out of the ground and tending to the avocado grove. I liked spending time in the dirt. The dirt was safe. My life slipped between two worlds. I had the capacity to enjoy the garden in the hot summer sun while knowing I had to survive real horrors late at night.

When evening came and the adults were too preoccupied to pay attention, my grandpa forced his tongue into my mouth like a ravenous dog. I was attacked.

Groped.

Pinched.

Molested.

Raped.

My grandparents' house was under construction when I was Seven, and they lived in a camping trailer on the property. A small, cramped space, it was dark and held onto the scents of my grandma's cooking and the grease from my grandpa's work clothes. There was a staleness in the air akin to a forgotten attic or cellar where no light enters.

It was not uncommon for my mom and stepdad to leave my siblings and me at my grandparents' house for the night. Although the trailer was snug, it could accommodate all of us. My brother always took the single bunk over the master bed.

My sister and I shared the twin bunk folded down over the couch. After spending the night, we were collected on Sunday afternoon and returned to our dad's house to get ready for another week of school.

Although I remember many assaults, there is one attack that stays especially fresh in my mind. It occurred during an overnight stay. My grandma cooked dinner while I played outside until she told me to come into the trailer.

"Becky, you can sleep with your grandpa tonight in the big bed. I'll sleep with your sister."

"Why?" I asked, looking down at my feet. It was not the first time she'd made such a request.

"My back hurts, and it's better for me," she replied, never bothering to look at me. She knew what she was asking. My stomach twisted into knots. I lost my appetite so much I didn't even enjoy the homemade, hand-cranked ice cream for dessert. As the night grew later, I tried to brace myself for the inevitable.

I was Seven and preparing for rape.

Around 10 p.m., I put on my nightgown and climbed into bed where my grandpa waited. He slept on the inside of the bed closest to the small window, likely because he could not be seen by the others. I slept on the outside closest to the narrow hallway running the length of the trailer.

Mentally and physically exposed, I lay in full view of my brother, grandma, and sister. I tried getting into the bed but not under the top sheet.

"You can't sleep like that," my grandpa barked as he forced me to get under the covers next to him.

I was Seven and trying to be safe.

Everyone fell asleep and the trailer grew quiet. The gentle snores signaled we would not be disturbed. My heart pounded as his enormous, calloused hands pulled my nightgown up above my belly and yanked off my underwear. Draping his heavy, strong arm over my waist, he pulled me against his body. His erect penis stabbed my buttocks and lower back so much I flinched. Lifting my left leg up over his own, he created a gap between my thighs.

His bare, erect penis began to thrust back and forth between my tiny legs. My grandpa, the patriarch of my mother's family, and father of three, penetrated his granddaughter's innocent sex, my sex, just on the surface of my labia so his penis could move freely. My "too small" vagina, as he called it, required a different environment to be fully penetrated.

He breathed heavily onto the back of my neck and grunted quietly as he thrust back and forth against my body. Raping me. My mind scrambled. Was anyone else in the trailer watching? Did they think I was a dirty girl? Did they think I wanted it? Did they look at the tears in my eyes and wonder why I didn't say anything?

I remained silent. Barely breathing. I left my body that night, watching it all happen to me from a distance. I watched myself stare out the window opposite the bed into the black night praying no one heard or saw us. In and out, in and out, he moved his large frame against mine while his hands brutalized my clitoris and nipples while his vile tongue invaded my ear.

Once he stopped moving, I came back to my body. His climax spread across my buttocks and between my thighs. He quickly released my leg and let go of my waist to roll onto his back letting out a long exhale mixed with a sickening soft moan.

I grabbed my underwear and jumped out of the bed, leaping into the adjacent bathroom. Sitting on the toilet for a few minutes, I felt "grateful" he hadn't pushed into my sex deeper with his penis or fingers.

I was Seven and grateful the rape wasn't too bad.

As the adrenaline wore off, fear took over. If I slept with him, he would certainly rape me again. There was no limit to his perversion. While I wiped his semen off my body, I decided I wasn't going back to his bed.

I opened the bathroom door and walked quickly to the front of the trailer, never glancing over to the left where he lay in bed. I couldn't stand the look in his eyes after he raped me. They were evil. Not human. His gaze always reminded me that his sexual appetite was insatiable.

Waking my grandma, I told her I couldn't sleep with him anymore. She didn't ask any questions and joined my grandpa for the rest of the night, and I climbed into the bunk with my sister.

My mind broke off a fragment of myself that night so the rest of me could survive.

I was Seven and I rescued myself.

Born Saturday night in the summer of 1977, Seven was a despondent piece of me, forever frozen in time. She held tightly onto the sights, sounds, and smells of all my rapes, which became my triggers. As the assaults continued, Seven became my Sadness.

I never said a word about any of the assaults. His violence escalated and became more frequent as he stole me away to run "errands" or "help grandpa" in the trailer. He used to take my siblings and me swimming in a public pool and enjoyed launching us into the air from the depths. There were many times when it was my turn and he would put his large hands under my swimsuit to assault me before shooting me out of the water and across the pool. As the years passed, my body began to build a sort of tolerance to the rapes and my vagina became "easier." Yeast infections set my sex on fire regularly as I got older.

In the fourth grade, I was ten years old, and all the girls were taken into a classroom to learn about our impending menstrual cycles. We learned babies could be made once a girl got her period and had sex. Most of my classmates focused on the impending periods. But not me. I understood my grandpa was having sex with me. The concept of rape had yet to develop. I became terrified. I prayed to an unfamiliar God that my period wouldn't come.

My prayers didn't work very long. When I was eleven and in the fifth grade, my cycle started. Sitting outside of class on a warm, sunny day, I felt a strange pull in my groin. I went to the bathroom and sat on the toilet to pee and saw thick, dark blood on my underwear. When I bent over to look between my legs, I watched a bloody mucous trail flow out of me into the toilet.

I was sure I was pregnant. What else could it be? They didn't tell us during our special talk that periods could be thick, clotted, and look like gloppy red threads running out of our bodies. When I got home, I sat on the toilet some more and prayed the blood would stop. I stared at the red globs lying at the bottom of the bowl, looking closely, sure I would see baby parts.

My mind became erratic. *Grandpa just had sex with me. So I must be pregnant. Do I have to have the baby? I don't want a baby with my grandpa. Would it kill me to have a baby? What would happen to me? Can I get rid of the baby? How do I do that? How do I make it so I can't get pregnant?*

I was eleven years old.

The next day, the bleeding continued, and I reasoned I wasn't pregnant. It was my period. It became a new monthly layer of dread and it was always incredibly painful. I used to pass out, run a temperature, vomit, and suffer severe cramps only prescription painkillers would relieve.

I was Seven's host. I wasn't able to cry out or scream during the assault in the trailer, or during any other assault, so Seven filled my head with her cries as I got older.

When I started to blend with her in high school, flashbacks from different attacks took over my mind. They were tactile. Visceral. I could feel the sweaty sheets sticking to my skin and my grandpa's hot breath burning my neck. The thick, wet mess he ejaculated between my thighs and across different areas of my body reminded me of the glue we used for arts and crafts.

Amelie and I spent a lot of time talking about Seven. I was certain that I had to connect with her first. It was intuition guiding me. She wasn't the noisiest, but she was the most methodical. She always sounded and felt mature beyond her years. I needed to tell Seven she was safe. The abuse was over. She was loved. Protected.

More than forty years after Seven was created, I sat in Amelie's house and relaxed into a deep, meditative state, ready to meet her face to face.

"Where are you?" Amelie asked.

"I'm in a meadow. It's full of green grass and tall pine trees. The sunshine feels good on my face. It reminds me of where I grew up. It's a safe place. I'm comfortable here."

"Sounds beautiful. Is anyone there?"

I looked around and I spotted a young girl hiding behind a tree.

"Yes. She's here. Seven. She has long, blonde hair and short bangs. She's wearing a dress. She's afraid and shy."

"Ask her if you can talk to her."

"Hi, can I talk to you?" I asked, standing about ten feet from her. I wanted to walk toward her, but something told me to be patient and wait for her to come to me.

She came out from behind the tree and stood still, staring at me for a few minutes.

"I'm here to talk with you if it's okay," I said. "Do you know who I am?" I asked, thinking she might not feel safe speaking to a stranger.

"I know you. Where have you been?" she asked, looking down at her feet and breaking my heart.

"I was lost. I heard you, but I didn't know how to find you for a really long time. I am so sorry I didn't find you sooner."

"Yeah. It was long."

"I'm so sorry. I didn't know."

"It's okay," she said, shrugging her tiny shoulders while still looking at the ground.

"Can we sit down and chat?" I asked.

"Okay," she replied. She walked over and we sat next to each other on the soft grass. The sun warmed both of us as a breeze danced through the treetops.

"You know," I said to her, "you were really little when Grandpa first hurt you."

"Yeah," she said, "it made me scared and sad."

"I know, and I worry about you."

"Why?" she asked, looking at me for the first time.

"I worry you think it's your fault," I explained.

"Kinda," she answered.

"What do you mean?"

"Well, it's like I was bad, so he hurt me," she said.

"You weren't bad. He was bad. You were good. It was never your fault," I said to her.

"I don't know," she said, scratching the ground with her tiny fingers. I wanted to hold her, but I knew it was too soon.

"What don't you know?" I asked.

"I don't know if I was good. Like maybe I broke some rules, and he got mad. It was like a spanking."

"No. Please don't think that way. You were never bad. He was a monster. You don't ever need to think it was your fault. You are good," I said to her with tears in my eyes.

She stared at the ground for a minute, and then looked up at me. Her eyes swelled with tears.

"They saw us," she whispered as her lips trembled.

"Who saw us?" I asked, filled with dread.

"People saw him do that to me. They think I'm bad."

"No. You're not bad," I repeated. I had to convince my Seven-year-old self she was good and deserved to be loved. I deserved love.

"It's my fault," she said flatly.

"No." I told her.

"I didn't tell," she said, and her shoulders dropped. She was so brave and yet so tiny. I wondered if she ever felt any joy.

"It's okay you didn't tell. You were too little to tell. You were very brave. You did nothing wrong. I'm so sorry."

"Where were you?" she asked.

"I wasn't able to be there," I said. "But I am here now. I am here to keep you safe. I'm grown now."

"Yeah. I missed you. I didn't have any grown-ups to keep me safe."

"I know. I'm so sorry. I'm here now, and I love you."

"Yeah," she replied. Her voice suggested she didn't completely believe me. We both took a few deep breaths.

"You wanna play?" I asked her. I thought adding a bit of fun to our time together would help us get to know each other.

"Maybe. Can I twirl?" she asked. "I like to twirl."

"You sure can," I said, standing up with her. "But before you twirl, it's really important you know that you were never bad."

"Hmm, okay, I guess," she said, walking away from me. It would take time for her to trust my words. She started twirling in her dress and bare feet.

"Are you okay? Do you feel safe?" I asked.

"Yeah, I'm okay. She watches me," she said.

"Who?"

"You know," she replied. "The angry one," she mentioned casually as she twirled in the sunshine.

I knew she was talking about Thirteen. I didn't know they were together forming some sort of social club in my mind.

"Okay. I'm glad she's here."

"She's waiting for you. You have to talk to her," Seven said with a serious look on her face as she stopped to look at me.

"I'll look for her soon."

"Yeah. She gets angry when she has to wait. I'm gonna spin some more," she announced as turned in the meadow.

"Okay," I said. "I have to go, but I'll be back soon. I love you, you know. I love you very much."

"Okay, see you later!" she shouted, spinning in the meadow.

When Amelie first introduced the idea of meeting the fragments, I didn't appreciate the process and how it would make me feel. Her words came full circle when I met Seven for the first time. It was incredible, but it was also painful. Seeing myself so young, fragile, and innocent made the memory of the assaults much more vivid.

Seven and I continued to meet often. It felt like we both needed to share our memories of the abuse. I remembered my grandfather's diver's watch scratching my body. She remembered him biting different areas of her flesh. The details we shared bound us together in a safe space where we could talk about all the unthinkable things our bodies endured.

*"There were lots of times he hurt me,"* Seven said. *Every time she talked about being assaulted, she looked down at the ground.*

*"What do you mean?"* I asked. *"How many times?"*

*"Every time,"* she said, *and my body filled with ice.*

*"Do you mean you remember all of the times Grandpa hurt us? Like when we were really little and when we got older?"*

*She looked at me and nodded yes. Horrified, I understood that the burdens of every attack sat with her on her delicate shoulders.*

*Every grab.*

*Every pinch.*

*Every penetration.*

*She was Seven, and she carried it all.*

*"Yeah. All of them. It's all my fault,"* she said. *I could hear a change in her voice, and I tilted my head down to see she was crying. She and I both cried a lot.*

*"No. It's not. None of it is your fault,"* I told her over and over.

*"I'm tired,"* she said, *lying back on the grass. "I just want to sleep all of the time."*

*"Well, that's okay. I promise you are safe. You can rest as much as you want."*

*"Am I really safe?"* she asked, *looking up at me with wet eyes.*

*"Yes,"* I reassured her. *"Get some rest, and I'll be back soon." I watched her doze off peacefully and wondered if she had been too terrified to sleep before I arrived. I left her in the meadow.*

## It Won't Hurt None

The pain and sadness weighed her down like heavy chains tied around her body, cutting deep into her flesh. I remembered how my seven year-old body bore the signs of trauma. I had a "nervous stomach" making me feel nauseous most of the time. Oozing, flaking, painful sores surrounded my mouth and took months to heal. Disastrous, rampant inflammation filled my body.

My mind and body reflected the truth, but I wasn't seen.

I was, after all, a star student. I couldn't possibly have any serious problems. The troubled kids couldn't sit still and never did their homework. I sat still, kept a clean desk, and did all my homework.

At a time when I felt invisible, my father's mother, my amazing Granny Chandler, was my solace. My grandpa and granny Chandler lived in a house next to my father's, and I spent most weekdays playing card games and studying with her after school.

Standing at maybe five feet tall, she had gorgeous, soft, long, white hair and spent most of her adult life sleeping tending to her sick husband. I never once heard my granny complain. Rather, she saw good in everyone and wrote letters daily to remain connected to friends and family. The cards she mailed us for holidays and birthdays always included a dollar bill.

A decent Monopoly player, she was devoted to crossword puzzles and she dominated every Scrabble game with her limitless vocabulary. She was a loving distraction from the trauma I faced. I don't think I would have survived if Granny hadn't lived just a few steps away.

*I thought about Seven's chains and visited her in the meadow a few more times, eager to unload her burdens and stop her chatter in my mind. Our relationship changed, and I sensed she finally trusted me. The next time we connected, Seven wanted to talk about the divorce.*

*"Hello," I said to her. We always met in the same spot in the meadow near a massive oak tree covered in bright green leaves. "It's good to see you again."*

"Yeah," she said shyly from behind a small sapling just a few feet taller than herself.

I waved at her and invited her to sit down with me in our favorite spot on the grass in the sunshine. She walked over and plopped down.

"I have a secret," she told me.

"What secret?" I asked, bracing for more hard truths.

"Dad left us because I'm bad," she let out. I never took time to think about how the pain of the abuse bound with the hurt of divorce.

Seven's burdens were doubled.

"No," I replied and felt my heart break for her once more. "He left because Mom and Dad didn't love each other. We went back to Dad later, remember? We lived with Dad because it was better for us. So, you see, he didn't leave because of you."

"It makes me feel sad," she said, looking at the ground.

"I know. Mom and Dad both let us down. And you got hurt," I said. "But I don't want you to feel sad anymore. Can I give you a hug?" I asked her. I had been very careful not to try to touch her during all our previous encounters. But I felt like we trusted each other and I could finally hug her, but only with her permission.

"Okay," she said and started to cry. I lifted her up and put her in my lap.

"You're not bad," I told her, squeezing her tight. "None of it was your fault. I know you hurt. Mom and Dad didn't take care of you. People ignored you, and Grandpa hurt you. Dad left, and it hurt. I am so, so sorry that no one kept you safe."

"Yeah," she said with her head buried in my chest close to my heart. Her whole body was heaving up and down as she tried to catch her breath between deep sobs.

"But, you know, it's all over now," I told her lightly, stroking her beautiful hair as tears ran down my face. "The bad man is gone. I'm an adult. I'll protect you. You're safe."

I held her for a long time. When she stopped crying, she took a deep, cleansing breath. As she exhaled, her shoulders sagged a little, releasing the tension from her body.

"I'm glad you came," she told me. I felt her hug me back, and it was glorious. "Can I go twirl?" she asked as she revealed a cheeky grin.

"Yes! You can twirl as much as you want! You can have as much fun as you want! Laugh out loud! Be super silly!" I exclaimed.

"Okay!" she shouted as she jumped up. "Come on! Come twirl! You can have fun too!" she yelled.

Seven gave me permission to have fun.

I stood up, and we twirled in the meadow on the soft green grass and giggled. After a few minutes, she stopped and a bit of her sadness washed across her face.

"Why didn't Mom and Dad love us?" she asked, looking directly at me.

I took a moment to catch my breath. The meadow was reassuring. I needed to choose my words carefully.

"They did love us. They do love us. They just don't always love us the right way."

"Yeah. It kinda makes me a little sad. It makes me feel tired." I appreciated how drained she must have felt. Trying to stay alive despite all of her pain must have taken every ounce of her energy.

"It makes me sad too. Why don't you lie down? I'm going to go while you sleep, but I'll be back soon."

"Promise?" she asked.

"I promise," I said. "I told you. I'm taking care of you now. You're safe. Take a nap, and I'll be back soon." Time was irrelevant in the meadow and 'soon' was relative. She never complained when it took days, or even weeks, for me to return to her.

"Last time, I didn't think you were gonna come back," she said, lying down in the shade of the great oak.

"I know. But I come back every time. Remember that, okay?" I asked. "I'm not leaving you. We're a team."

Seven stared up at the clouds dancing across the beautiful blue sky. "I miss our family," she said, her voice barely above a whisper.

"It's okay. But, you know," I said to her as I lay beside her on my back to enjoy the sky, "our family wasn't always good."

"Why?" she asked, lying next to me, her tiny hand lying in my palm.

"Because people get hurt in bad families. You got hurt. Your grandpa hurt you. Mom and Dad hurt you. Our family was bad," I told her. When I reminded her our family was bad, I was really reminding myself. We both had to accept the betrayal, pain, and disappointment. I wondered how we, I, would ever accept and find forgiveness for my family.

"Yeah," she said, "Grandpa hurt me a lot. I kept waiting for Mom and Dad, but they didn't come."

"I know. But none of them can hurt you ever again. I'm here now. I'm your parent. I'll protect you."

"Okay," she said as she closed her eyes. "I love you."

"I love you too," I told her as I watched her fall asleep. It was the first time she ever said she loved me.

In exchange for my promise to keep her safe, she gave me her love. I've heard over the years, "kids don't come with instructions." That's true. But Seven taught me that if you just keep them safe, they will hand you their heart. I left her in the meadow knowing we loved each other and I was determined to keep her safe and happy.

Seven was the child I never had.

Our shared memories triggered all the pieces of me that felt defenseless. Weak. Unsafe. I began to feel Thirteen's angry hypervigilance rising to the surface. After my final session with Seven, I opened my eyes, and I was back in Amelie's office. It was time to meet Thirteen—the angry one.

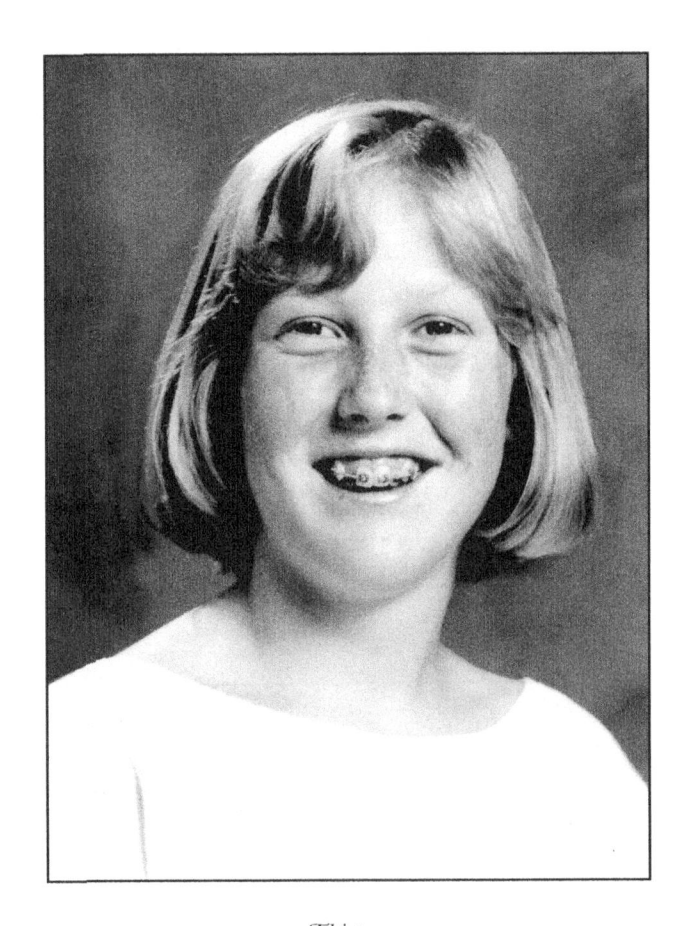

*Thirteen*

## Chapter 14

When I was thirteen, my life was all about the color purple. During one special weekend in the summer, I was the only one who went to stay at my mom and stepdad's house. It was officially a "Me Weekend."

My mom bought me a purple top at the flea market. The purple shirt had a neckline almost as wide as my shoulders. She also bought me some new white pants. Wearing white meant I probably shouldn't roll around in the mud anymore, or at least, not very often.

I felt stylish in my new clothes. It was one of the best weekends ever.

It's difficult at times to appreciate the great moments when there were so many that were poisoned by trauma. Not long after the amazing Me Weekend, my brother and I were dropped off to stay with my maternal grandparents for a few days during summer vacation. The house construction was completed and they no longer lived in the trailer that remained on the property. The scent of fresh paint lingered in the air of their enormous new house.

My grandpa growled I was getting to be "too much trouble" as I got older and the threat of pregnancy loomed. His deeply penetrative rapes had nearly stopped by the time I put on my purple top and white pants and we arrived at their house. I was feeling particularly confident that weekend and I believed the worst was behind me. It was a misguided sense of security.

Saturday night, I set the table in the new kitchen. The red brick-patterned flooring curled up against the dark-brown cabinets. My grandmother hated those cabinets. It was all she talked about for weeks after they were installed.

An excellent cook, my grandma had a copper-bottom Revere Ware set that hung from the ceiling. Just about everything she cooked benefited from a dollop of bacon grease collected in a cast-iron jug on top of the stove.

The round, wooden dining table sat next to the refrigerator in the corner opposite the sink. After we cleared the dishes, all of us sat around the table and listened to my grandpa's stories. Eventually, my grandma and brother went to bed and my grandpa and I sat alone.

He continued to tell stories until well after midnight when I finally decided it was time to go to bed. Saying goodnight, I stood up from the table, and my grandpa lunged at me, causing his chair to crack so loudly I thought it broke.

Throwing an arm on either side of me, he caught me in a savage, powerful grip. My hands frantically scratched at his to pry his greedy fingers off me.

He jerked me back toward him and my feet left the floor. His arms were strong around my waist and he forced me onto his lap. I felt his erect penis push into the back of my white pants. His left arm remained wrapped around my waist and his right arm went across my chest, pulling me harshly against him.

"Let's go to the trailer," he whispered. "It won't hurt none."

The world went silent.

Time stopped.

I looked down at his right arm and watched his hand harshly squeeze my left breast through my favorite purple top.

At that moment, I detached and watched myself from the corner.

Corners were safe.

An unknown force swelled inside of me. I felt a raw, explosive sense of power for the first time since my abuse started at Five.

The only thought I had was, *Oh, fuck no. Not tonight, motherfucker.*

I watched myself grab his strong, heavy arms, and push them off me. I launched out of his lap and landed on my feet. I turned around to face him, still seated in his chair. Stepping forward between his legs, I slammed both of my hands onto his barrel chest with such force his chair slammed into the wall.

Staring directly into his eyes, I leaned down to face him. My voice was controlled and sinister. "Don't you ever fucking touch me again, you fucking monster."

Silent, he stared back at me with big, wide eyes. No longer watching events from the corner, I rejoined myself as I turned to leave the kitchen. I ran up the stairs leading to the bedrooms on the second floor and bolted into the bathroom. I slammed the door shut and locked myself inside.

I vomited into the toilet as the adrenaline overwhelmed me.

Flushing the toilet, I lowered myself to the floor and crawled on my hands and knees to the door. I didn't know what to do. Was he coming to my room to rape me? Would he drag me outside to the trailer where we would be entirely alone? What would he do to me now that I threatened him? I was more terrified at that moment than at any other time in my life.

Drenched in sweat, I felt every single second of my terror. My heart pounded. I couldn't breathe. I stayed on the floor paralyzed by fear and listening for any signs he had chased me up the stairs.

After waiting for what must have been twenty or thirty minutes, I opened the door slightly and called out to my brother. His room was just a few feet away.

"Hey! Wake up!" I shouted.

"What do you want?" he asked, annoyed.

"I think I hear something in my bedroom. Go and see if there's someone in there," I said.

He got out of bed and walked by the one-inch gap in the bathroom door. After searching the bedroom at the opposite end of the hallway, he passed by the bathroom on his way back to bed.

"There's no one there," he said. "You're so weird."

I took some deep breaths. The cool floor grounded me. I had to think. A door at the top of the stairs kept the noise from our antics out of the rest of the house. If I could leap out of the bathroom, lock the stairwell door, and get to my bedroom, I might survive.

I was convinced if I made even one mistake, I would be raped.

Leaping out of the bathroom, I slammed the door at the top of the stairs and locked it with shaking hands. I fell into my bedroom onto the floor. My body shuddered violently as I scrambled to push the door closed and turn the lock.

I stood up and wasted no time as I shoved the two twin beds and the dresser against the door. The clothes rod from the closet became my weapon. I pulled out the window screens. If he came through the door, I was going to beat him to death or jump through the second-story window before enduring another assault.

I sat in the far corner of my room all night waiting for him. Every creak in the new house, every sound from the garden, intensified my vigilance. When the sun started to rise, I delayed going downstairs until I heard my brother leave his room.

We found our grandma cooking bacon and eggs. As we walked into the kitchen, she looked up from her stove.

"Don't make too much noise this morning. Your grandpa is in his photography studio," she mentioned casually. "He's in a bad mood. Becky, why don't you go tell him it's time to eat?" she said to me as her gaze returned to the cast-iron skillet. Why would a grown woman ask a young girl to speak to her angry husband? She's a coward, I thought to myself. They're all cowards.

"No," I said sternly as I sat down at the table.

She turned to look at me. I glared back. I was done taking instructions from her.

When my grandpa finally came into the house to eat, he sat in the same seat where he'd launched his attack on me the night before. He barely looked up from his plate and didn't say a word to anyone. We ate in relative silence, save for the sound of forks scraping against the restaurant platters we used for every meal. I sat up straight. Tall.

I knew it was over.

He never grabbed or tried to assault me ever again.

My mind protected me, once again, when he grotesquely cooed *"it won't hurt none"* into my ear. Another fragment broke off. Born Saturday night in the summer of 1983, Thirteen was a traumatized, hyper-vigilant, ferocious piece of me designed for battle. She became my anger and defender against the world.

But Thirteen was a hydra. A two-headed beast. She attacked and defended me in equal measure, whenever she perceived a threat. I hated her and I used her. Needed her. Our relationship was confused and unhealthy. Some days, her power helped me and I would summon it. Other days, I wanted to permanently extinguish her.

Just a few weeks after the final attack, I heard an angry voice in my head shouting "Fuck you" at just about everything.

*"Fuck you if you think you look good."*
*"Fuck you if you think I'm wrong."*
*"Fuck you if you don't like what I'm saying."*
*"Fuck you pretty girl who has nice clothes."*

Much like Seven, the feelings trapped with her blended into my daily life. I knew her voice wasn't the real me. I felt awkward when my response to a banal situation, like a server bringing me an order two minutes too slowly, ignited a wholly unnecessary rapid-fire verbal assault. I hated blending with Thirteen. Her anger felt wholly unnatural.

"I've spent thirty years trying to tame her," I told Amelie when she asked about Thirteen in our next session. "I want to silence her. I've paid a price for her anger. I didn't get promotions, lost clients, and ruined relationships because my anger is the first emotion I present to most people."

"You have to convince her to stop. She can't torment you forever," Amelie coached.

"I know," I replied, a bit frustrated. I took a deep breath and said, "I'm not really sure how to do that."

"Well, talk to her and explain why you don't need her anymore. She needs to be released from her role as your protector and shown love."

"I'm a little afraid to tell her to stop," I admitted, "because I still rely on her when I need strength or courage."

"Rebecca, you're a powerful, intelligent, fearless woman," Amelie told me firmly. "You don't need her. She's not real."

Sitting back on Amelie's sofa, I watched her light a candle. We set the intention to meet Thirteen and started with some simple breath work to ground ourselves and still our minds. After closing our eyes, the sounds from outside the window grew quiet, and we started our meditation.

"Okay. Where are you? What do you see?" she asked.

"I'm in the meadow."

"Great. Now picture the top of your head is open like a door and bright light is entering your body through this opening. What color is the light?" she asked.

"It's white. Bright-white light," I said.

"Beautiful," she said in her reassuring French accent. "Take a few more deep breaths and focus on the light coming through the top of your head and filling your entire body," she instructed. "Now look around. Tell me, is anyone with you?"

"Yes," I said. "A girl. I know it's Thirteen. She has her back to me."

"It's okay. She's a difficult teenager, but remember she has no power."

"She's sitting under a tree. It's the tree I sat under with my mom when I told her I was abused. Thirteen's body is still turned away from me."

"Great, introduce yourself. Remember, she's stuck in time. She might not know you are an adult."

*"Hi. Do you know who I am?" I asked Thirteen nervously as I stood to the side and a few feet away from her. She had long, blonde hair and wore white pants and my favorite purple top.*

*"Why should I care who you are?" she snapped with her arms folded across her chest. She turned around and stared through me with an angry gaze.*

*"I'm Rebecca. I'm here to talk to you."*

*"You've gotten old," she sneered, keeping her arms crossed. She stood up. Adjusting her stance, she squared her shoulders and let me know she was ready to fight. "Why are you here?" she asked forcefully, knocking me well off-center.*

*There was no use in trying to explain to her the nature of our complicated relationship. The way that I needed her at times and hated her at others. The past wasn't going to help me in the present. I decided that I needed to accept full responsibility for our dynamic. I had to be the adult and offer the first olive branch.*

*"I'm here to apologize and thank you," I said. "I didn't take care of you. I didn't protect you. I let you be my guardian, and it should never have been your job."*

*She glared at me. "No shit. But it was my job, wasn't it? I had to fight him all on my own. I had to be strong. There weren't any adults around to do the job," she punched back.*

*"You're right," I said softly. "You fought him off all on your own. Thank you for being so brave. For helping me so much over the years." Thankfully, her arms relaxed by her sides as I spoke. "There's a lot we need to talk about. I'd like to come back if it's okay."*

*"Come back whenever you want. I'm always here," she said in a way suggesting she stood watch. Part of me wondered if she felt obligated to stay.*

*"Thank you. I promise I'll be back. I'm not leaving you."*

"I'm done for now," I told Amelie, keeping my eyes closed. I felt tension throughout my body. Thirteen was going to be tough to manage.

"Okay, picture yourself alone in the meadow. Take a deep breath and imagine the open doorway in the top of your head is closed shut and locked. Now open your eyes."

My eyes opened. I knew there was a lot of work ahead of me.

"Welcome back," she said with a smile, "that was intense."

Amelie and I worked together for several more months, and I continued to meet with Thirteen.

"Hey, how are you?" I asked Thirteen as we met again in the meadow. It was a relief to see she no longer crossed her arms when I appeared. I felt I slowly was gaining her trust.

"I'm fine," she replied, her standard response. She was never great or happy. Just fine, like every other surly teenager.

"I want to talk to you about the night you fought him off. I didn't know it was possible to feel that much rage," I said to her. I thought some words of appreciation and respect might create an opportunity to talk more freely.

"It had to end. My body couldn't take any more rape," she said flatly. She was curt. Precise. In her vigilance, there was only room for hard edges.

"You know I'm really grateful for your courage, right? You saved me."

"Yeah, I know. I had to keep us safe. All of us."

"How many are there?" I asked. "I've met Seven. I sometimes hear a small voice who's afraid. I think she's Five."

"Yeah, Five is always fearful. The other is Six. She stays away from the rest of us. I've watched over them all this time," she explained with a layer of resentment, and pride, in her voice. I knew she believed she was the only one who could have ever done the job properly. "Are you here to tell me you don't need me anymore?" she asked. Thirteen was always two steps ahead of me.

"Yes, I am," I said. "I can take care of all of you by myself."

"I doubt it," she scoffed. "You've never met Five and didn't know about Six. How can you protect us if you don't know us?" Her defense mechanisms were well fortified.

I wasn't sure how to scale her walls. My walls. They felt like a permanent part of my design.

It was a precarious moment in my negotiation for peace. I started to feel frustrated. Impatient.

"I will meet Five and Six," I pressed. "It all takes time. But how do I convince you I can take care of all of you? How do we get there? I can't stay angry forever. Your anger doesn't help me. It hurts me. You're hurting me. What do I need to do?" I asked her, feeling vexed. I was out of ideas and patience with this stubborn teenager. "You have to stop. I don't need your protection and neither do the others."

"Right," she said and crossed her arms. "So you don't need me anymore. Is that right? Are you sure? Because just a few months ago, when things got a bit rough, you nearly asked me to help you," she growled.

Thirteen geared up for battle. I watched her clench her fists. She had one script, but I knew her bravado was bullshit. We were playing a game of chicken, and I was about to call her bluff. I reminded myself she was just a young teenager.

"You're right," I said, "and it was a mistake. But let's remember, I didn't ask you to help me in the end. I proved I can handle my own life," I explained. "I'm an adult. I'm telling you to stop. I've had enough. Turn. It. Off." Maybe it wasn't the perfect choice of words, but I was tired of her unruly abuse.

Thirteen looked shocked. She bit her lip and looked at the ground to avoid my eyes. I knew I'd hurt her feelings. She was just a child. I felt bad for digging my claws in too deep.

"Okay, I'll stop," she finally agreed, and then started crying.

I realized I had never once considered her sadness or pain. I had never asked how she felt. I only ever focused on and resented her rage. Thirteen, my warrior, hurt inside. She looked exhausted.

"I'm really sorry. I'm not being fair. You've been hurt enough. Please, don't be sad. This is a good thing. You should have never had this job," I said, hugging her for the first time. I forgot to ask permission and wondered if she would push me away. When I felt her hug me back, I started to cry. Our fight with one another ended. There was no winner. Both sides bore too many wounds to claim victory.

"It's been too much," she said. "It's been really hard. I was so afraid that night." She stopped hugging me to wipe her tears away with her sleeve. When she looked up at me, dark circles framed her eyes.

"I know. You were afraid, but you still found a way to be so damn brave. I will never be as brave as you."

"He really hurt them, you know. He hurt all of us," she said from her heart. She was, despite all appearances, fragile.

"He did. But he's dead. And it's over," I told her. The time to break the cycle had come.

*"Do you forgive them?"* she asked. *"Grandpa, Grandma, Mom, and Dad? Do I have to forgive them?"* I struggled to answer her because I felt conflicted about forgiveness.

*"No,"* I said. *"You don't owe anyone anything. But consider accepting them and all their failures. It doesn't mean you condone their behavior. But if you accept their faults and release them, you can stop resisting the truth and heal. You can stop feeling like you have to fight back all of the time."*

*"I'll try. It's hard. I never felt like I could relax,"* she admitted as we both sat down.

*"I understand. But you're safe now. It's time to rest. Close your eyes. I will protect you. And thank you. Thank you for trusting me and letting it go. I love you,"* I said while she lay back on the grass and closed her eyes.

Seven and Thirteen finally embraced a new sense of peace. My sadness lifted and my anger began to ease.

"Thirteen and Seven are softening," I told Amelie once our session ended.

"Great. You're ready to meet Five and Six. What do you think they're going to say?" Amelie asked.

"I don't know. Five is so little and terrified. I don't want to say the wrong thing. I don't know who Six is—I'm not sure what she sounds like."

"You'll be fine. Just remember to keep it simple. Kids their age aren't complicated," Amelie coached.

She was right. It was time to meet Five and Six.

*Five*

## Chapter 15

As a five-year-old child, my family called me "Becky." I was the height of a typical kitchen counter and weighed about forty pounds. Obsessed with animals of any sort, I had a favorite "doggy dress" that was white with plaid trim. Scottish terrier dogs adorned the pockets.

My best friend was an old, white, fifteen-pound cat named Bert whom I lugged around as my trusted sidekick.

We lived in the woods and used to walk to the lake near our house where my brother, sister, and I skipped rocks. Playing with my siblings was the best. We were inventive and made sleds out of cardboard boxes from the grocery store and rode them down hills covered in pine needles.

A bit of a daredevil, I flew down our steep road on my tricycle one afternoon and hit a rock, flipped through the air, and collided with a telephone pole. When the doctor asked me which part hurt the most, I pointed to my palm scraped from the asphalt, completely ignoring the small hole in my forehead.

My Kindergarten teacher, Mrs. Parks, was wonderful. She used to give me a big hug every morning and told me I was an excellent reader.

I was precocious, adorable, funny, sassy, and innocent.

Like a lot of young children, I was keen to be close to my maternal grandma and grandpa. They made me feel special when they told me funny stories, called me beautiful, and took me for swims in the creek close to their house. We made delicious, hand-cranked, homemade vanilla ice cream in the summer. I thought they were the best people on Earth until my grandpa betrayed me and extracted a fleshy sacrifice from my innocence.

The first time his fingers penetrated my five-year-old sex I became his victim. Becky ceased to exist and "Becky the Survivor" emerged. To this day, my stomach lurches when I am called Becky by anyone. The association with my abuse is too sharp.

When I took a ride with him in his work truck to get gas, he pulled over on the side of the road. Pulling me close to him, his hands reached under my dress and dug inside my underwear. I was confused when his enormous, calloused fingers penetrated my sex and I left my body.

Born in the spring of 1975, Five, the youngest fragment, became frozen with fear whenever he pulled her underwear down. Disappearing during each penetrative assault, Five held her breath and remained silent while he stuck his large fingers into my vagina. Five held onto the terror and it took root in my body.

Every time he jabbed his tongue into my mouth, sucked on my ear, or pinched my nipples, I winced. He taught me to play a game called S-T-O-P and G-O. I used to say "S-T-O-P S-T-O-P" when I wanted him to stop because things were too painful or scary. He would interrupt me and say "G-O G-O," ignoring my pleas. He rarely wanted to stop. I hated the game.

"Go give Grandpa a kiss," the adults ordered me. I used to ball up my hands into tiny fists when I approached him. Some of the adults laughed when he stuck his tongue into my mouth, and I jerked away. I was embarrassed and confused when he reached out and grabbed at my crotch through my clothes, behaving like a monster in front of family members. They all pretended not to see him.

What was I supposed to do?

I was trapped.

I was afraid to tell. I was Five and wanted to be a good girl.

At six feet tall and over two-hundred pounds, he was a big, powerful man. He scared me.

After every assault, my mind slipped sideways, and I disappeared as my child's mind spiraled. Would he hurt me if I told my Dad? What would happen to my brother and sister? Was I a bad girl?

I never got any answers.

I heard Five off and on once I entered high school but Thirteen was noisier and usually drowned out her voice. I met her for the first time when I forty-nine years old.

"What's the intention for today?" Amelie asked.

"Let's meet Five. She has so much fear and anxiety."

"Okay, let's see what happens. Let's start with some deep breaths," Amelie instructed. We settled into a relaxing meditation and began to work.

"Okay, are you in the meadow?" Amelie asked.

I was in a new part of the meadow on the edge of a great forest.

"Yes. There's a small child here, but it's not Seven. She's standing next to a large pine tree pretending to scribble on it. I used to pretend to paint pictures on pine tree bark when I was little."

"Say hello," Amelie nudged me. Her guidance always helped me when I met a fragment for the first time.

"Hello," I said, standing in front of her. I immediately noticed how much smaller she was than Seven. "I'm happy to see you."

"Thirteen and Seven say I can talk to you," she said. "They say you're big now, and you're not a stranger."

"I'm glad. Would you like to sit down on the grass? It's really nice," I said, motioning for her to join me in the sun.

"Okay," she said.

As she walked toward me, I knew it was Five. She wore my favorite doggy dress. When she stood beside me before sitting down, I wanted to cry. She was so tiny. I had forgotten how small I was when I was first assaulted. We sat down together in the warm sunshine.

"This is a pretty place. Do you like it here?" I asked as we settled on the ground.

"It's scary," she answered. "Where is the bad man? Is he coming?" she asked. Did I need to tell her my grandpa was dead?

"Oh. I'm sorry you're scared. It's not nice," I told her. "But you don't have to be scared anymore. He's gone. He died. So you're safe."

She became still. "I don't know. I'm still a little scared," she said, breaking my heart. Tiny and innocent. Fragile. She was just a baby.

"I'm so sorry. I'm sorry it took so long to find you."

"Yeah," she said. "He made me hurt here," she said pointing to her tiny sex.

"I know. And I'm sorry. I didn't keep you safe. No one kept you safe. It's not your fault," I told her. "You were really brave, you know."

She looked at me through her brilliant blue eyes, and enormous tears rolled down her pink cheeks onto her dress. Instinctively, without asking permission, I picked her up and held her in my arms. She wailed and soaked my body with all her fear and isolation. I cried with her. The horror of rape sat on her five-year-old shoulders for nearly forty-five years, and they couldn't hold it any longer.

When our tears stopped, I wiped her face with my shirt and told her, "The bad man is gone. You will never be hurt again. I will keep you safe. No one will ever hurt us again. It's over."

"Promise? Cross your heart?" Five asked.

"Cross my heart."

"I'm tired," she said, crawling out of my lap and laying down on the grass. They were all so tired from maintaining their traumatized energy for decades.

"Okay. Why don't you take a nap? It's safe to sleep now," I said as I watched her body curl up in the sun.

"Are you leaving me?" she asked.

"Only for a little while. But the others will watch over you. You're safe," I reassured her. "How about I tickle your back until you're asleep?"

"Okay. Come back soon," she whispered as I stroked her back, grateful to see her body relax.

"I sure will. I'll be back very soon," I replied with tears in my eyes.

My heart broke for the little girl who so bravely absorbed all the fear while she survived so many assaults. Being able to comfort the true source of my anxiety was a gift. I was determined to soothe her pain.

Thankfully, a five-year-old is a lot less complicated than a prickly teenager. Our chats moved along rather quickly, and it didn't take her long to accept I was older and would keep her safe. I checked in on Five a few more times, and she seemed happier. Brighter.

"Hey, how are you? How do you feel?" I asked her while standing in the meadow.

"Good. I like playing here," she said as she ran in circles. "Have you met her yet?" she asked after stopping to catch her breath.

"Who? Thirteen? Seven?" I asked, unsure of who she was talking about.

"No. Six. She isn't allowed to play with me. She's alone. You need to find her," she said to me with a serious expression before walking toward one of her favorite oak trees. It had perfect, low branches, making climbing easy.

"I will. I will find her. I promise. Be careful, please. Don't go too high," I cautioned her. I worried but told myself to relax. Five was finally freed of her burdens and now she was fearless. It was wonderful to watch. "I'm going to go now. I'll see you later, alligator!"

"Okay. After a while, crocodile!" she shouted before bursting into giggles.

A few days later, I meditated at home and set my intention to meet Six. The other.

When I finally settled my mind, I wasn't in the meadow. I stood inside an unfamiliar stone building. A single door was open, and I walked through to find myself standing at the end of a long hallway. Walking down the corridor, I stopped just opposite a lone, open door. I couldn't see into the room. It was pitch black and smelled like mold. Decay. It all felt and smelled oddly familiar.

It had the same smell as my grandparents' trailer and my grandpa's photography studio. It had a cement floor and very few windows. It was his private space where visitors were not particularly welcome. He assaulted me in that space many times over the years. He used to take nude photographs of various women when no one else was home and showed me the images. They were tucked away in the top drawer of his metal desk. He made me promise never to tell anyone about the women.

I felt, I knew, another fragment waited in the room. I walked cautiously across the stone floor and knelt down on my knees. Stopping at the doorway, I focused my eyes and noticed a small figure hiding in a dank, rancid corner furthest from the door. Vines tangled around her, holding onto her like a prisoner and binding her to the damp walls.

She looked feral.

"Hello," I said, "can you come here? Can you come out of this room?"

"I'm dirty," she whispered. "I'm not allowed to leave."

"Please, can you just come out of the corner," I pleaded with her. "I want to see you."

"No," she said firmly, "I'm a dirty girl and I can't leave."

"That's not true. You can come out. I would like to see you. Please. We can sit together in the sun and get warm," I told her. "I promise it's okay."

After a lot of coaxing and patience, she wriggled free from the vines and walked into the doorway. Into the sunlight. The vines squirmed and reached out at her like angry tentacles. They reminded me of my grandpa's hands grabbing at me. I stayed on my knees and she stood in front of me. Her gaze never looked up from her feet.

A disgusting, torn bit of cloth covered her body. Her knees were rubbed raw. Dark bruises formed a mosaic all over her skin. Every mark reflected her humiliation and the wounds buried in her flesh. Snot ran down her tear-stained, soiled cheeks. Her hair was matted and stuck to the sides of her face. Every inch of her skin was dry and cracked.

Filthy.

## It Won't Hurt None

*Bruised.*

*Broken.*

*I looked at her through my tears, doubting I would ever get her, get us, clean. She was the first to survive my grandpa's penis entering my vagina, tearing into my flesh until it burned.*

*Born during the summer of 1976, Six's body reflected the monstrous pain of every penetration. She was raw and stained by his perversion.*

"Sit down," *I said gently as tears still rolled down my cheeks. I draped my arm around her sickly body as she sat down next to me. I held her close. She smelled like sex.*

"You shouldn't touch me. I'm too dirty."

"No, you're not. I love you. I'm not afraid to touch you. I'm here to take care of you. I think we should leave this place. It's not nice. We can leave and get clean," *I told her, not entirely believing my own words.*

"How?" *she asked, still not wanting to look at me.*

"I don't really know," *I told her. It was the first time during one of my meditations I didn't have the answer.*

"I tried to clean it the best I could, but it won't come off. See," *she said, holding up her little arm.* "I can't leave. I'm still dirty."

"I understand. I can't get all the dirt off of me, either." *I took a deep breath.* "I think you are very beautiful," *I told her.*

"No, I'm not," *she said, angrily pushing herself away from me and pinning herself against the wall opposite where I sat.* "I am not."

"You are beautiful," *I repeated.*

"Stop. That's a bad word. He said it to me, and then he hurt me. He made me dirty. My insides are dirty. They hurt."

*I took another deep breath and remembered when he used to tell me I was beautiful while his body ripped my flesh. It took me years before I learned how to stop flinching whenever anyone told me I was beautiful.*

*I was our healer while trying to get healed. I wanted Six to know she was worthy of love and beautiful.*

"He told us that so he could hurt us," *I explained to Six,* "but he was bad. He was very bad. It was never your fault. You did nothing wrong. Ever. And I don't think we should feel dirty anymore. I'm tired of feeling this way. Are you tired?" *I asked her.*

"Yeah, I'm tired," *she replied.*

"Then let's go," *I said as I stood up and crossed over to her.* "Come with me."

*I held out my hand. She thought about it for a minute and then Six slowly grabbed my hand and stood up. We left the cold, filthy place she'd called home her entire life. We continued to walk away, never looking back. A flash of bright-white light shot across my mind, and suddenly we stood in a familiar part of the meadow.*

*The filth, blemishes, bruises, and sexual assaults staining both of our bodies disappeared. We were clean. The tattered cloth that covered her body was replaced with a pair of jeans, a hand-me-down shirt, and some sneakers. Six loved new sneakers, especially the kind we used to buy at Kmart before the new school year.*

*I stopped and kneeled down on the grass and looked into her eyes. "You're beautiful," I said, holding her face in my hands. "You are beautiful. And you are worthy of love."*

*She looked beyond my eyes and into my soul. She spoke directly to my shame when she cupped my face with her soft, tiny hands and said, "You are beautiful and deserve love," with a wisdom far beyond her years.*

*I closed my eyes. I took some deep breaths, and the words "beautiful and love" rose out of the ground. Rising up through my feet and legs, past my stomach and the lump in my throat, it flowed out of the top of my head. With every breath, beautiful and love filled me up, and some of my shame left.*

*When I opened my eyes, Six was still looking at me when Five showed up and walked over to us.*

*"Hi," said Five.*

*"Hi," said Six shyly, grabbing my hand.*

*"Wanna go climb a tree?" Five asked.*

*Six, unsure of her new surroundings, looked at me.*

*"Go ahead. Have as much fun as you want. You're safe here," I assured her.*

*Six revealed the most jubilant smile I'd ever seen. Letting go of my hand, she joined Five and they both giggled as they took off running into the meadow to climb a tree.*

*As I watched them leave, Six stopped for a moment to turn and look at me. I was crying for both of us. She saw my tears and ran back to wrap her tiny body around me.*

*"It's okay. Don't be sad," she said, squeezing me tight. "We're okay, and we are beautiful and loved."*

*"I'm okay," I said. "I'm not sad. I just don't know if all the dirt will leave us," I said to her.*

*"I don't think so. I think some of it will stay. But maybe it's okay. Maybe we just need to have fun."*

*"You're right. We just need to live. Now, go play!" I told her.*

*"Okay! See you later, alligator!" she shouted, running back to Five. The two held hands as they ran off into the woods.*

"After a while, crocodile!" I shouted.

When their cheeky giggles faded, I sat down in the meadow and cried for Five, Six, Seven, and Thirteen. For all of us. I mourned for the loss of our innocence and our pain.

They were courageous because they survived. They were courageous while they waited for me to come to make them feel safe. And they were courageous when they trusted me and believed me when I told them they were loved.

When I stopped crying, I looked up and saw Thirteen standing nearby. She was always watching.

"Where are they?" she asked me with a look of worry on her face.

"You know, you can relax. You're all safe here," I answered.

"Yeah, but I still like to watch over them," she replied.

"Okay. They're playing. They ran into the woods," I said, wiping my face. "They're both okay." Trusting me to protect the younger girls was new, and it still made her uncomfortable.

"Why did it take you so long to find us?" she asked. She was always so damn direct.

"Well, to be honest, I didn't always want to listen. It took me a long time to understand you needed me."

"You're going to be okay, you know. Just wait and see," she said to me, hinting there was more in the meadow waiting for me. Truth be told, I wasn't sure I could survive any more discoveries.

"Thanks. I hope so. I have to go. Why don't you go catch up with them?" I encouraged her, knowing she was bursting to find them.

"Yeah, okay," she said. "They love trees."

"I know. I love them too."

Thirteen took off into the woods.

I stood alone and wondered if I would ever truly feel clean, much less beautiful. I wanted to believe I could learn how to completely love myself. The trouble is I didn't know how it was done. Did I just need to decide that I would no longer feel any of my shame? What did that mean? I left the meadow with more questions than answers.

Melancholy overtook me just a few days later. I couldn't help but wonder what might have been had I not been abused.

What if I had grown up in a loving, safe home? What if my family had protected me? What if my mind had never fragmented, and I'd lived my entire life as a whole, happy, untraumatized person? What if I'd always believed I was beautiful and worthy of love?

Would I have had more confidence? Would I have become a pro tennis player? A judge? Kinder? Friendlier? More settled? Married? Would I have children?

I ran an inventory of my life's accomplishments, missed opportunities, and failures. Who would I be if I had simply been safe? What would have been had those who were abused by my grandpa before me chosen to put an end to his violence? Why did it have to be my burden?

Six added complexity to my healing. What was it about her that made it necessary for her to live trapped in a room with no windows? Why did I meet Five and Six last? Why were their voices the weakest? Did I ever hear from Six? What did she sound like?

Part of me believes Thirteen ferociously protected them. It's likely they only revealed themselves once Thirteen felt certain they were safe and gave them permission. The reconciliations between the fragments and me slowly lowered their collective chatter in my mind.

"Will they ever go completely quiet?" I asked Amelie one day during a phone call.

"Reconciling is the first step. They trust you and listen to you now. The next step is integrating them back into yourself. It's going to take time. Take a break for now. You've done a lot of powerful work."

I took Amelie's advice and began to live my life in relative peace and quiet. Listening to my pain, my messengers, left me feeling hopeful about the future and eager to take another leap. I began to imagine a life beyond Kenya.

# Freefall

*"A mermaid does not fear the depths, for she is no stranger of the darkness and the cold. It was the darkness that made her scales shine so brightly, and it was the cold that made her heart so warm. She does not fear the deep for she has been to the bottom and knows that she can rise."*
*(The Magic Crafter)*

## Chapter 16

LESS CHATTER.

More joy.

Living mindfully and in the present created space in my life to ask questions about the future. Was there a reason to call Kenya home for another five or ten years? What would I lose if I stayed? What would I gain if I left? Was I listening to my authentic self when I asked the question or was Flight involved? Honestly, sometimes it was difficult to distinguish between genuine intuition and when the fragments and their companions were running my life.

Eventually, I figured out that Flight told me to flee! Run! Get out of danger! But my strong Pisces instincts told me to imagine the world as limitless, full of possibility, and to look beyond my current borders.

Flight was fed by Trauma.

My instincts to explore came from my soul.

In 2018, I meditated on how I felt about Kenya and it became clear it was time to leave. A lot of my friends were moving on to their next expat destination. A recent relationship ended and I felt no desire to be open to yet another Kenyan man's interpretation of love. I thought through the decision carefully, as I didn't want to make the decision in some sort of trauma-infused mindset but with gratitude for everything that Kenya and Africa offered me over the years. It felt like it was time for a fresh start but where should I go next? I didn't have a clear answer until I spent more time with Amelie.

"I don't know where I'm supposed to live anymore. I don't think I'm meant to stay here, but I'm confused about what feels right," I said to her as we sat down on her cozy sofa.

"Okay. Let's do a simple exercise. Use these pieces of paper and write down the names of every city you will consider calling home. One name per piece of paper."

I wrote down London, Paris, Dubai, Nairobi, Los Angeles, New York, Manila, and Singapore.

"Great. Now place every piece of paper on the floor face up so you can see the names of the cities," Amelie directed.

It seemed odd, but I trusted her, laying the papers face up on the floor.

"Step onto each piece of paper, one at a time, and tell me the first reaction you feel."

I didn't even get a toe on Nairobi before I said, "No. Absolutely not," and she removed the paper.

I set my foot on Paris. "Fantasy. I don't speak the language and have no connections. I just love France." Paris was removed.

Stepping onto London, I said, "I'd love to, but I don't think I'm ready yet. It's expensive and complicated to get a work permit. I'll call it home one day, but not now."

"Dubai. I've done that already. I really hate the climate." Dubai was removed.

On to Los Angeles. "I have no desire to ever be back in Los Angeles. I don't belong there."

Next, New York. "It's too hectic. I already lived there. I can't do it again." New York was removed.

Manila was up next. "Beautiful, but no. It's as unsafe as Nairobi and impossibly chaotic. It's difficult for expats."

I stepped on Singapore and I paused to take a breath. My body relaxed and my shoulders softened. I had never even so much as passed through Singapore; but it was clear to me I was supposed to live there next.

"So," Amelie said, "Singapore."

After my session with Amelie, and spending late nights doing research online, there was no doubt in my mind Singapore was home. It was safe (they had almost no crime), modern, and work permits were processed without any of the corruption

I'd faced for so many years in Africa. During a trip to Manila for work, I decided to spend a quick weekend visiting Singapore.

It did not disappoint. A futuristic, beautiful, multicultural, safe, modern city and country I ignored the exasperating humidity and thought it was magical. I flew back to Manila more determined than ever to make my relocation a reality.

It took time to collate all the immigration, financial, and other information necessary to transition from a base in East Africa to Southeast Asia but at last, in March 2019, I was ready to move.

Change can be sad, scary, and exciting all at the same time. The softer, more subdued fragments roared back into my mind when I started to plan the final logistics of the move. They all had an opinion about my choices.

*"Moving is scary," Five and Six chattered over each other.*

*"I don't want to leave our friends. I'm sad," Seven chimed in.*

*"This is a huge mistake. Are you sure you don't need me to help sort things out?" Thirteen asked.*

Thankfully, the work with Amelie, and my own meditation practice, gave me the ability to close my eyes and address all of them.

*"Hey there! Remember, I'm in control now. We're safe. This is happening. Everyone, relax."* The friendly, yet firm, admonishment lowered their volume. I needed to focus, and I didn't want a second, third, fourth, or fifth opinion.

Seven was right. Leaving Kenya was rough. Apart from the years I spent growing up in the Southern California mountains, I'd never lived anywhere as long as Kenya. The idea of saying goodbye hurt my heart. Of all the farewells I had to endure in the final days, perhaps the toughest was saying goodbye to Nana. Once the movers packed all my prized possessions into a shipping container, I locked the door for the last time and cried. The love I felt living in the house next door to Nik, Lisa, Nana, and the kids, changed my life and my relationship with Africa.

The skeleton keys jangled in my pocket as I walked next door to the big house where Nana was waiting for me. I'd made that walk so many times to bring over a treat, have a glass of wine, or sit with Nana and all her animals. After handing over my keys and promising to return whenever I could, my eyes filled with tears and my throat clenched as I walked out the front door and headed off to catch my flight.

I landed at gorgeous Changi airport on a rainy Saturday afternoon. I collected four heaving suitcases and headed to a tiny, two-story house I discovered while prowling through property rental websites late at night. It was a charming, older house that served as officer's quarters many years earlier. It was the first time I had a large, fenced garden all to myself! The gardening possibilities immediately started forming in my mind as the airport shuttle pulled away and left me in the driveway.

Appreciating the sea breeze that gently tossed the bamboo trees side to side, I stood still for a moment and took a few deep breaths. Unlike my departure out of D.C., I didn't have my mentor Lynda greeting me with flowers, a card, and a hug to help me appreciate the enormous shift. It was all on me to stay present and let myself feel the moment. As I shifted onto the patio and opened the front door, a rainstorm began just as I started to cry. Leaving Kenya, and all my friends and family, finally felt real. And, suddenly, a wave of vulnerability crashed over me. *What have I done,* I asked myself.

For just a split second, I was tempted to summon Thirteen. A part of me felt like I needed her courage to figure out a new country, and life, all over again. I knew two people in Singapore. I was fifty years old. I felt weary of the work waiting for me. But I took a beat and slowed things down. Amelie was right, I gave Thirteen far too much credit. I was capable and talented.

I was real.

Thirteen was not.

My head cleared and I heard, *"We love this place!" Five, Six, Seven, and Thirteen sang out in a chorus once the suitcases were unpacked and I started to check out the house more closely. "It feels so safe here, and our new house is really cute! There are frogs in the front garden!"*

*"See,"* I replied. *"I told you I was going to take care of all of you. I'm glad you're happy."*

A month later my shipping container unloaded and I felt ready to branch out and start making new friends. After a few posts and replies in an expat Facebook group, I met Theresa and we immediately bonded. Just a few short weeks after our first meeting, we decided it was essential to purchase and ride bikes. Humidity and heat be damned! It became clear pretty quickly that neither of us was ever going to win a medal for our bike riding skills. After nearly crashing into more than one group of innocent bystanders along the beach path on a hot Saturday afternoon, she looked at me and said, "I think we need to get ice cream."

Theresa was not only one of the most energetic, beautiful, successful, and kind people I've ever known but she also spoke my love language.

Ice cream.

I knew I was going to be one of her best friends.

Between business trips and near-death experiences riding my bike, it took some time before I could make space for more healing. Some of my new Singapore friends encouraged me to book a session with a somatic healer. I didn't know what to expect when I walked into Natalia's office.

"What exactly is somatic work?" I asked her after we settled onto a couch in her treatment room.

"Good question. Somatic work resolves the trauma in our flesh. If you think about it, our tissue receives trauma first. Our minds then interpret the trauma and embed it as a memory. If the original source of the traumatic energy isn't released from our tissue, then we can't ever totally heal."

"The energy keeps recycling itself? Is that right?"

"Yes. Exactly. The original source of the energy, where you were actually injured, has to heal," Natalia explained.

Her words resonated with me. My trauma was embedded in my flesh and it created friction between my body and mind. Where my flesh could never forget the exact details of my abuse, my mind needed to forget, gloss over, or dissociate. The difference between my past talk therapy and somatic work became clear when I thought about Nana's cottage in Nairobi.

The house had wood floors. Over time, some of the floor boards buckled and warped and they needed to be repaired. I had two choices. I could have the floorboards mended, and they would probably stay flat and strong for a year or two. Or I could lift the floorboards and repair the source of the problem. Repairing the subfloor was a bigger investment and took a lot more time, but the repair would last forever.

Where talk therapy with Dr. D repaired and reinforced the floorboards, somatic work, much like my work with Amelie, would offer a permanent repair to every layer making my foundation sound. Five, Six, Seven, and Thirteen were warped floorboards that lifted away from me through trauma. I had to heal the foundation so that they could integrate their energy, lie flat once again, and return to me before I could feel whole.

## It Won't Hurt None

The sessions with Natalia were a natural extension of the work with Amelie. I started every appointment by lying down on a massage table and taking some deep, calming breaths. Next, I imagined there was a door at the top of my head and pictured it opening to allow energy to flow. Soon, I saw myself sitting in the meadow calmly gazing upon a large Buddha. The grand statue sent a healing white light into my body. Once the light stopped, one, or several, of the fragments appeared.

Working with Natalia I connected with Five, Six, Seven, and Thirteen more intensely than ever before. The fragments and I laughed and cried. I repeatedly apologized for not protecting them and for taking so long to find them and their trust in me grew.

"You know," I said to Five, Six, and Seven, "You don't need to be here anymore. My body is safe. I'm safe. You can come back to me." It was nice to speak to just the three of them without, Thirteen looming nearby.

"Well, we like it here," Six said.

"I know. But it's better for me if you leave the meadow and return to me. I'm happier if we're together. It takes a lot of time for me to come here to be with all of you. Are you afraid to come back?"

"Yeah. It's a scary place," Five said. "It's bad."

"Well, it used to be scary because we got hurt a lot. But I don't get hurt now. I'm safe."

"What about Thirteen?" Seven asked. "Does she want to go back? Will we be together?"

"I'll talk to Thirteen. You'll all be together. You don't have to worry."

"I don't know," Seven said. Five and Six looked at her, unsure. She thought about it for a few minutes before she agreed. "Okay, we'll come back, but only if Thirteen says so," Seven said.

Thirteen was older. Complicated. A teenager. She resisted the idea of coming back. Integrating sounded claustrophobic and she was going to have to give up control. When patient, soothing conversation didn't convince her, I decided it was time for some tough love.

"Hey," I said to Thirteen. "Let's sit down."

"I'm good," she said standing in front of me with her arms crossed. "I know why you're here."

"You know I'm really grateful for all you've done for me. And I'm sorry for all of your pain and anger," I said softly.

"Yeah, okay," she said a bit impatiently. "We've already talked about all of that. What do you want?"

"It's time for all of you to come back to me. Your time here, apart from me, has to end. I need you to integrate," I said to her. We stood in silence for a few minutes. She didn't immediately say no and that was a good sign.

"What do you mean by 'integrate?'" she asked. "That just sounds like another way of saying you want us to go away. Why do we have to leave? I thought you liked us. What happens to me if we go?"

"I do like you. I like all of you. I love all of you. I'm happy we met and we understand and respect each other. Listen, I know you love this place, but this isn't where you belong. You're a part of me. I need you to integrate because I've been living with all of you as pieces of my soul outside of myself for too long. I want to be whole again. It's time for you to come back. The others are ready."

"I don't trust you," she said with her last bit of fight.

I was beyond frustrated. I immediately gained a whole new sense of respect for anyone who survives raising a teenager. I decided to be true to myself and push back.

"You don't have a choice. If you refuse to leave, you'll be alone. I'm not going to listen to you anymore. I won't visit. The others will be gone. I am not negotiating this point with you. It's time to go."

She glared at me. "Fine. But if I feel like we're in any danger, and you can't handle it, I'll bring us all back here and we'll never leave." Her threat didn't surprise me. She only understood hypervigilance. I reminded myself that through her tough exterior, she was actually afraid.

"I hear you. I get it. I know you're worried. You just have to trust me when I tell you it's over. None of you will ever be hurt again," I said firmly. "Enough," I barked before leaving her in the meadow.

---

It took a few weeks before Thirteen relented. As I prepared for my final session with Natalia, I wasn't sure how they would all integrate but trusted the process as we got to work.

Once I entered into the meditation, I stood in the meadow. Five, Six, Seven, and Thirteen appeared. It was only the third time I met all of them in one meditation. I sensed a bit of tension with Thirteen. Something about her was off. I wondered if

I'd missed a step. In the past I spent all of my time talking at Thirteen. I "jumped over" her anger and never actually gave her, me, the space to feel and release it properly, which is why it vented out of us like steam erupting out of boiling kettle. Did I need to give her permission to release the final layer of her anger? Was she waiting for a cue from me?

"Thirteen," I said. "You seem really pissed off. What's the problem?"

"I can't let it go. I'm just so fucking angry," she said through clenched teeth.

"Okay. Why don't you just let it all out then, yes? I will absorb all of your rage today. I'm sorry I never gave you the space to do it before. Please, let it all out. I can take it."

Standing just a few feet away, she turned with the others to look directly at me. When she opened her mouth, she let out a primal scream that evolved into a roar. It nearly shattered my bones, but I stood my ground.

It was a test, I told myself. Do not flinch.

Thirteen wasn't going to leave if she didn't believe I had the courage to stand on my own and keep us all safe. My flesh felt like it would tear away from my body as she roared, but I wasn't afraid. Her anger made me sad. Every single time she let out another roar, my sadness grew.

When she stopped, I gave her a minute to catch her breath.

"It's okay," I said to her. "I'm glad you got it out. And I'm so sorry that you still hold so much anger. So much pain."

"It wasn't for you. It was for him. He's the reason I can't let it go," she said as she pointed at something behind me. "He won't leave us alone."

I turned around and saw a younger version of my grandpa, identical to a photo of him when he was in the Navy, walking towards us in the meadow. My meadow. He dared to come to my safe place. The metaphor was clear. The fragments might leave the meadow, but his energy remained. They weren't the actual source of my trauma, they were merely a symptom. This was a part of the healing journey I did not expect or welcome. I never wanted to see him or be near him ever again.

"Quickly, all of you get behind me," I ordered. Thirteen, Seven, Five, and Six shuffled behind me. I squared my shoulders, widened my stance, and stood straight and tall. I was ready for battle.

"Stop," I ordered. He stopped walking and stood about ten feet away from me. "What do you want?" I asked in a calm, assertive tone. There was no trace of fear in me.

*Casually, as if speaking with a long-time friend, he said, "They'd like to talk to you. Your grandparents."*

*"Ah, I see. You're just a messenger. You're nothing at all, are you? Well, take this message back to them," I said as I prepared for war if he took another step closer to us. "Don't ever fucking try to contact me ever again. If either of them try to come here, I will fucking destroy them. I am not afraid. Now get the fuck out. You don't belong here."*

*He immediately disappeared.*

*In that moment, I proved I would stand my ground and protect the fragments and myself. I was strong enough to keep us safe. When I turned to check in with Five, Six, Seven, and Thirteen, I watched them fold into me and felt them return back to my body. We were finally integrated. I passed the test.*

"They're all gone. They're inside of me now," I told Natalia. "I can see them inside my body. Thirteen is literally elbowing for room. She's trying to make space."

"It's a good thing," Natalia reassured me. "You might feel nervous, agitated, or sad during their acclimation process. It's a brand new environment for all of them. Just give yourself some time and be aware of how you feel," she said.

After our session ended, we walked to the office lobby. A new sense of "wholeness" started to take over. It was disorienting. I wasn't sure how to feel. Would I hear from the fragments ever again? How would we relate to each other? Would it be different than when I met with them in the meadow?

"Take it easy. It's going to take a bit of time for all of them to settle down," Natalia offered sympathetically, pressing the elevator button to send me back down to the street. When I walked out of the clinic and into Singapore's hot, humid air, I entered the nearest café. I sensed the visualization wasn't finished. I could feel it. There was more to the story. I worried I would lose the connection if I waited to continue the meditation once I got home.

Packed for the lunch-time rush, I felt some pangs of hunger as I entered the café, noisy with shouts of "Pick Up!" Somehow, I ended up in a vegan hot dog restaurant. I stared at the menu and found it impossible to pretend a carrot with toppings was somehow equivalent to the hot dogs of my youth.

I skipped ordering any food and asked for some iced tea. Scanning the room, I grabbed my drink and sat down at a table as far away from others as possible. I noticed my mouth was oddly dry. After drinking a few gulps of tea, I took some deep breaths, thankful my eyes were disguised behind dark sunglasses. For the next forty-two minutes, I focused while a vignette played out in my mind, my eyes wide open so I could type notes into my phone.

*Thirteen was back in the meadow. She stood apart from me. What or who was she looking for? Did she need to confront my grandpa? How did she know he was there?*

*And then I saw him. A much older version of my grandpa sat like a lump on the ground. He looked exactly the same as the night Thirteen fought him off and stopped the abuse. Thirteen walked over to him and stood in front of him. She took a moment to stare down at him and then she started shouting.*

*"Motherfucker!!! You are a disgusting beast! You're a monster!" she screamed as spit shot from her mouth and her hands balled into fists.*

*Thirteen's anger didn't scare me. It wasn't happening "outside of me" anymore. It wasn't directed at me. The rage was coming from within and it felt good to watch her release our anger. He was motionless. He sat like a useless sack of garbage and absorbed all her rage. His face was turned down. I stood near her but I didn't try to contain or stop Thirteen because she was part of me. I was strong and ready to validate her rage. We were on the same side of the battle. She vomited anger and hate all over him and held him accountable.*

*"You hurt them! You broke them! It's all your fault!"*

*Slowly, he tilted his head up so his eyes could meet hers. Fear replaced the smug look he carried on his face. A man who lived life without consequence, no one ever dared to question him, and certainly never yelled at him. Now, a thirteen-year-old girl publicly shamed him.*

*I watched to make sure he didn't look away. He had to see her. Hear her. She started punching him hard with her fists and he fell onto his back where she kicked him in his groin repeatedly. I felt her power. Her fight was my fight. Her anger was my anger. She was covered in sweat and her knuckles were bleeding. She wanted to destroy the man who tried to destroy us.*

*Five, Six, and Seven appeared. Five wrapped her tiny body around one of my legs. She was afraid but still watched as Thirteen pummeled my grandpa. Our rapist. Any time he moved, Thirteen* punched or kicked him. I sat down and Five, Six, and Seven claimed space in my lap and next to me.

Seven was quiet. I noticed her hands were in fists. Thirteen looked at her and they exchanged a curious nod as if Seven was giving Thirteen permission.

Thirteen turned back to him and shouted, "Look at them! Look, you coward! You hurt the babies!" as she pointed at Five, Six, Seven, and me.

He started to cry. His tears disgusted me. I did not feel any pity for our rapist. Our attacker.

Thirteen ignored his tears. She launched a series of rapid jabs to his body. Five, Six, and Seven stayed close to me. "It's okay. It's over. We are safe. It's over," I told them.

I stroked Five's beautiful hair.

"Are you sure we're safe?" she asked, sitting in my lap.

"Yes, I'm sure. It's over. You're safe. Stay with me."

Through swollen, bloody eyes, he looked at us. He struggled onto his hands and knees and reached out like a monster. His big, rough hands were still hungry for our flesh.

He was a pedophile.

A man sexually satisfied by a child's innocence.

He was evil.

I told Thirteen to step aside as I leapt up and stood in front of him blocking his view. He was still on his hands and knees. Still reaching out. I kicked him in the face and watched as blood shot out of his mouth as he fell onto his back and shrieked like a wounded animal before crumpling onto the ground. I towered over him, careful to shield Five, Six, Seven, and Thirteen, and kicked him violently. "No! No! No! No! No! Motherfucker! No! You will not hurt us anymore! Keep your fucking hands off of us, you disgusting monster! You will never hurt us ever again!"

I felt it, at last. The purity of the anger I'd avoided to be a good girl. Anger I never understood. I no longer resented or judged it as it released with every kick. My foot met his body with such force that I felt his ribs snap. His bones broke. My powerful legs assaulted every inch of his body. His tissue gave way as rage flowed through me. All my anger, pain, sorrow, and fear released while I destroyed his body.

Curled into a fetal position, he was a bloody, broken heap when I finally stepped back to catch my breath. Looking at Five, Six, Seven, I knew I had to give them permission to release whatever they were holding onto. It was time to put an end to him.

"I want you to share your feelings. Do whatever you want to him. There are no rules here," I said to them. Five stepped forward. Her courage overwhelmed me.

"I can do what I want? I won't get in trouble?" she asked.

"Yes, whatever you want."

## It Won't Hurt None

Five, who sat in her Kindergarten class in chairs about fourteen inches tall, at tables about twenty-two inches high, stood before him in all her courage. He may have looked small lying half-dead on the ground in the meadow, but when he forced his fingers into my tiny five year-old sex, he was a towering giant. A grown man.

Five stood strong, balled her hands into fists, and stomped on his head shouting, "S-T-O-P! S-T-O-P! S-T-O-P! S-T-O-P!"

Thirteen, Six, and Seven watched. I took Five's hand as she became enraged. For her, it all started one day in his work truck when he shoved his fingers inside her body and broke her. He stopped being her grandpa and became her abuser. She continued to kick him in the head and shouted, "Bad! Bad! Bad! Bad!" When she was finished, she was covered in sweat and joined the others.

He remained useless, wretched, on the ground.

"Seven, come here," I prompted.

She calmly walked forward and stood over him. She studied him lying on the ground, bloody. I watched Seven and marveled at the little girl who so bravely absorbed the horror of every grab, pinch, insertion, thrust, and tear. Over the years, Seven's limitless courage took all the pain for herself, sparing me the torment of a new fragment forming during each assault. The math could have been overwhelming. I endured over two hundred instances of abuse over eight years. Had it not been for her miraculous bravery, my mind could have easily created dozens of fragments. I was forever in her debt.

"Whatever I want?" Seven asked, taking my hand.

"Yes, whatever you want."

Thirteen held Five and Six close to her and nodded at Seven. She turned back to look at the rapist. Grandpa.

"You're nothing," she said to him flatly before releasing a guttural, beastly wail. Five, Six, Thirteen, and I joined her. Our collective cries were a single, ear-splitting song of indescribable pain, anger, and shame.

Suddenly, Five, Six, Seven, and Thirteen returned to me and left me alone with him in the meadow. I felt powerful.

"Look at me!" I shouted at the limp man on the ground.

He looked up. His face was swollen beyond recognition. I felt no remorse for his wounds. They would never compare to my own.

"My body knows the truth and my body will never forget. You are nothing to me. You have no power."

*Lowering myself onto my knees, I met his gaze face-to-face. I was not afraid.* "We are finished. I am finished."

"I will be lonely," he mumbled. His jaw was broken.

"I don't care."

"Where do I go?" he asked.

"Go wherever it is men like you go to rot. It's not my job to help you. It's my job to take care of myself. Leave. You don't belong here."

He reached out at me one more time. Black-hearted and damnable, he was beyond redemption as he tried to grab me.

Grab, grab, grab. He was always grabbing.

Five, Six, Seven, and Thirteen reappeared. They weren't quite convinced I could keep them safe. They stood behind me. I felt their fear. I understood we could not remain integrated if they didn't feel safe. I stood strong. I knew I would protect all of us at any cost.

"Stop! Leave now. You will never hurt us again. Ever. There is nothing for you here."

My words penetrated him. Violated him. My power destroyed his energy. He withered until he disappeared. I proved beyond any doubt I was their protector. I kept my word and they finally trusted me. Five, Six, Seven, and Thirteen returned to my body and I stood alone in the meadow.

Holding my arms out wide in the sun, I smiled as I breathed in the air with new lungs. My legs tingled. I let out a cry. Five, Six, Seven, and Thirteen cried inside me. I fell to my knees and rested on the cool, soft grass taking time to get my bearings. When I finally stood, I placed my hands on my hips, sensing that Five, Six, Seven, and Thirteen were permanently settled. I spent a few more minutes in silence and then I left the meadow.

Sitting in the café, I suddenly felt heavy. My breath was labored and I wondered if anyone could see me struggle. My skin felt new, thicker. Forty-four years after my house and foundation were fractured by rape and abuse, the foundation was repaired. My shaky house and tower were finally on solid ground. I made it home and slept through the night for the first time since the surgery. I wondered if I could trust that my grandpa was gone forever or lurking, once again, in the shadows.

A week later, I booked an online session with Amelie. I thought it would be a simple, restorative conversation building on work with Natalia. After we practiced some breath work, I was back in my meadow but surrounded by darkness. I may have viciously beaten my grandfather but I had yet to extinguish the source of his energy. My fight wasn't over.

"Amelie, he's here. My grandpa is here. He wants me," I told her. I felt evil all around me. "I don't know what to do."

"You have to put an end to him. Look around. Your mind will help you. What can you do to him?"

"He's standing on the edge of a cliff. I will push him over the edge. I know I have to kill him," I said.

"Do it. It's time to end this," she said.

I thought of Thirteen's bravery in the kitchen. Without saying a word, I walked up to him and pushed against his chest with all my strength. As he fell back, he threw a rope around my waist. I panicked. We were both going over the edge.

"He's got me!" I told her. "Amelie, he has a rope around me and he's taking me with him."

"Okay. It's okay. I'm going to summon the Archangel Michael to come down right now. He's going to cut the rope. Do you see him?" she asked.

"Yes. He's on a horse. He has a large sword and he cut the rope," I replied. "I'm free. I'm on my hands and knees on the edge of the cliff. My grandpa is lying at the bottom of a deep canyon. But I don't feel like he's dead. I'm going to send boulders over the edge to pulverize him into dust."

"Good. Do it and tell me what you see," she instructed.

"He's buried under huge rocks. I'm still on my hands and knees. I'm vomiting a thick, black liquid. It looks like tar. It's burning the grass in front of me and making a hissing sound."

"Good. Let it out. Let it all out of your body," she encouraged me.

I felt the black ooze come from deep in my core as I vomited several more minutes. Collapsing on the unburnt grass behind me, I focused on bringing my breath back to normal. I started to cry as I left the meadow.

"There is so much sadness about all of this," I said to Amelie. I was tired and felt overwhelmed.

"You're right." Amelie said to me. "And it's okay to be sad, but it has to be over. You've been fighting this war for too long," she said. "I think your grandpa was a demon. He was wicked and cruel."

I agreed. My demon was real and scary. He was also persistent. I felt his energy lingering around me as we finished the session. Evil that strong wasn't going to just disappear. It had to be purged by powerful healing and pure energy.

I never confessed to Amelie that at the very end of our meditation, I saw my grandpa's fist push through the dust and rocks. He let me know our fight wasn't over. Some of his energy lingered. He wasn't dead, yet, but he was much weaker. I never forgot the image of his fist. I knew he would return one day and the next time we met, I would end him forever. I vowed to prepare for more healing after the holidays and once we rang in 2020.

## Chapter 17

Festivities for the Year of the Rat took over Singapore in January 2020 while reports of Covid-19 crept into everyday life. Singapore announced "circuit-breaker" lockdowns, ordering us all to stay home, and I booked an online session with Amelie.

"What's happening?" she asked.

"We're in lockdown. Everyone has to wear a mask whenever we go outside. Social distancing is in place. No gatherings of any kind are allowed. They're serious. This is bad, Amelie. I'm certain all my contracts will be canceled. If there are no film shoots, then they don't need me to consult."

"Don't get ahead of yourself. It's early days. They're saying it's just the flu," she said, trying her best to calm me.

I did my best to ignore my anxiety but the instincts that served me well as a producer told me life as I knew it was ending. My intuition was correct. All my contracts were canceled in late February 2020. I had to leave Singapore and began compiling relocation quotes. I put together a plan to close my company and cancel my work permit.

As the world grinded to a halt, I felt my mind shutting down and I chose to sit firmly in denial. I couldn't say the actual words, "My company is closing and I have to leave," out loud. I booked a session with Amelie in March. I was feeling a lot of anxiety about moving back to America. "I'm afraid to go home," I said to her.

"Why? What is it about going back to America that makes you so uncomfortable?"

"I am the worst version of myself in America. I spend too much. I eat bad food. Everything my PTSD inspired compulsions want is waiting for me at home. You don't understand what this feels like. I'm having several panic attacks every day just thinking about it. I am a disaster when I am in America." In hindsight, my panic had as much to do with returning back to the geographic center of my trauma as it did with my impulse control issues. We talked some more and Amelie reminded me to breathe and be present.

"Do you think it's possible I'm being sent back to complete my healing?" I asked her once I settled down.

"Yes," she coached. "It's time to go back for healing. Time to write the final chapter about the trauma. You're ready to push through it."

When our call ended, I finally said the words I had avoided for weeks out loud. "I'm going home," I said to myself staring into my mirror before curling up and crying the rest of the day.

Scheduling an international move as Covid ramped up was complicated and it took two months to finalize my plans. As mid-May approached, and my departure grew near, I locked in the last piece of the L.A. logistics with the help of Aparna, my wonderful friend from my days working in Egypt. She helped me arrange a studio apartment in Hollywood I would call home while I self-isolated. Once my exile was over, I planned to stay with my older brother and his wife.

I spent the final few days in Singapore alone and worried about my career, expenses, getting out of Singapore, shutting down my company, settling back into American life, and avoiding Covid. I also had to contend with a last-minute case of Dengue fever also known as "bone break" fever.

It was a lot to process. Thirteen grew noisy as my flight out of Singapore loomed.

*"We're just going to leave? Give up?"* Thirteen asked.

*"Yes. I can't stay in Singapore without work and I have no idea when Covid is going to end. We're going home."*

*"What if we get Covid and can't fly? What if they won't release our container to come to Los Angeles?"* Thirteen asked.

*"It's all going to work out. Calm down. I don't have the energy to deal with all this right now. Please, just let me handle things. Trust me, please,"* I implored. To her credit, she went quiet.

The difficult work of integrating her paid off.

When the movers arrived in late May 2020, I watched largely in silence as all of my things went back into a shipping container. None of it seemed real. I thought I was going to call Singapore home for at least three to five years. I was just getting started. Suddenly, it was over.

Two days later, after loading my suitcases into the airport taxi, I said goodbye to the little house in Katong and closed the door for the last time. I placed my hand on the cool cement wall and I thanked the house, Singapore, and the universe for a glorious but far too short fourteen months. My legs felt heavy as I climbed into the taxi. I put on my darkest sunglasses and cried all the way to the airport. The life I loved was officially over.

In all my years as an expat, creating a life in Singapore was my crowning achievement. I was proud to have a fenced, private yard fragrant with the jasmine I planted. The frogs and I enjoyed the sprinklers in the front yard, and I loved listening to them sing late at night.

I would miss my friendly neighbors, particularly the Belgian couple who lived across the street. They were artsy, eccentric, and wonderful. They made one of the world's best gin and tonics. I longed to walk around the corner from my little house, taking time to stop and inhale the incredible fragrance from my favorite frangipani tree. Most of all, I would desperately miss time with my excellent friend Theresa. It broke my heart not knowing when we might meet again for more bike ride failures and ice cream.

But most profoundly, I grieved the loss of the version of myself who had a successful business, worked with amazing clients, and felt free to chase success. I mourned Rebecca the Expat's enthusiasm for adventure and her future.

My Pisces self is wired for life outside of the United States. I grew accustomed to flying nearly 400,000 miles a year between Africa, the Middle East, Europe, and Asia for work. Sitting in a plane at 35,000 feet felt natural. My flight to Los Angeles, however, was a trip I did not want. The tower was down. A new house was being built and I didn't feel like I had much say in the design. I had no sense of control over any part of my life.

As the plane lifted out of Singapore, I was one of thirteen passengers on the plane and I felt restless for the entire seventeen hour flight. I walked into a bizarre, dystopian scene as I entered the completely deserted immigration and baggage claim areas at Los Angeles International Airport.

I still couldn't believe I was actually back in America—to stay. I took an Uber to my apartment. The streets were empty and the city felt eerily quiet. The entire world was on Covid lockdown and I immediately felt trapped. I pushed my suitcases into my studio apartment and collapsed in a heap to cry.

After a week in Los Angeles, I stopped crying. "Reverse culture shock" took over. I knew it was going to take a long time to adjust to full-time American life. Even familiar things felt confusing. Grocery stores were alien lands. The sheer number of choices for hummus left me riddled with anxiety. After staring at all the brands, I backed away from the chickpeas like they were radioactive. I didn't dare look at the cheese section for fear I would collapse. When I approached the cashier with a few meager items, I pushed my cart toward the counter and just sort of hoped I was doing it right.

"Do you have a store savings card?" the cashier asked.

"Yes," I replied, "but I forgot to bring it with me." I used to get a new one every time I came home for a visit. Somehow I'd managed to put all my cards in an envelope. The envelope was in a container, on a ship, currently in the middle of the Pacific Ocean.

"It's fine," she said. "Just type in your cell (not mobile) number on the keypad."

*Which number did she want*, I asked myself. Kenya? Dubai? Pakistan? Singapore? No! America! Get it together!

"Hmm. I actually don't remember my number. It's new," I said pathetically.

"Okay," she said, exhaling deeply. I prayed she would take pity on me through the Plexiglas barrier as I smiled at her through my mask.

"Can I get a new card?" I asked, sounding a bit pathetic like a character out of a Dickens novel. "Please, miss, may I have yet another card? I've only got fourteen of them stuck on a ship somewhere between Singapore and America. I'm just a bit useless as I repatriate, you see, and I really need the five-cent discount on my tomatoes." All of that raced through my head while I reminded myself that I needed to try to sound like a local. It was "toe-may-toes" and not "tow-mah-toes." My language was just one of many quirks to sort out after years spent living and working in former British colonies.

"I'll just use the store card," she replied mercifully. "Did you bring your bags?"

Shit. "No. I'll buy three," I replied. They would go nicely with the entire box full of bags that were, of course, on a ship. I left whatever few strands of dignity I had left in the grocery store. I walked home eager to exploit the mercy of online grocery shopping.

Former Expat 0 – Reverse Culture Shock 1

After two weeks of life in Hollywood, I reached out to everyone I knew from the good old days of advertising. I was eager to find some work. Any work. I needed a solid distraction because Darkness, my depression and nemesis, was most definitely not on the ship. That bitch flew shotgun with me from Singapore and was getting a little too comfortable.

There were, of course, no jobs as the global economy came to a catastrophic halt. Without work, my mind faltered and Darkness worried me. It felt sinister and eager to exploit my circumstances. Everything about my life was unpredictable and I was in a permanent state of freefall. As my mental health slipped, I clung to the notion that all the therapy, meditation, and healing fortified my walls from any serious intruder. I triple locked all the doors and windows in my mind and hoped I was protected.

Yes, the fragments were integrated. And yes, it simplified things in my mind. There was far less chatter, and I had more peace. But their energy lingered inside of me and all the upheaval made them glow like an ember after a roaring fire. Hot and dangerous, they could still set the house on fire.

In the past, I recovered after my house, and the tower, collapsed because I had one thing in my life to help me feel grounded. Work. When I was twenty and first went to therapy, work kept me focused. The consistency of my schedule aided my recovery. In D.C., I may have felt like I was in a hurricane, but the overwhelming demands of my job eventually pulled me through the storm. After moving back to Los Angeles from New York, and then Cairo, work kept me attached to the real world, even when my mind did its best to slide off the rails.

2020 was different. There was a global pandemic. Work didn't exist. I became completely unhinged. I made job hunting a full-time job but it wasn't enough to prevent Darkness from pushing deep into my mind. I spent most of my life beating depression back and, at times, falling victim to its toxic urges. This time, Darkness felt stronger because it had a partner. A new accomplice added greater complexity and challenge to my mental health. As the days and weeks of isolation pushed on and Covid spread, I couldn't see my way through unemployment, loneliness, financial struggle, my ongoing health issues, and the dark cloud filling my mind. My house was about to collapse.

## Chapter 18

"*You are never going to get a job.*"
"*You are a failure.*"
"*You blew it.*"
"*You can't even get a house.*"
"*Everyone is tired of You.*"
"*No one loves You.*"

Darkness opened the door as my life spiraled, and a voice teeming with self-hate walked through. Unlike Thirteen who used to shout at me about everything she disliked, the new intruder felt distant, much more personal, and sounded full of hate. I assumed it was Six. Always focused on sadness, fear, and anger, I never provided Six any release. I wondered if there was something incomplete between us.

Why didn't I invite her to pummel my grandpa in the meadow with the others? Why didn't she ask to take her turn? Was she restrained? I didn't know how to answer the questions and it felt like I couldn't connect with the fragments as I'd done so many times in the past.

As I battled with life and my mental health, the voice I assumed was Six unleashed a new level of torment.

"*Your life is a disaster. You've totally fucked it up. Yes, you traveled the world. Yes, you had adventures. It doesn't matter. You're fifty and you can't pay rent. Can't get a second interview much less a job. You should feel humiliated.*"

I took time away from job searches and other distractions and I sat down to meditate. Once I saw myself in the meadow, I called out to Six. She appeared immediately and stood in front of me.

"Six, why are you so angry? You're nasty. Where is all this hate coming from? I thought you were happy to be with the others."
"Hate? I don't hate you," she replied softly.
"Then where is it coming from? I hear your voice, and it's getting louder."
"That's not me," she replied cryptically.
"If it's not you, then tell me who it is," I pushed back.
"I don't know who it is. It used to hurt me until you found me. Now it's gone," she replied before leaving the meadow.

Who was it? I stayed focused and continued the meditation. I pictured Six the day I found her alone in the dark room. She had so many scars, bruises, blemishes, and sores. The vines wrapped around her like they were feeding off her.

Was Six some sort of host?

If Five was my fear, Seven my sadness, and Thirteen my anger, did Six represent or play host to my shame?

Was it possible the voice wasn't Six? Was it a hitchhiker and not a fragment at all?

Did Shame attach itself to Six like a parasite and feed off her over the years while holding her hostage? When Six was set free, did Shame latch itself onto me? I didn't have any answers to any of my questions. I didn't know much about the lingering effects of survivor's shame. The meditation ended and I felt vulnerable.

In late December 2020, I suffered from a constant, hateful barrage of thoughts and I lost all perspective. Desperate to silence the venomous attacks, I listened when Darkness offered me a permanent solution.

"You know, if you just killed yourself, things would be much simpler. All of the noise would stop," Darkness hissed like a giant serpent preparing to crush its prey.

Weak, isolated, and vulnerable, I couldn't figure out how to get free of Darkness's death grip. I lost all hope and sight of the good in my life. I surrendered to the idea that it would be better to kill myself and so I completely detached from the world around me. Like a good producer, I researched the best method to end my life. I wanted a pragmatic, cost-effective, final solution. As I devoted more of my time to producing my death, I felt relieved. Death, just as Darkness promised, was a solution to the torment in my mind.

I laid out a timeline for killing myself and decided to wait until after the holidays. It seemed somehow more hurtful to end my life during a season of celebration. I cared just enough about my friends and family to delay ending my life but not enough to stop the effort entirely.

The calendar turned over into 2021, and the day to die grew near. I was ready. I had everything I needed to execute the plan, but I kept encountering small distractions. As I finalized my suicide note, an urgent email about nothing in particular came through, pulling me away from the planning. A text message from a friend the next day turned my attention away from death once more.

I thought about my grandpa forcing his way into my body and raping me. The pain and damage he left behind. The wounds and permanent scars that would never entirely heal. My discarded womb and ravaged body. All my suffering was about to end in suicide.

My grandpa's fist rising out of the dust was a sign. He was stronger. He won the battle. I'd fought for nothing. My death was inevitable, and I didn't care.

My life was nothing.

I was nothing.

Every day, Shame's malignant voice reminded me of a million reasons why I should end my life.

*"Your body isn't healing. You're unhealthy. You can't even walk up a flight of stairs. You know this will never end. Not a single doctor you've seen can help you. You can't even look at yourself anymore. You're disgusting. No one wants you. You're an out-of-shape, middle-aged, single woman. You don't deserve love. You're filthy."*

I edited my suicide note while mapping out another piece of the logistics. It didn't matter that I had friends and family who loved me. I felt completely and utterly alone. I didn't want to struggle anymore. Death offered a permanent silence I craved.

The universe never gave up on me, while I made plans to give up on myself. Wanuri, the master storyteller, friend, and mother of my wonderful niece and nephew in Nairobi, unwittingly pulled me out of the depths for a second time. She had no idea that just two days separated me from the end of my life when she offered me work. A lifeline.

"I'm working on a new project," she wrote in a text. "And I need an assistant. Would you be willing to do it?" she asked.

I looked at her text for several hours and cried. Did I have the strength to rally? Giving up was easier. Simpler. I read my suicide note one last time and went to bed, knowing I would not reply to her text and take my life.

That night I dreamed my Granny Chandler visited me in the meadow. She held me, and I felt her love fill my depleted soul. We didn't need to speak. I knew she loved me no matter what I decided. When she left, I sat down on the grass and thought about my brothers and sister, mom, and dad. I saw my nieces and nephews, friends, and my global family all over the world and recoiled, just for a moment, at the thought of leaving them.

I woke up from the dream and wrote back to Wanuri. "I'll do anything if it means working with you," I replied. "And if it doesn't work out for some reason, I'm here to help no matter what."

I chose to stay alive for the sake of others, and that was enough at the time. Hour by hour, and then day by day, I found a new pocket of fresh reserves and started believing I could rebuild the house—the tower—one more time. After all, starting over was my specialty. I just needed a hand.

I signed the contract to work with Wanuri and went from planning my death to planning a temporary relocation to Austin, Texas. During the final few weeks in Southern California, I stayed with my sister and her family. Our lives could not be more different.

My sister is an incredible wife, mother, daughter, friend, and leader in her field. Oftentimes, she's the glue keeping my entire family together. Glue was always too sticky and far too permanent for me. While I bounced around the world, she took care of everyone except, maybe, herself. Armed with a gloriously cheeky sense of humor, when she tells you to "hold my hoops," step back and watch her inner warrior take charge.

We went out one night, just the two of us, a few days before my departure for Texas. Our adventure wasn't particularly sexy or exciting. We were making a nighttime run to buy boutique dog food for their latest rescue, Dexter. "He's a champion," my sister explained when I asked why the shepherd/hound mutt required premium dog food.

As we drove to the shops, we talked about our lives and I started crying. My near suicide wasn't so far behind me. I was fragile and still hovering precariously close to the edge.

"This has all been very embarrassing. Me having to stay with family. I really screwed up my life," I said to her as we took a minute in the car to sit in the parking lot. I couldn't face her. My shame was too real, and I stared at my feet while biting my lip.

"Don't think that way. Why would you think like that?" she asked.

"You did it right," I said through tears. "You made the right decisions. You have a beautiful home. You're married. You have a family. You did it all right. You know, all I have is a storage unit full of boxes and a bunch of passport stamps. I have no security. I blew it."

"You have to stop. Stop thinking that way." Her heart was in the right place, but she didn't know that Shame would never let go of me. Shame told me I was a *burden* to my family. That was Shame's word, not theirs. It took me a long time to figure out that asking for help meant that I hadn't given up on myself. I still had hope.

Shame was unlike any other torment. It sat entirely alone and, *". . . did not provide a shred of light or path at all. It was undoubtedly one of the most corrosive emotions. It made me think I was a failure, I didn't belong, and the trauma I survived was my fault. None of it was true, but that little voice inside my head was very convincing and hard to ignore."* [1]

I sat in bed late at night, wondering if I was condemned to carry Shame's pernicious voice with me the rest of my life. Was there any hope to reconcile?

The long drive to Austin helped me mull it over. I-10 wasn't the most interesting stretch of road between Los Angeles and Texas, but every mile I drove added a layer

---

1 https://questpsychologyservices.co.uk/

of clarity. A little bit of my dignity returned, and a little bit of Shame was left on the side of the road. When I finally drove into Austin, I moved into a condo I called home for the next four months. It was a wonderful sanctuary.

Nothing is as cleansing and clarifying for me as work and payday. Clear of depression and Shame's death grip, and with some money finally flowing back into my savings, I was able to settle into a stable rhythm a year after coming back to America.

Austin is a charming, albeit relatively small city, and the entire film crew got to work quickly. Days usually started around 8 a.m. and ended whenever Wanuri was ready to go home. When not busy working with her to prep the shoot, I was entirely devoted to having fun with my niece and nephew.

After about a month, the rest of the key crew arrived, and the final prep phase ramped up as the shoot approached. Feeling focused and clear, I was too busy to give Shame a lot of my attention, and my producer's instincts were in fine form. I knew I was going to be unemployed the moment we wrapped the final shoot days in Los Angeles and I needed to figure out where I would live and how to make money. I was well aware of how easily it was for my mental health to slip once the demands of the workday disappeared.

My job search odds improved after I added a few months of freelance work with a major film studio to my resume. Recruiters danced when my CV no longer read as some bizarre, irrelevant foreign odyssey. Just a few weeks before the film wrapped I booked remote contract work with a Big Tech company.

When we left Austin and shifted back to Southern California, I moved into my younger brother's empty apartment at the beach. Although we didn't spend much time together when he was growing up, we got to know each other well once we got older and family politics were pushed aside. My little brother is intelligent, funny, and loving.

His house became my oasis. Each day, after sitting in front of a computer screen and consulting for Big Tech for ten hours, I logged off and walked to the ocean. The salt air and exercise was a tonic and made me feel optimistic about the future. The water's energy connected with me and fed me wave after wave, day after day, until my soul felt replenished. After a few months at his place, I felt ready to settle and let some roots grow. I still heard Shame in my head, but I was able to ignore it most of the time as work and life kept me busy.

The renewable energy in the ocean let me feel cautiously optimistic about some progress I'd made with a new functional doctor. My new approach to my health included taking higher doses of progesterone, testosterone, estrogen, and various supplements. My sleep was slowly restored. I took time to feel proud, and grateful, for pulling through the early months of 2021 alive.

In October 2021 I briefly rekindled my producing skills and pulled another move together. Ten short months after standing on the edge of oblivion ready to end my life, all my boxes were moved into my new apartment. My mom, sister, and niece helped unpack. I was unprepared for the feelings that rose to the surface as we opened each box. I think I stored some of my sadness in the storage unit along with all my treasures.

"Where did you get this chair? It looks like it's made out of twigs," my niece asked.

"Oh, a basket weaver made it. He used it as his work stool. I didn't want to buy a basket, so I bought the stool. I love it because it's simple and handmade."

"And this, what about this brass?" she asked.

"That's from Iraq. I was in Baghdad a few years ago for work," I replied.

"What about this?" my sister asked, pointing to a hand carved, wooden stool.

"It's from Cameroon. A medicine woman used it for birthing. I bought it from her during a shoot," I replied, and then I started to cry.

"What's wrong?" my sister asked.

I stared out of my dining room window. I couldn't look at her. "I had a life," I told her through my tears. "I had an incredible life I loved very much. It's all gone. I'm grateful for everything I have but this new life is still really hard for me."

I was excited, and profoundly grateful, to have my own place and to feel more settled, but I still hadn't fully processed my feelings about my move to America. My reverse culture shock would take at least another year before it settled down just enough so that I stopped missing my past life. I promised myself I would focus on processing my feelings. It simply wasn't fruitful to continue to swirl in sadness. I reminded myself to feel happy. Despite all the challenges, I was blessed.

Practicing gratitude helped me whenever Shame circled back with fresh venom.

*You could lose your contract.*
*You're not quick enough.*
*No one else will hire you.*

*You will lose the apartment.*
*You shouldn't eat that.*
*You shouldn't wear that.*
*You should save more.*
*You don't have any friends.*
*You're ugly.*

I grew to understand that Shame was the source of my compulsive habits, self-doubt, hate, and the feeling I was "defective." It was a major breakthrough but I didn't know how to deal with the horrible, looping insults in my head. It was time for more healing.

*I set an intention to meet Shame. I had no idea what it would look like, but I was eager to find out. I closed my eyes, took some deep breaths, and I transported myself to the meadow. Shame was waiting for me. She was a faceless twenty-year-old version of myself.*

"You don't scare me," *I told the disfigured being in front of me. It was true. I didn't feel fear. I was curious.*

"Yes, I do. I scare you every day," *Shame replied.*

"Wrong. You annoy me every day. I'm not scared."

"I control you every day. You almost killed yourself because of me," *she hissed.*

"That's partly true. You ganged up with Darkness. I wanted you both to shut up. What do you want from me?" *I asked curtly. I wasn't in the mood to be friends. I was tired of the journey and had little patience left for this chapter.*

"I don't want anything."

"Then why are you here? Why now?" *I asked.*

"I've always been here. You're just listening now," *Shame replied. I knew she was right. I spent my entire life listening to Thirteen, Seven, Five, and Six. There was no room to hear Shame until the others were quiet.*

"I want you to stop," *I pushed.*

"Then stop me. You're the reason I exist," *she barked. So clever, I knew ending our relationship was never going to be that simple.*

*She stepped toward me and her face came into focus. I'm safe, I told myself. And then I* remembered that every other fragment really just wanted to feel love. Their anger, sadness, and fear was a mask.

I stepped toward her, wrapped my arms around her, and said, "You are beautiful. I love you. You are safe. You are clean. I love you." I hugged my physical self while I repeated the phrases out loud. I kept repeating, "You are beautiful. I love you. You are safe." I hugged Shame, my words filled the meadow, and Shame became younger.

We were back in the trailer. Shame lay on her side while he raped her Seven-year-old body. I kneeled down on the floor and looked straight into her face, into her eyes, and held her hand.

"I love you. It's okay," I told her.

"Make it stop, please," she begged me.

"I can't. But I'm here with you. I love you."

"I want it to stop," she cried. "Why won't anyone help me?"

"I'm sorry. I love you."

I couldn't stop him, but I saw Shame. I understood her humiliation and helplessness.

We left the trailer and stood in a familiar house. I watched my grandpa pull down Six's pants and underwear. When he picked her up and forced her onto his lap where his erect penis waited for her tiny sex, tears ran down her face. He held her tightly against his chest, crushing her lungs and ensuring she could not meet his gaze.

He was a coward.

He entered her for the first time. Six's body was pierced with pain she never knew existed.

"You're beautiful," he whispered into her ear. His breath made her sick as he thrust into her and ripped her innocent flesh.

I kneeled down on the floor and looked straight into Six's eyes. Shame was waiting for me in her gaze.

"What if someone comes in?" she whispered through tears of pain while he grunted behind her.

"No, they won't. They're too busy," I explained.

"Make him stop," she pleaded.

"I'm sorry. I can't. It's almost over," I whispered to her.

"He's breaking me," she cried. "He's breaking me inside."

"I know. I'm sorry," I answered. I cried with her as I relived the horror of the first time he raped me with his penis. When he climaxed, his depravity filled my womb. Evil took root inside me and festered in my body filling it with rot.

Shame and I left. When we came back to the meadow, she was an adult once again. She stood in front of me. I didn't know what to do. Integrating her like the other fragments didn't feel right.

*"Will you ever leave me alone?"* I asked.

*"No,"* she replied quickly without any expression on her face.

*"Then how do we live with each other?"* I asked. I couldn't imagine listening to her acidic tone for the rest of my life.

*"I don't know,"* she replied.

*"You hurt me,"* I said, looking at her.

*"I am hurting,"* she said. *"My humiliation and pain last forever. I can't stop sharing it with you."*.

I cried for a long time once the meditation ended. I was sad for Shame's burdens but I was also tired of the struggle. My resilience waned. I didn't know if I could accept that Shame needed help, but I also didn't know if I could step into yet another healing journey. I spent a few more weeks trying to resolve Shame's corrosive nature but to no end. I wondered if I would ever find harmony with myself. Would I ever totally recover and finally feel whole?

# Recovery

*"Healing is fucking messy. It's alienation. It's detachment. It's batshit crazy. It's jet-black, inky Darkness. It makes you ache for the void and mundane. You want to quit everything, but you can't. You won't. Not now. No, baby, not ever. Because even though it aches the mother of all aches, you've changed. Underneath all that bullshit, there you are. Brand new. Born again. An angel of earth who's woken up to their cosmic mission. And you ain't ever going back. And there's more like you out there. We're waking up right next to you in the dark, wild one. So don't worry about fixing any part of you, and let your wicked shambles raise the goddamn roof on this whole thing."*
*(Author, Tanya Markul, theshebook.com)*

## Chapter 19

**H**EALING NEVER STOPS.

It evolves.

I survived eight years of sexual abuse. I spent thirty-nine years healing. Nearly my entire life has been lived as Rebecca the Survivor. I've grown accustomed to the heaviness of being courageous. I almost can't imagine myself free of its yoke.

Five years after my partial hysterectomy, I remained at odds with my mind and body. I meditated on the disconnection and pictured myself sitting in the meadow with both of them. There was no joy between the three of us. Our bonds were broken. When I asked them what they needed to heal, their response was singular.

They needed me.

I had to stop being impatient as they continued to recover from the surgery and the lingering effects of trauma and complex PTSD. They asked me to accept and love myself. I agreed to try. There was a part of my body that needed to heal before I could indeed love all of me. My vagina and pelvis were the epicenter of the sexual violence and the traumatized energy trapped in their tissue powered Shame.

In the past, I refused to consider that it was possible some trace amount of my grandpa's dark energy remained embedded in my most delicate flesh. It became clear to me that I couldn't avoid it any longer. If I was brave enough to survive rape for eight years and find healing, then I had the will to summon courage once more to speak to myself about the trauma in my sex.

## It Won't Hurt None

The conversation wasn't entirely new. I first started talking to myself about my vagina in high school when I had to outwit culture's obsession with "purity."

My grandpa ripped my virginity away long before my sexuality was in full bloom. In high school, I wanted to fit in, and that meant being part of the "I've had sex and I'm grown up" crowd. But I couldn't very well sit around with my girlfriends and say, "Oh yeah, my first time was with my grandpa when I was Six."

To fit in and survive yet another teenage initiation, I had to produce a virginity cover story. If I could convince my girlfriends, and the occasionally inquisitive teenage boy, my "first time" was somehow similar to their own, then the truth about my brokenness would remain a secret locked away in a forgotten cellar in my mind.

As the summer of 1986 approached, a lot of my girlfriends were all planning to "meet the right guy" and "lose" their virginity over summer break. I implored the universe to send me the right guy for my "first time." In early August, Mohawk appeared. He was nineteen, tall, handsome, charming, spent weekends in the mountains at his family's house, and he liked me.

That was enough. A week after first meeting him, it was time for my fake rite of passage. After ending my shift at the local Chinese food restaurant, I went home and showered to remove the scent of BBQ pork from my skin and hair. When I got to his house, he assured me we were alone, and we made out on the couch. Eventually, we pulled all the cushions off the couch and laid them on the floor. After adding a blanket to our nest, we stood in front of each other in near-total darkness and giggled as we removed each other's clothes.

I don't remember feeling afraid. I think I was more mesmerized. Perhaps it was a rare time I stayed in the present moment rather than dissociating. When he actually entered me, I closed my eyes and held onto the fantasy that I was a virgin and the wondrous act was the beginning of womanhood.

The physical sensations I longed to enjoy faded just as he climaxed. I was relieved, I mean ecstatic, when it ended. Rolling off me and onto his back, he pulled me close and we embraced. I let myself experience the intimacy of the moment. I didn't know sex could be kind and gentle, even if it was a lie.

I left Mohawk and it was a quick drive home before I walked through the front door of our house and headed straight for the bathroom. Part of me hoped for the bloody show some of my girlfriends talked about after they'd had sex for the first time. Blood would prove I was a good girl. After sitting on the toilet for a few minutes, I had to accept I wasn't bleeding. There would be no show for the filthy rape survivor. I wasn't a good girl and the entire charade ended in tears.

All of it was totally unnecessary, of course. The only reason I went through with the travesty was because I was taught, like all other girls in my culture, that my virginity was my value: something to keep until it was deemed ready to "lose."

But my sex isn't currency. Like the rest of my body, it belongs only to me. I spent years after my hysterectomy wondering why I didn't protect the most vulnerable part of myself from The Cutter. Why wasn't I more discerning? More cautious?

The answer came to me when I closed my eyes during a meditation and tried to picture my pelvis, vagina, and the space where my womb once resided. I wasn't able to send love and acceptance into my body to heal. Instead, resentment took over. I felt my body tense when I admitted that I felt bitterness towards my body for the pain and trauma it still carried. As the resentment welled up within me, I let myself feel all of it. The darkness of my feelings took over and I was confronted with an unspeakable truth.

The surgery was my unconscious attempt to castrate my grandpa, and my Shame, out of me.

I still don't know how to completely recover from that revelation. How do I forgive myself? More importantly, how do I learn to trust myself? If I don't trust myself, I cannot possibly learn to trust anyone else. I'll never experience real love and intimacy.

I don't want to continue to live life with the shameful notion I should just be grateful to be in the room with someone. But, time feels fleeting and at fifty-two, I can't help but wonder if I've missed the window of opportunity for true partnership and intimacy.

Should I have just somehow ignored my trauma and married someone who was "pretty nice" to me? Would pretty nice have been enough? I can't imagine any relationship or marriage built on a foundation of "it'll do" lasting more than a few miserable years. Perhaps I avoided intimacy to protect myself, knowing deep down I didn't have the tools, and self-love, to nourish someone else.

Did the Universe protect me and stop me from becoming tethered to the wrong person? Did it know I would run myself in circles trying to make a partner happy no matter what, like I did with The Geek? Would I have spent every day with my husband grateful to be in the room, believing I never deserved respect and happiness?

How was the love and intimacy I wanted and deserved possible when Shame told me I wasn't worthy? If I kept hugging Shame, and myself, and proclaimed love for us both, would the curse of loneliness and humiliation be lifted? And then what? Who will I attract? Who is worthy of all my gifts?

I had a lot of questions in 2022 and realized that more work was needed for me to find peace, intimacy, and love with myself and a future partner. I decided to search for the same sort of healing environment I found with Amelie in Nairobi and Natalia in Singapore.

I found Hana in Beverly Hills.

There was a quiet calm that filled the treatment room in Hana's office and I felt welcome and safe. She reminded me of Amelie and Natalia as she spoke in a calm, confident tone invoking a strong sense of trust when we sat down and started to talk.

"I'm feeling sad and overwhelmed. I already deal with depression and other mental health issues and Covid makes it all impossible to manage," I explained to her.

"That's understandable," she replied. "It's been a really rough time."

"My whole life was turned upside down by Covid and now I've got this running loop in my head," I explained.

"What does the loop sound like?" Hana asked.

"It says stuff like 'You're an idiot, you're a failure, you're ugly. No one wants to be with you.' I thought I was just being self-critical. But now I know it's connected to my childhood abuse. It's my Shame. I don't know how to get it to stop."

Hana didn't seem surprised by my story, and she didn't push me for more details about my trauma.

"Well, let's focus on an exercise that will help you repel the voice which is really just misguided energy," she said. "The first step is to recognize that any statement in your head starting with 'You' is unkind, unnecessary, and unwanted. I think you should practice shutting down that voice and then we can discuss the abuse, the depression you mentioned, and other issues in future visits."

I loved her direct nature. I always appreciated healers who didn't feel the need to make things overly complicated.

"Close your eyes and let's focus on the energy you call Shame. Picture it as an energy force trying to attack you." The description worked because it sounded like a scene out of a movie. "Remember, you're dealing with energy so you control it. Do you see it?" she asked.

"Yes, it's circling towards me," I replied, my eyes closed. I saw a ball of energy propelling towards my chest.

"Great. Now I want you to push both of your hands out from your chest in unison along with a deep exhale. As you're pushing the energy out, away from your body, say the word 'NO' out loud. Repeat the movement until you don't hear or see Shame anymore."

I practiced the movement several times until Shame retreated and there was silence in my mind for the first time in several months. I felt enormous relief but worried it was a temporary fix.

"Will I ever be entirely free and clear of it?" I asked Hana after we finished practicing the movement.

"No," she replied clearly. "It will never completely leave you."

I'd heard it before, but for some reason, I never accepted the prognosis until it came from Hana. Perhaps truths become easier to accept as I get older.

Hana and I focused on self-love, attracting intimacy, and family dynamics over the next several weeks. If I was going to have any success in love, I had to learn how to establish healthy boundaries around my house, and in my life, without feeling boxed in. It was complicated. I struggled with accepting people close to me while staying true to myself. After all, a gate cannot be open and closed at the same time.

How do I receive love from people who hurt me? Am I required to accommodate their own challenges, which may have confused or clouded their ability to prevent my trauma? Every time I speak to a doctor, healer, or close friend and I share how I feel my parents failed me, I am almost always met with the same response.

"Yeah, I get that your parents didn't protect you. But I'm going to play Devil's advocate. Have you ever considered that they did their best despite their own issues?"

I work really hard not to become enraged when I hear that reply—and I hear it a lot. Once I breathe through the moment, I ask, "Why do people give the Devil more advocacy than you're willing to give me? Why can't you just say, 'There is no excuse. It was a horrific betrayal, and you have every right to feel what you feel. I'm sorry. I am completely in your corner.'"

They never have an answer.

It leaves me to wonder, am I somehow so grotesque and offensive that I am relegated to sit subordinate in a dark corner, groveling for emotional scraps? Why are so many eager to lay a banquet of grace for my parents, family, and friends? What about me makes it acceptable to never make my feelings the priority?

Why is it so difficult to put me first?

I decided the answers are irrelevant because I don't want to get stuck in resentment. If I continue to live my life latched onto grudges and false hope, then I'll wake up every day attached to the bad parts of people who are inherently good. And so, every day I practice holding onto the knowledge that my mom and dad love me, even when they hurt me. It is by far the most complicated part of my journey and it will take a lot more time to practice before I create space to forgive.

When I choose forgiveness, does it mean I have to condone their failures? No. I retain my right to all my feelings and my truth. I do not forgive to ease the pain of others. Rather, I choose to forgive others so that I may also forgive myself. I choose to accept, forgive, and release the betrayal, understanding I will never again tolerate bad behavior.

The legacy of abuse ends with me.

I am the only one who decides my truth and if I am truly healed. It's always been completely up to me. I stood on the precipice of a seismic shift and I could feel a shockwave coming.

I was about to see Hana for our last appointment, setting the intention to permanently release Five, Six, Seven, Thirteen, Darkness, Fight, Flight, Shame, and all the other torments from my mind and body as much as my heart, body and soul would allow.

"Are you ready? I have a good feeling about today. I know it's time for you to release all of it," Hana said as we walked into the treatment room.

"I'm ready for it to all end. This has been a lifetime of hurt, discovery, and healing. I'll be glad when I can just be myself," I replied. "I have one chapter left in my book to write so it feels like good timing."

"That's great! Have you written about your future yet?" Hana asked me before we started our final meditation.

"No," I said laughing. "It never occurred to me to write about the future. I never even considered what that looks like."

"Think about it," she replied with a smile as I closed my eyes. I settled into a deep state of relaxation, and I was in the meadow for just a moment before I saw my core. My body's center.

"I see black dust, particles, inside me where my womb used to sit," I told Hana. "It's the final specks of trauma. The last time I saw it, I vomited it out of my body. It was like thick, hot tar. This is different. I can barely see it. It has almost no energy or power left in it."

"It needs to be released. I'm going to insert an acupuncture needle into your belly through your shirt," Hana said. "I want to give it a way for your body to expel it."

As soon as she inserted the first needle just above my navel, she started coughing uncontrollably. When she finally stopped, she asked, "Did you feel that? I put the needle in and energy came out and my throat immediately tightened. My eyes are watering."

"Do you feel safe? Are you okay? Tell yourself you're safe," I said urgently, understanding the power and toxicity of my grandpa and the trauma.

"I'm fine. The needle itself pushed back against me. There was resistance," she told me. "Like something didn't want to be removed." We continued the session and I cried as Hana massaged my stomach.

"Why are you crying? What's happening?" she asked.

"It's about the surgery," I told Hana. "This is about letting go of my womb, the trauma, hurt, and pain. All the resentment." Hana continued the massage until my tears stopped and I felt like all the anguish surrounding the hysterectomy was released.

"I think you did a lot of work today but something tells me there's more to discover and heal. Take some time today and tomorrow to ask yourself what you're avoiding. What have you overlooked as part of your healing? It will come to you," she advised. "Call me tomorrow and let me know what you discover."

After the session ended, I spent the rest of the day revisiting the idea of resistance. As the moon rose over the lagoon just opposite my house, I sat down in my meditation corner, lit some palo santo incense, and closed my eyes. Who, or what, was resisting?

I saw myself standing alone in the meadow patiently waiting for some insight to come my way. I thought about Fix, Six, Seven, and Thirteen. Their combined stories were linked. Thirteen may have been a fierce protector, but Seven was the thinker. She was the planner.

And then, it all became clear.

The resistance Hana mentioned was Seven.

She held more than just my sadness and her healing was incomplete.

Seven had rage.

Too young to fight, Seven transformed her rage and ignited Thirteen to finally fight back.

In the end, it was Seven who ultimately rescued me that night in the kitchen and ended the abuse. I had to wonder, did I owe Seven anything? Did a debt stand between us and the final stage of my healing?

*I meditated about her the next morning, and then I got into the shower. When I closed my eyes, I saw Seven waiting for me in the meadow. Without saying a word, she turned toward the horizon and every second of every horrific assault, including those I had entirely forgotten, flashed across the sky. His hands, mouth, penis, and the full force of his weight tore into my flesh over and over for eight years. Too many assaults to count. I couldn't look away. If Seven was strong enough to remember, then so was I.*

*When the vignettes ended, she looked at me and screamed the finale to her terror before embodying all her rage. Instinctively, I stood in the shower and kept my eyes closed. I was safe. Opening my mouth, I screamed with her. The steam from the shower continued to rise as I released a low, guttural, long, angry roar.*

*The final vestiges of sadness washed off me and I finally felt all of Seven's rage.*

*My rage.*

*The anger I avoided for decades, the anger I denied like a good girl, was releasing. None would remain once it was over. We roared together. Our lungs were powerful. Our hands were in fists. Our howls filled the meadow.*

*And then he appeared. My grandpa. Lying in a heap on the ground at our feet. Pathetic.*

Seven stood over him in all her power and her voice boomed. I watched her fury blast across his body and he started to decay. Crumble. Seven, the strongest of all my selves, thundered over his rotting corpse until he was nothing but dust. And then he was no more. The image I kept of his fist rising through the rubble vanished and my entire being knew he was finally vanquished.

She looked at me and was immediately joined by Five, Six, and Thirteen as if they were summoned.

"I'm sorry," I said to her. "I didn't give you credit for saving me. I didn't know you had to face him one last time."

"It's okay," she said. "It's over."

"Is it really over? Forever?" I asked her.

"Yes. It's time for all of us to leave."

As she said those words, my Granny Chandler appeared and joined us in the meadow.

"I'm going to take them," she said. "They belong to me now."

"Wait. I don't know if I'm ready," I replied. The hot water in the shower continued to cascade over my body and felt like a purification. A baptism.

"You're ready," Granny said. "You're whole. Complete. It's time to release them."

She could see on my face that I was nervous. I didn't know who or what I was going to be without the fragmented energy rattling around inside me.

"Before you go and get romantic about them, remember one thing," Granny admonished me wryly. "They nearly pushed you over the edge more than once. It's time to let them go. Let it all go."

"Will I ever see you again?" I asked my Granny. I missed her every day and wanted to know I could connect with her in the future.

"I'll check in on you," she said with a smile.

I looked at Seven and started to cry. How would I learn to stand on my own?

"You're going to be okay," Seven said as she joined the others. "You don't need us anymore. We're ready to go." They held hands, and I watched them walk into the woods until I was alone in the meadow.

I stood in the hot shower with my eyes closed. The water washed over me. The filthy shame was gone.

"It is over!" I shouted out loud.

And for the first time in my entire life, I knew it was true.

I was clean.

I was finally whole.

I started living life as a fragmented version of myself at the age of Five. For years, no one actually knew me. I didn't know me. Who was I without all my traumatized layers?

The person who used to love taking control over large film sets, directing teams of people, managing complex budgets and schedules, doesn't exist today. I don't need to exercise so much control in my life because I'm no longer stuck in fight or flight. I am not wearing Trauma's chains or carrying PTSD's burdens.

The crushing urge to uproot and move constantly to try to outrun my trauma is gone. I still love the idea of being a global citizen, but I also equally love the idea of settling down and creating a true home base from which to launch a thousand adventures. I am no longer host to detachment. Instead, I live life in the fullness, vibrancy, and complexity of the present. I can do that because I am safe. I am strong. I am healed.

"A hysterectomy is a simple procedure," The Cutter said five years and thousands of words ago. Perhaps I should thank her. I'm not sure I would be getting to know my true, untraumatized self, had I not sat down in my post-surgical spiral and started to write.

The next time I tell anyone, "I was sexually assaulted as a child, but I've done a lot of work, and I think I'm in a good place with it," I'll be telling the truth.

My truth. I am Enough. Right now.

Not when my body changes, when I make more money, or fall in love. I will no longer design my life based on the false promises of the future. I am happy and content today. At this moment. Seeing my life evolve into a profound sense of abundance and gratitude leaves me feeling more empowered and excited about the future. I am in control, and I alone choose how I respond to every situation.

So, what lies ahead for Rebecca the Survivor? Am I allowed to stop being a survivor? Do I have the right to live my life simply as Rebecca?

The answer is, Yes!

Rebecca *was* a survivor.

## Chapter 20

In the future, Rebecca Elizabeth Chandler lives on several acres along with a menagerie of rescued sheep, pigs, goats, chickens, ducks, horses, cats, and dogs. Injured and sick animals always seem to find her for healing and love. In return, they give her peace.

She attracts a partner later in life than most. She wakes every day knowing he puts her first and stands firmly in her corner. He is her most trusted advocate.

She radiates a warmth that speaks to her healing and acceptance of her past as well as a joyous celebration of her present.

Most days, Rebecca is up just as the sun peeks over the horizon, save for Sunday mornings when staying in a warm bed with her husband is far too tempting. The house is still as she gets dressed and gently styles the soft, pure, white hair she inherited from her late Granny Chandler. She stops her morning routine for just a moment to admire her reflection in the mirror. Her body is her friend and feels strong. Supple.

She radiates a warmth that speaks to her healing and acceptance of her past as well as the joyous celebration of her present.

Rebecca enjoys walking down the long hallway running the length of the house adorned with various pieces of art procured from a lifetime of traveling. Inside a small, cozy room with a limitless view of land and sea, she meditates on gratitude and love.

She grounds herself every day in her practice as she sits in a doula's hand carved stool she treasures, giving birth to a life of vibrancy. She returns to her husband, who offers her love, acceptance, and security. Intimacy. He is kind, patient, and funny, and they giggle under the covers like love-struck teens. Rebecca disappears into his reassuring embrace and they make time for love often and relish in the joy of their life together.

Celebrating every day, she is humbled by the affection of her family and friends near and far. Her foundation is fortified by their kindness, patience, and acceptance. The global network of lifelong friends continually expands and she is made richer with each new connection.

After checking in with the various creatures that call her house home, Rebecca sits down at her computer and turns on some relaxing music. Crafting new stories with rich themes, she is grateful for the prose filling every page. The words flow with ease as she encourages her readers to find healing and stand tall and proud in their truth. A few more pages complete the chapter she left the night before when her husband kissed the back of her neck and led her to bed.

As the sun rises overhead and midday approaches, she seeks inspiration and Rebecca finds it in the meadow next to the house. Wildflowers celebrate and show off their colorful display as they line both sides of the sandy path leading into her sanctuary. She heads toward the giant oak, relishing the late-morning sun that warms every cell in her body. Stopping to twirl barefoot on the soft, damp grass, she ends her journey climbing her favorite tree.

She loves trees.

Listening to the wind sing through the branches, Rebecca is at peace with the world. Her house, and tower, no longer crumble. They are complete and strong. The keystone is forever locked in place as she continues to practice forgiveness and patience each day.

Her empathic, Pisces gifts come easily. Naturally. She looks forward to spending time in the afternoon sharing encouragement, and wisdom, with other souls who feel lost, confused, curious, and are in search of healing. She advocates for survivors around the world and is humbled by their willingness to share their truth one story at a time.

Night comes and her partner, her champion, offers her a glass of her favorite wine as they settle before a fire after dinner. There's something pure and wonderful about snuggling into her husband's embrace as they watch the flames dance and talk about their next adventure to far off destinations.

Rebecca Elizabeth Chandler is a woman, partner, friend, sister, aunt, daughter, author, speaker, and guide. A listener and healer. Harnessing the limitless power of her courage and truth every day, she stands fearlessly in love with herself and the world as she writes the next chapter.

## Author's Note

When I first started writing this story, I viewed every day through Trauma's lens. It was narrow, inflexible, and in control of my future. Five years later, I'm grateful, and surprised, to be on the other side of the most harrowing parts of my healing journey. I didn't know sharing my truth would mend my deepest wounds and create room for love.

I still hear occasional whispers from Trauma. In moments where I feel particularly vulnerable or frustrated, my mind slides just a bit before I catch myself. Eating and spending continue to be compulsions that challenge me, but the good news is I am slowly winning the fight. With daily practice and the support of the people I love, I gain more confidence and control of my life.

I've started a new journey to explore trust. I want to understand what trust is and how I can develop it within myself and with others. The fundamentals of trust were stolen from me early in life and I'm excited to learn how to repair it during the next phase of my healing journey.

Practicing forgiveness and accepting my flaws, and the flaws of others, remains complicated. But I'm patient and kind with myself. I hold fast to the truth that it's impossible to dance on a beautiful carpet full of nails. I won't give up. I work each day to remove resentments, one nail at a time. I want my joy to flow freely so I can dance carefree and barefoot through life.

My physical self continues to struggle but slowly things are starting to shift. In acceptance, I find grace and the ability to settle into my health journey with more hope than ever before. I still find sleep elusive at times and wonder if I will ever lose some of the 80 pounds I gained since the surgery but choose not to spend too much time dwelling on all of it. I'm learning to accept that recovery will take longer than I'd like and patience is needed.

I meditate most mornings and I visit the meadow often. It will always be a place of peace and healing. I look forward to exploring myself more and pushing deeper into the forest, and my mind, to discover new sources of inspiration and healing.

Some close to me have read my story and reached out to tell me how sad they feel I went through so many difficult experiences alone. They ask why I didn't reach out when life became unbearable. I'm grateful for their love and kindness but I don't have an answer except to say, sometimes, it was difficult to remember that people loved me. In the pitch black depths where there was no light, their love was, sadly, irrelevant. I cannot explain it any more than that.

And in that revelation, I am reminded to be more understanding, kind, patient and more attuned to everyone. I can do more to make sure they feel loved and supported, no matter what life is throwing their way.

I can do more.

We can all do more.

Now that Trauma no longer defines me, I find myself strangely comfortable in my newfound vulnerability. In my new skin, I am grateful to be living in the Present and excited to see where this unexpected adventure will take me next.

# Epilogue

EVERY SIXTY-EIGHT SECONDS, an American is sexually assaulted. And every nine minutes, that victim is a child. One out of every six American women has been the victim of an attempted or completed rape in her lifetime. About three percent of American men—or one in thirty-three—have experienced an attempted or completed rape in their lifetime.

One in five women and one in thirteen men report having been sexually abused as a child aged 0-17 years. One hundred twenty million girls and young women under 20 years of age have suffered some form of forced sexual contact.

The United States has one of the worst records among industrialized nations—losing on average five children every day to child abuse and neglect. A report of child abuse is made every ten seconds in the United States.

Every year, more than 4 million referrals are made to child protection agencies involving more than 4.3 million children (a referral can include multiple children).

Nationally, neglect is the most common form of abuse. Three out of five (nearly 61 percent) of victims were "only" neglected, more than 10 percent were "only" physically abused, and 7 percent were "only" sexually abused. Yet the statistics indicate a more complex problem where children experience multiple forms of abuse simultaneously. In 2018, more than 15 percent of kids were poly-victimized (suffered two or more forms of abuse).

Call or text the Childhelp National Child Abuse Hotline at 1-800-422-4453 or visi https://childhelphotline.org.

# Special Thanks

A SMALL GROUP OF friends supported this effort and I'd like to take this opportunity to specifically acknowledge:

Julie Adams (UK) for a gorgeous cover design. Thank you for your patience, advice, creativity, and wonderful sense of humor.

Sara Volle, Development Editor (USA) for all of your support to develop the early manuscript. You were kind, patient, supportive, and turned 130,000 words into a proper draft.

Kate Bassford Baker, Final Development Editor (USA) for your willingness to not only beta read the draft but to also jump off the cliff with me and help me fine-tune the final version. You are an incredible talent and I am so grateful that you said yes to my request for help.

My beta readers Magda Travis, Cindi Crane, Laurie Chittenden, Alicia Snyder, and Jana Russon. Thank you. All of your feedback created a richer, fuller story.

Aparna Ramakrishnan, beta reader, confidant, friend, co-author of the companion journal *Hurt No More, Grow a Foundation for Healing*. You listened, encouraged, understood, and inspired me over the years. Thank you.

Nadene Seiters, Proofreader (USA) for your attention to detail, patience, and creativity.

Carrie Hollister, Editor/Proofreader (USA) for your sharp lens adding the final finish.

Bryan Daniels, Designer/Creative Director, (USA) for your notes, encouragement, and inspiration.

Denise Dhillon (USA) for listening to me talk about the writing process, share the ups and downs, and explore the catharsis and the pain throughout 2022. You were always available and willing to listen, offer advice, and make me laugh. I didn't know I needed a writing cheerleader until I met you. Your encouragement made it possible for me to complete the journey.

# Resources

**wwww.rebeccachandler.com**
Please visit my website and check out the companion journal, *Hurt No More – Grow a Foundation for Healing*.

**My Healers:**
Amelie Muthundo, Healer and Coach
www.ameliemuthundo.com

Natalia Rachel
Author, Speaker, Trauma-informed Educator & Practitioner
https://www.nataliarachel.com
Book: '*Why am I like this? Illuminating the traumatised self*'
Penguin Random House SEA

Hana Doustar LAc
CEO and Head Clinician of The Clinic for Pain and Anxiety
www.clinicforpainandanxiety.com

**Reading**
"*The Body Keeps the Score: Brain, Mind and Body in the Healing of Trauma*"
by Sean Pratt, Bessel A. Van der Kolk, et al,
Penguin Publishing Group, 2015

"*The Body Never Lies – The Lingering Effects of Hurtful Parenting*"
by Alice Miller, Translated by Andrew Jenkins
W.W. Norton and Company, 2006

"*Expectation Hangover – Free Yourself from Your Past, Change Your Present, & Get What You Really Want*"
By Christine Hassler
MJF Books, 2014

*"Healing the Fragmented Selves of Trauma Survivors – Overcoming Internal Self-Alienation"*
By Janina Fisher
Routlege, 2017

*"The Sum of my Parts: A Survivor's Story of Dissociative Identity Disorder"*
By Olga Trujillo
New Harbinger Publications, Inc., 2011

**Online**
https://www.isst-d.org/
International Society for the Study of Trauma and Dissociation

https://988lifeline.org/
National Suicide Prevention Hotline (USA)

https://childhelphotline.org/
The Childhelp National Child Abuse Hotline

https://www.childwelfare.gov/topics/responding/reporting/how/
U.S. Department of Health & Human Services Child Welfare Information Gateway

https://www.psychologytoday.com/us/therapists
Find all types of mental health professionals near you

Made in the USA
Monee, IL
11 March 2023